What Could
He Be
Thinking?

Other Books by Michael Gurian

PARENTING

The Soul of the Child
The Wonder of Girls
The Wonder of Boys
A Fine Young Man
The Good Son
What Stories Does My Son Need
(with Terry Trueman)

EDUCATION

Boys and Girls Learn Differently
(with Patricia Henley and Terry Trueman)
The Boys and Girls Learn Differently Action Guide
(with Arlette Ballew)

MEN'S STUDIES

The Prince and the King
Mothers, Sons and Lovers

PSYCHOLOGY

Love's Journey

YOUNG ADULT

Plugged In: From Boys to Men
Plugged In: Understanding Guys

FICTION

The Miracle
An American Mystic

POETRY

Emptying
The Odyssey of Telemachus
As the Swans Gather

What Could
He Be Thinking?

A Guide to the Mysteries of a Man's Mind

MICHAEL GURIAN

Element
An Imprint of HarperCollins*Publishers*
77–85 Fulham Palace Road,
Hammersmith, London W6 8JB

The website address is: www.thorsonselement.com

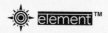

and *Element* are trademarks of
HarperCollins*Publishers* Ltd

First published in the US by St. Martin's Press 2003
First published in the UK by Element 2004

13 5 7 9 10 8 6 4 2

© Michael Gurian 2003

Michael Gurian asserts the moral right to
be identified as the author of this work

A catalogue record of this book
is available from the British Library

ISBN 0 00 717698 8

Printed and bound in Great Britain by
Creative Print & Design (Wales), Ebbw Vale

For Gail, my love

Contents

PART IV: WHAT COULD HE *REALLY* BE THINKING . . .
ABOUT HOME AND CHILDREN?

Acknowledgments

S ince this book has been twenty years in the making, I
hope that all the researchers, clients, friends, and col-
leagues who have inspired me will know my gratitude even if there
are too many to name on this page.

First and foremost, my thanks go to my wife, Gail, who has, more
than once, asked me, "What could you be thinking?" My philosophy
is inspired by her encouragement and her own work in family therapy and attachment issues. She has also been my "boss" over the last
five years as she organizes the work of the Gurian Institute. Without
her efforts, both professional and personal, this book would not be
what it is.

Diane Reverand, at St. Martin's Press, has inspired me greatly
during the process of writing this book. I appreciate her vision, her

wit, and her ability to keep me focused on what is most important. Many thanks also to Melissa Contreras, her able assistant.

Candice Fuhrman, my agent, has shepherded this book from its beginning. I cannot thank her and her staff enough. Elsa, I couldn't have done it without you!

At the Gurian Institute, special thanks are due Kathy Stevens and Terry Schwartz, our codirectors in Colorado Springs, and many thanks to the people who have allowed me to touch their homes, schools, and workplaces over the years.

Many thanks to the professionals in brain development who make my own work possible. Among them are Ruben Gur, M.D.; Laurie Allen, Ph.D.; Anne Moir, Ph.D.; and Phon Hudkins, Ph.D.

Whenever I had an anecdotal question about women's perceptions, I turned to focus groups in Spokane. Special thanks to Pam Brown, Carla Jakabosky, Stacey Mainer, and Christine Barada. My thanks also to Leslie Huppin, Rita Yaegar, Bobbie Corbin, Peggy Reid, Carol Bellinger and Marianne Pavlish.

Thank you also to the following men who have not only given me friendship, but helped me evolve my public conversation about male development: Terry Trueman, Bob Cole, Gene Dire, and Richard Dalke. A hearty thank you to my brother, Phil, for his friendship and his Web and design work.

My thanks also to the many clients who, in my therapy practice, let me help them to understand men, women, and intimate separateness. They cannot be named, but they are very important to this work.

My thanks are also due those physicians and other medical professionals who have allowed me to ask them questions of science. Thank you to Lloyd Halpern, M.D.; Jeff Hedge, D.O.; Michael Mainer, M.D.; Peter Fern, M.D.; Donald Howard, M.D.; Darl Van Der Linden, Ph.D.; and Ross Coble, M.D.

My work sits on the shoulders of work done by many others over the last decades, both professionally, in brain development, and nonprofessionally, as all of us together create the kind of world we would be proud to leave to our children. A philosopher is only as worthwhile as his readers, thus I thank you for helping this work to have a positive impact on the world.

Introduction:
What Could He Be Thinking?

I hold nothing alien that has to do with human nature.

—Terence, Roman poet

The title for this book comes from a conversation I had one Saturday with my wife, Gail, and four of her friends, following their monthly women's lunch. Gail had invited her friends to our house for tea and dessert. Three of the women were mothers, two were married, two were in long-term relationships, the other dating, all were professionals, two were presently stay-at-home moms. Their ages ranged from thirty to sixty.

I was about to leave them alone when Carly, one of Gail's best friends, a woman in her early fifties, said with a wry smile, "So, Mike, come sit down with us and explain a few things about men."

Ah, the dangers of this particular moment! One must tread carefully, even among friends. It is so easy to appear to be rationalizing or making excuses for men, especially if a husband or boyfriend has recently behaved badly.

I laughed. "You know, Carly, I think I have to go fix the car now. Then I have to clean the garage."

After a few chuckles, Gail said, "We were talking about men, and we just want you to put on your biological 'male brain' hat for a second." I wasn't going to be able to get out of this conversation!

"Not that men are all we ever talk about!" Carly joked. "But will we *ever* figure you guys out?"

It was one of those "What could he be thinking?" lunches, Gail told me. This phrase had emerged over the last few months in the women's group. Often it was used in humor, other times with poignancy, as when Gail came home from the lunch having learned of a marital conflict or of a family in pain.

I sat down with these women and we got "down and dirty."

Danielle, thirty-one, referred to her boyfriend. "Okay, Mike, explain this to me: Last night Jeff and I were watching *Charlie's Angels* on video. After it's over he says, 'Danielle, that was a great movie.' He really meant it! I'm going, '*Charlie's Angels*? A great movie?' What could he be thinking?"

Katherine, mother of a ten-year-old boy and herself an urban planner, said of her husband, "Larry and I started talking about Timothy McVeigh and whether he should have been executed. Larry was just cold about it. 'I'm glad they killed the guy. Just forget about it,' he said. I thought, I've been married to him for twelve years, but I don't understand him. 'At least it's worth thinking about the implications,' I said, but he said, 'The implications mean nothing. Kill the guy and move on.' I know he had deeper thoughts and feelings about it but wouldn't admit it. I'd like to know what he was really thinking."

Sandy, a single mother of four, told a story about her ex-husband, who had kept the children the previous weekend. "Logan is only six years old, but his father let him ride his bike to the park unsupervised. I mean, really, what could that man be thinking?"

Carly, recently remarried, her children grown but her stepchildren still in their teens and living with her, recalled an incident a few days earlier. Her husband would not back down in a conflict with another man over his place in line at the grocery store. "He's fifty-two years old and wouldn't let this other guy get a word in edgewise,"

Carly reported. "He made this other guy's little slight into such a big deal, such a blow to his pride. What could he be thinking?"

I think in those two hours we must have covered countless questions about men and male behaviors. Here are just a few—some humorous, some quite serious.

"Why is it, when he's staring into the refrigerator, he never sees what's right in front of him?"

"Why does he just leave his laundry lying around?"

"Why does it seem like men are on some kind of quest?"

"Do men and women think about ethics differently? Are there biological sources for this difference?"

"When a man's development is wounded in his childhood, is his brain actually altered? If so, what emotional adjustments should a woman expect to make in order to keep a marriage strong?"

"Does the male brain experience as many feelings as women do?"

"Why do men seem to leave their kids behind and start a new family more easily than women after a divorce?"

"How can men remember all the pitchers' names and World Series scores, but they can't remember yesterday's conversation?"

"Why is 'romance' such a primal thing for women but not as much so for men?"

"Do men have more sexual fantasies than women?"

"When men get angry, it's difficult to get them to 'talk about it.' Why?"

"My dad worked himself to death for his family, and we never really appreciated him—now my husband does the same thing. Why do men put so much into work?"

"Men seem to think about 'honor' a lot—at least it seems so from the movies. What does 'honor' mean to them? Is there a biology to male honor?"

"Can men actually be more fragile than women, at least in a lot of ways?"

"What is it with men and cars?"

"Are women afraid of commitment, or is it only men who are?"

"Why are men obsessed with getting control of the TV remote? In fact, what is it with all the gadgets in men's lives?"

"Is it healthy for men to cry as little as they do?"

"It seems like men bond with women differently than women bond with men. Is this true?"

What had started as a "dangerous" moment for me became one of great learning. This conversation was more than just the individual anecdotes expressed. There were certainly answers I could give about males, yet throughout the discussion I was as much a listener as a teacher, realizing the existence of questions and comments these women couldn't express—the deeper confusions we all have about men. When a woman asks herself a question about a man in her life, she is most probably asking a question about all men.

Discussing the encounter with Gail that afternoon and on into the night, I knew that I wanted to address these questions and answers in a book. Women, like men, are asking very loudly today, "What is a man?" and all of us are seeking solid answers, not just some new trend of images or ideas.

During the afternoon's discussion, some of the women put this need into words. Danielle said to me, "When you talk about men, you talk about neurobiology and that kind of thing. It's as if there's a 'science' about men. That's good to know."

"It's such a revelation," Katherine said, "to learn how the male mind *actually* works."

"It's a relief," Sandy agreed. "I didn't have any brothers, and I barely knew my dad. It helps to know what men *really* think."

These comments reveal our readiness to look for solid identities. Danielle, Katherine, Sandy, and many others are ready to absorb social-trend theories into their thinking. But in intimate relationships, they want to rely on what is natural and altogether real.

THE SCIENCE OF MANHOOD

The research base of *What Could He Be Thinking?* is primarily the "science of men." Just as the sciences of physics and astronomy are charting our universe now as never before, the biological sciences are charting human nature, both female and male.

As a social philosopher who specializes in neurobiology, I utilize an approach I call nature based. Its basic idea: Since society originates from nature, studying what is going on in human nature itself is the clearest base for social thinking. Though our culture presently uses the dichotomy of "nature vs. nurture" to attribute different elements of human development, nature-based thinking posits very little distinction between the two. In real life no biological organism exists outside its environment, thus the organism and the environment actually work in tandem, not in opposition. When we talk in this book about male biological trends, the male brain, and male biology, we will be looking at nature and nurture together.

In *What Could He Be Thinking?* the "nature" we will most frequently consult is the nature of the human mind: the brain and the many human mysteries that interact with the brain, as science can help us understand them. In the last decade, scientists have learned so much about the human brain that many of our past assumptions are being completely discarded. We can now grasp a great deal about the nature of the human mind if we ask the right questions. "What could he be thinking?" is one of the right questions.

In this book I'll help answer it with the assistance of a number of kinds of research, and with a special emphasis on scientific approaches. In the note section for this introduction, you'll find resources that enable you to read much of this material yourself, if you so desire. I will use three categories of research:

1. Hard science. In this category are scientific studies into the male and female brain, conducted on all seven continents over the last three decades. These involve cutting-edge technologies for studying the human brain. Research from the following fields of hard science will appear in these chapters:

- neurobiology
- neurochemistry
- neuropsychology
- genetics
- endocrinology

2. Soft science. In this category are the social sciences. We will match hard science with soft as we proceed, checking results of each with the other. This research includes the fields of:

- psychology
- sociology
- anthropology
- ethology

We'll pay specific attention to historical and anthropological studies of biological trends in men and women from all ethnic and racial groups. By "biological trends," we mean inborn tendencies that predate social influences and inborn tendencies that are modified or enhanced by social influences. We'll also utilize psychological and social studies on male and female development. I have chosen, among these, mainly the cutting-edge studies that include human biology and human nature, and I've avoided psychological studies that are mainly the social opinion of the clinical psychologist.

3. Supporting anecdotes. Both hard and soft sciences give us a credible and secure base for understanding human nature, but they are dry and lifeless without real life as an illustrator and critic: real people living real life, men and women in everyday relationships. I have selected a variety of sources for anecdotal support to the biological research, including:

- A focus group in Spokane that was formed from Gail's women's lunch group.
- Action research from the Michael Gurian Educational Institute, with anecdotes and stories.

- Illustrative letters and E-mails I've received during the last decade from men and women.
- Research from my family therapy practice (I have changed clients' names and withheld certain details in order to protect confidentiality).
- Examples from historical literature.
- Examples from contemporary books, movies, and other media.
- Personal life experience.

Supporting anecdotes and stories from individuals who have lived out the biological trends are crucial, I believe, to the understanding of the male brain. When we put hard sciences together with soft, then combine these sciences with diverse life stories, we can investigate the mysteries of a subject—in our case, the male mind—with greater confidence.

In each chapter of this book, you'll find an in-depth presentation of what the sciences say about men, the male brain, and male nature, in research corroborated on a world stage with diverse cultures; you'll find this presentation illustrated by psychological and sociological studies; then, in turn, you'll find all the scholarly research from the sciences reflected in everyday examples from lives just like your own. With this approach, I am striving to make the new sciences, by which we can finally understand men, highly accessible; I am hoping to bring scientific wisdom about men, women, and relationships to everyday life. When this happens, we have established a new field of human study called gender biology, one that enables us to understand men and women from the inside out.

We'll look at how the male brain differs biologically from the female brain.

We'll explore how male biology affects a man's thinking about emotions, communication, sex, romance, marriage, morality, and other keys to the journey of human life.

We'll wonder together if a man could really be serious when he says, "What do you mean the house is a mess?" or even more frustrating, "You worry too much. The kids are fine."

With this approach and material, we'll not only discover the secrets of the male mind but also investigate "maleness" as an essential element each of us must encounter fully in our lives if we are to advance our humanity.

Throughout this scientific process, we should keep in mind that one book is not the whole person—so we are striving to see what he *could* be thinking.

In presenting this information to you, I hope you'll find inspiration and vision that is life changing. I have set that high standard for this book, a standard based on the idea that human nature is always adapting. In our time now, we are striving for adaptation as passionately as people of any other time have. One of the key pieces we've been missing in our discussions of men and women has been the knowledge of male and female nature itself. I hope in this book that key piece will fall into place.

THE NATURE OF A MAN

I decided to write *What Could He Be Thinking?* after the inspiration of that Saturday afternoon encounter, but its journey into print began at the start of my twenty years of research into the biology of males and females. At that time I noticed that basing one's theories on actual human nature ran counter to the trend in psychological literature, self-help, and the social philosophy of relying on the opinions of clinicians in the fields of sociology and psychology for wisdom. Still today, much of what we read about men, women, relationships, family life, and education is primarily based on the study of social trends, not biological ones—society blind to human nature. When the subject of men and women is broached in most popular and academic literature, it is viewed from the lens of "how our society has affected a man" or "how our culture has affected a woman."

My own research over the last twenty years compels me to make that approach secondary, not primary, in my books. Though social opinions and expert studies of social and personal trends are certainly of value, hard science generally provides an even more compelling and accurate base for answers to questions about male and female development.

From deep within our biology we gain a most powerful sense of who we really are.

Personally and professionally I did not always understand this. I was a child of my generation, looking toward social ideology and psychological opinions about men and women for truth about human identity. When I was a college student in the seventies, a course was offered called "The Nature of Man"—a philosophical study of human civilization, past and future. I searched in it for hard data about men. Despite its wisdom about "Man," I didn't learn from it what a man (or a woman) was. In graduate school, I still searched, learning that whatever a man was, he was socialized to be dangerous and defective. Manhood was really "masculinity," a social construct that needed to be deconstructed.

Earlier in my boyhood, my family had lived around the world, so I had learned some important things about what men were both in my own culture and in others. Everywhere we traveled, I observed, I modeled, I listened. In any country of the world, the topic of manhood haunts a growing boy. Over the years, and when we returned to the United States, I learned a lot about what people thought the male role should (or should not) be. During adolescence I grasped at manhood by doing dangerous and provocative things and by watching the men.

Neither my professional development nor my growing up showed me the nature of a man—something from deep within that I could hold on to. I matured in a time that lacked consistent messages about the nature, goals, and responsibilities of men because all the human messages about males were in transition. At one point, in my twenties, I decided that it must not matter if I "became a man." Being an "adult" and a "person" was enough.

But it wasn't. I, like all males, knew at some deep level that there is a biology of manhood—internal frameworks that drive a man just like female frameworks drive a woman. I sensed something organic and naturally male in me. I could not discover what it was. I came to believe there was no useful male nature. I was in a kind of limbo and, often, in despair. I looked in the mirror many times and wondered, "Who am I?" I formed relationships with women who wondered why we men didn't value our love relationships enough to explain and share ourselves. These relationships ended more quickly than I wished. I rarely understood why they ended, and only later did I realize that I did not understand the full breadth and depth of how I, as a man, could carry on these relationships.

When I became a practicing family therapist, I helped married couples through their pain and hurt. Sitting in the little room talking, all of us knew that marriages, families, and lives were at stake. Who were these men sitting in these rooms trying to talk? Over the years, many of us came to realize that we had to understand men from the inside out or we would not be fully able to live or love. Many men live and die without understanding who they are. Millions of relationships and marriages die in confusion.

Twenty years ago, during graduate school, I became intrigued by new sciences—neurobiology, sociobiology, neurochemistry, biochemistry. I couldn't find full courses about them, but there was burgeoning literature available. These sciences were very wise. When combined with common sense and a spirit of wonder, they revealed to me the inner world of the human being. Their revelation of our human nature is even more advanced today, providing nature-based research that answers, in this book, the very question: "What is the nature of a man?"

In the last twenty years, I have surveyed scientific literature from thirty cultures on all continents, and no matter the culture I study, I discover what early brain scientists (some of whom you'll meet in this book) already knew: Socialized differences between men and women exist, but there is a primal nature to "man" and "woman" on which culture has only a minor effect. This nature holds keys to better life, work, parenting, and especially, the success of all intimate relationships, including marriage.

Science, at its best, is of practical use to human beings living their everyday lives. In *What Could He Be Thinking?* I plan to provide you with practical, useful, and inspiring science.

A NOTE OF GRATITUDE

Though this book is primarily about men, it could not have been written without the help of many women. Gail's help, guidance, and encouragement have been invaluable. From Gail, my daughters, and all the women who have guided me, I've gained a gift that deeply enhances this book: In presenting the nature of men, I must try to think like a woman. The women in my life have helped me focus on the primary questions women and girls are asking about men. The many possible chapters in this book were honed down to eight with their wise assistance. Gail, my daughters, and all the women I know possess amazing wisdom about the nature of a man.

"Don't just write another book about relationships," a friend said to me when she heard what I wanted to write. "Don't write what we already know. Help us see the future."

Another friend said, "Don't apologize for this book being about men. There are gobs of books and magazines and talk shows about and for women. Help us women understand you men!"

My intention in this book is to fulfill those charges: to provide a new vision of men. Now let us begin that vision with a look into the place where so much of the human journey begins—in the male brain itself.

PART I

The Male Brain

—⟨᳃⟩—

Is there really such a thing as a "male" brain? Of course there is!
How strange that we even have to ask the question.

**—Nancy, seventy-two, widow, three children,
six grandchildren, retired teacher**

Hermann Hesse said, "To be a human being is to try to link my
own small soul with the great soul of the eternal."
For me as a man, this is the standard I live by.

**—Jim, fifty-two, married, one child,
two grandchildren, financial planner**

1

What's in His Head:
A Friendly Look at the Male Brain

One of the most amazing things I've learned in my life is that there really is such a thing as a male brain, and my brain is not quite that.

—Sunny, thirty-one, married, three children, a lawyer

It was a night like any other. Gail and I had a child, Gabrielle, who was just two years old. After putting her to sleep, we took a moment to plug a videotape into the video player. It was 1992. We had been fighting on and off for months. Neither Gail nor I felt supported or understood. Our communication had broken down more than once. We loved each other and loved our child, but we had spoken the word "divorce" recently. A number of our friends were divorced, but we didn't want to divorce after only six years of marriage and were looking for any help we could get. One of our friends, a fellow professional in the mental health field, had given us a videotape series called *Brain Sex* to watch. Tonight was our night to fit it into the routines of work, a young child, marriage, and overall exhaustion.

There were three tapes in this series. The words "Brain Sex" were emblazoned on the front. Gail looked at me wryly, saying, "So two brains can have sex?"

We started the first tape. Its subject was the differences between male and female hormones and how those differences, begun in the womb, actually form a boy's and girl's brain. The videographic research involved babies, children, teens, and adults. At every age studied, men and women exhibited distinct differences. The second tape covered similar research worldwide on how the brain works and how the male and female brain differ. Gail and I had read some of these studies, but we had never seen what the videographers had captured on this videotape.

About ten minutes into the tape, Ruben Gur, a neuroscientist at the University of Pennsylvania, smiled at the camera as he showed MRI and PET scans—color pictures of the brain at work—to the videographer. Those pictures clearly showed that women's brains looked very different from men's, even when doing the same tasks. The female brains were significantly more lit up and colorful than the male brains. (Researchers have since learned that the female brain has 15 percent more blood flow than the male.) When processing emotions, for instance, far more cortical areas (physical areas in the brain) of the women's brains were active than of men's. Whether talking, thinking, remembering, or relating, the female and male brain significantly differed, and we could see it. Ruben Gur's pioneering work has now been corroborated by scientists all over the world. (Please see the notes to the introduction for access to this research).

We studied the brain scans on the videotapes several times and then finished watching the third of the *Brain Sex* tapes (which I highly recommend to everyone). In our professional lives, Gail and I had read material on "the male brain" and "the female brain," but we hadn't seen this kind of concrete proof before. After six years of marriage, we had come face to face with human reality.

I said, "We thought we knew a lot about each other, but maybe we haven't known enough." Gail said, "There really is such a thing as a 'male' brain. It's hard to argue with an MRI." We realized that our communication, our support of each other, and our under-standing of our relationship were just beginning, after six years of marriage.

Accepting the reality that we were significantly different from each other was unavoidable now and marriage saving. We were both human, and it was time we learned to accommodate human nature.

CAN WE *REALLY* KNOW WHAT HE'S THINKING?

People say, "That's so male."

Or: "That's a guy thing."

Or: "Why do men do that?"

With different gender words, the same can be said of women.

These phrases articulate our intuitive knowledge of a fact that the new sciences now actually show us: Females are "female" and males are "male," not only because of their physical and sexual anatomy, but because the brains inside their heads are profoundly different.

Each chapter of this book will explore different aspects of the male brain (since this book is primarily a vision of men's minds), but a great deal of the ever-mysterious female mind will clarify itself, too!

How do we *know* the male brain is different from the female? Pictures, as the saying goes, speak a thousand words. PET scans, or positronic emission tomography, are pictures of the actual brain at work. MRI scans (magnetic resonance imaging) and SPECT scans (single photon emission tomography) can also look inside our heads.

Much of the material in this book is based on the work of scien-tists who take pictures of the male and female brain while the sub-jects think, feel, live, relate, act, and even sleep. These pictures are accessible to all of us now, which makes talking about human nature all the more possible than it was even a decade ago. Before these neural scans, we could say, "There's no such thing as 'human nature.' There's just a blank slate, and then the culture shapes you." Taking it further, we could say, "There's no such thing as 'male nature' or 'female nature.' We all have the same brain, which gets shaped into 'masculine' and 'feminine' by culture. We'll just change the socialization and thus change the man."

We could convince ourselves that our partner could be just like us.

Because of what we've learned from PET scans (as well as SPECT scans and MRIs), this sort of thinking is no longer valid. Though societies, cultural influence, and what is broadly called "nurture" do have much to do with the psychological costumes men and women wear, the male and female brain are "male" and "female" regardless of the culture or the continent on which the men and women are raised. Culture matters, but biology matters much more than we had previously realized.

Given the scientific material we now have, there is great potential for a new understanding of the sexes. I hope you'll find an exciting vision in this book, new insights you can apply toward making your relationships more harmonious and fulfilling. Our first step begins with a clearer picture of what a brain is, and especially, what the male brain looks like.

A FRIENDLY LOOK AT THE MALE BRAIN

Every human brain, whether male or female, has 100 billion neurons, the same number as there are stars and planets in the Milky Way. Just like the light that shoots from a far-away star to our vision in our night sky, signals between the cells in our brain shoot toward each other at the speed of light. When people say, "There's the outer world and the inner soul, and they are mirrors of each other," they are intuitively understanding the fact that our human brains are, in a mysterious way, the mirror image of the cosmos, a concept I developed in more detail in *The Soul of the Child*. I believe the rapid, electromagnetic interactions of cells in the human brain to be one of our most obvious biological reflections of what religions mean when they talk about the "soul."

This amazing brain is formed in utero, and therein begins its journey into a "male" or "female" brain. The tissue and neurons are genetically wired to form in certain ways, and then hormones act on the fetal brain to make it a male or female brain.

Here's how it works in a nutshell:

In the mother's womb, hormones surge at different times to catalyze brain growth. Specifically, at between three and six months in the womb, the human brain of the fetal girl or boy is being bombarded with different hormones. When a forming brain gets bombarded with testosterone, certain cortical areas grow and become connected to other areas. Connections between cortical areas occur in what are called neural pathways. When a developing brain gets bombarded with estrogen and progesterone, certain other cortical areas grow and connect.

If the child in the womb is a chromosomal male child (XY), the mother's hormonal system reads this as "male" and makes sure the child's brain is bombarded with higher degrees of testosterone. If the child in the womb is a chromosomal female child (XX), the mother's hormonal system makes sure her brain is bombarded with higher degrees of female hormones. In the womb, the brain of the child is already being sexualized—feminized or masculinized—by hormones.

Boys and girls and men and women share the same hormones. The fetal boy does not only get testosterone and the fetal girl only estrogen. The brain development of all babies, no matter their sex, is stimulated by all the hormones, just as grown men have some estrogen and grown women have some testosterone. But the signals sent between the mother's ovaries and the fetus depend to a great extent on the XY or XX chromosome. A boy baby is going to get more testosterone, and thus a more "male" brain; a girl baby is going to get more estrogen, thus a more "female brain." By six months into the mother's pregnancy, the boy's and girl's brains have formed and will be mainly affected by his or her own sex hormones from then on.

The development of the male and female brain in the womb can be affected by the stress the mother experiences during her pregnancy. If an expectant mother is under considerable stress—for example, physical abuse, illness, or significant emotional distress—the surges of testosterone and estrogen can be affected. For example, if she is under overwhelming stress, the mother's stress-hormone (cortisol) levels may be very high, which could cut off some of the testosterone surges a male fetus needs for normal development. If this occurs, a chromosomal male child, a boy, might be born with a penis, testicles, male muscle-to-fat ratio, and other physiological male traits—but with a female brain. As he grows, this boy may report feeling like a girl trapped in a boy's body. A PET scan of his brain may well show that he has a female brain system but male physiology and hormones.

Recently, a set of similar cases have been reported on *20/20* and other television and print media. In a natural anomaly, some children are born with both male and female genitals. In the past—and still to a great extent in the present—physicians were not taught in medical school that male and female brains are different. So a doctor might say to parents: "Boys and girls are formed by parents and culture, so let's just pick one gender and surgically change the body to fit." In a famous reported case, the doctor surgically removed the male genitals, making the child a girl. Unfortunately, that "girl" struggled with gender identity and suicidal depression throughout life. At fourteen, the girl was told by her parents and doctor what had been done to her at birth. Finally understanding who she was, she got a sex change. He now lives a life free of suicidal depression and other side effects of having a brain and body that are not in sync.

A great price is paid by the individual whose brain and body are out of sync. Nature keeps the number of individuals who must pay this price to a minimum by helping males develop a male brain and females a female brain before they are born. Cases like the aforementioned demonstrate that though the human brain is definitely plastic and flexible and deeply affected by upbringing, nurture and environment, the maleness and femaleness of the brain is not as malleable as some people would like us to believe. Men and women acquire new neural skills throughout life, but this does not mean the way their brains are set up changes—just as a person's basic personality structure does not change significantly through life. If a person is shy, he's shy; if assertive, she's assertive. People are who they are.

We can teach them new skills, but we shouldn't expect to change the fundamental nature of who they are. In fact, to attempt to do so can be very damaging.

AVOIDING STEREOTYPES

Equally damaging is the perpetuation of stereotypes—whether stereotypes of traditional masculinity and femininity or other new trends in pop culture. As we move forward to explore exactly what we mean by "male" brain and "female" brain, it is important to recognize that human biological sciences don't aim to stereotype people. Biologists have proven a huge spectrum of brain difference among men and women. Within the parameters of the typical male brain is a wide spectrum of possible behaviors. For example, while many men are uncomfortable talking about their feelings, some men can discuss their feelings easily. The male brain (like the female brain) is multifaceted and is capable of doing and being many things at many times.

When we talk about men, we will avoid stereotyping. We will discuss *biological trends* lived by men and by women relating to men. In exploring these trends, we will often generalize about "men" and "women," but in each chapter of the book, we'll also consider exceptions to the rule. We'll explore how these exceptions happen in human evolution. I call them *bridge brains*—male brains and female brains that cross the genders. While biological trends help us to talk about men and women as biological groups, the bridge brains have much to teach us, for they often don't quite fit the group. Nature has always liked the exception as much as the rule.

HOW DO WE RECOGNIZE A MALE BRAIN?

Having glimpsed how the brain grows in the womb, let's now explore an answer to the question, "What do we actually mean by *male* brain?" To do this, we'll look at the structure and functioning of the brain, then specifically detail differences between male and female brain structure and functioning. Toward the end of this chapter, I'll provide a questionnaire that will help you identify qualities of the male and female brain. Your answers will provide you with a personal sense of a man's brain biology and understanding of to what extent a man you know lives life from the perspective of a "male" brain; and also to what extent he, and even you, might be a bridge brain. You can fill this in for yourself, your spouse, your sons, and any other male you know.

Before you fill out the questionnaire, let's look briefly at the brain itself.

The Human Brain

Our brains are divided into three parts.

The brain stem, at the place where neck and spine become skull, is the oldest part of the brain. It handles digestion, breathing, and fight-or-flight muscle responses.

The limbic system, wrapped around the brain stem, is a part of the brain that developed later in human history. It has two primary jobs: to handle our emotional responses to the world and to organize our sensory responses to our environment. The amygdala and hippocampus, which house major differences between males and females, are located in the limbic system. So is the hypothalamus, the part of the brain that primes our hormonal responses.

The four lobes at the top of the brain—occipital, parietal, temporal, and frontal—are wrapped around the limbic system. This *cerebral cortex* or *neocortex* is the newest part of the brain (less than 2 million years old). It is divided into two hemispheres, the right and the left. The neocortex handles our thinking, speaking, moral reasoning, reading, abstracting, designing, idealizations, goal orientations, and more.

The Male Brain

Male and female brains are both set up with these three basic parts. Difference lies in the size of certain parts, as well as how they connect and function. Since the 100 billion neurons talk to each other differently in the male brain and the female, certain parts of brain tissue look different on PET scans.

What follows are some very interesting areas of male and female brain difference. Each of the eight chapters of this book will explore these differences much more fully, but this introduction will give you a basic picture of the male brain.

Differences in spatials. The male brain has developed over millions of years toward a bioenvironmental trend of hunting and building. Even though a man you know may not hunt animals or build buildings in his everyday life, male brains tend toward more development of such complex spatial skills as mechanical design, measurement, direction, abstraction, and manipulation of physical objects. It is because of this that a man is more likely than his wife to spend his Saturday in the garage, using a circular saw to cut wood for a doghouse. Surges of testosterone in the womb and then again at puberty are partly responsible for the male's increased reliance on spatial and mechanical strategies in the brain. These surges have a special effect on spatial functions in the right hemisphere of the male brain.

Differences in verbals. Because the male brain is devoting more cortical areas to spatials, it tends to devote less cortical areas to word use and word production than the female. This is why a man will tend to spend his free time tossing a football or playing a video game, whereas a woman might chat on the phone or curl up with a book.

Connecting the right and left hemispheres of our brains is a small bundle of nerves called the *corpus callosum*. This set of nerves allows cross talk between the two hemispheres. In men, the corpus callosum is, on average, about 25 percent smaller than in women. Because of this, men don't connect as many feelings to words, or even thoughts to words. If the feeling or thought needs to move from the right to the left hemisphere, a man has 25 percent less chance of moving it over. This is crucial because the male brain does its language in the left hemisphere, while women use six or seven cortical areas for language in both hemispheres. The end result is that men have a more difficult time making language out of experience than women do. In fact, they use, on average, about half the amount of words that women do.

Differences in brain chemicals. This difference in word use is connected not only to the structures in the neocortex, but also to differences in the way our brains secrete their chemicals. The secretion of *serotonin* and *oxytocin*, two very powerful chemicals, is stimulated in the hypothalamus. Serotonin calms us down. Men have less serotonin than women. As a result, men tend to act impulsively to a greater degree than women. For example, a man might react to a perceived threat by using physical responses, whereas a woman might try to talk her way out of a situation.

Oxytocin is one of our primary bonding chemicals. When humans feel very connected to someone or something, this feeling comes, to a great extent, from oxytocin. Oxytocin is part of what biologists call the "tend-and-befriend" instinct, often contrasted with the "fight-or-flight" instinct. The higher the oxytocin levels in a brain, the less aggressive the person is likely to be. Furthermore, the person with higher oxytocin levels will tend to be more immediately and directly empathic, and more likely to link bonding and empathy with verbal centers of the brain, asking, "How are you feeling?" or, "Is everything okay?"

Recently, scientists learned that men have less oxytocin than women. Little girls will tend to bond with dolls while boys tend to spend more time spatially, moving balls in real space or moving video figures in virtual space in video games. Girls and women will spend more time relating to others and objects in sedentary, calmer, and more verbal ways, while boys and men will tend to seek quick physical tension release. It is due to lower levels of oxytocin that a man might take longer than a woman to bond, for example, to an adopted infant.

Different bonding strategies. When you drive by a park and see men playing basketball, you are seeing a group of men relying more on "spatials" than "verbals." They are moving an object, a ball, through space, and gaining their bonding pleasure through the task itself, not as much through the use of words. When you drive by a coffee shop and see three women chatting together, you are seeing a group of women relying more on verbals than spatials. They don't tend to want to move an object through space in order to feel good. They don't tend to want a ball—a mediating hunting object—through which to bond with each other. Six to seven language centers in their brains are lighting up as they talk with each other, and their bonding pleasure comes from that. Their brains rely on the quieted impulsivity of serotonin, which gives them the willingness to sit calmly for hours, and the complex bonding chemistry of oxytocin.

Action first, talk second. If there is a "bottom line" of difference in these observations, it can probably be summed up in this way:

Lower levels of serotonin and oxytocin contribute to the male brain's biological tendency to choose action first and talk second.

It is somewhat the opposite for the female brain. Adding to this is the fact that the male brain also does not hear as well. Rather than rely on subtle aural signals, like talk, the male brain responds more quickly to more obvious signals, in action. In the actions of men, you can see the male brain more impulsively moving around, looking for external objects to encounter, than the female. Men are less inclined to stop, be patient, listen, communicate emotions verbally. So if you have a fender bender, for instance, and your husband or partner seems more interested in fixing the car than in listening to you explain how it happened, he's not necessarily being insensitive. It may just be the male brain at work.

Hormones. The hypothalamus signals the secretion of our hormones. Men have a hormonal system that is dominated by testosterone, the sex and aggression hormone. Men have up to twenty times more testosterone than women. Even the most buff woman has lower testosterone than the least muscular man.

Testosterone affects the formation of the male brain, the size of the corpus callosum, the spatial activity in the right hemisphere, and hundreds of other qualities, including increased aggression in males. This aggression might show up in actual physical violence or simply in greater social ambition. For example, corporate CEOs, whether male or female, have high testosterone levels in relation to the average for their gender. Sometimes you see testosterone operating when you pass a video arcade. The kid playing NASCAR is increasing his testosterone levels as he yells at the screen and tries to go faster, faster. Increasing his testosterone level feels good. The man or woman playing soccer is increasing testosterone, and even all the people in the bleachers are increasing theirs as they watch the competition. Competition and testosterone are directly linked in the brains of participant and observer. Testosterone is an important part of human life energy.

The amygdala. Deep in the limbic system is the amygdala, which handles many of our emotions and aggressive impulses. The amygdala is larger in men than women, leading to increased aggression. In the male brain, there is less of a link from the amygdala to other parts of the brain that regulate emotions by moving emotive impulses to the frontal lobe, the thinking part of the brain in the neocortex, for translation into impulse control and moral decision making. As we'll explore more deeply in the next chapter, men and women think differently about ethics, empathy, and morality, in large part because of differences in the amygdala as well as in the neural pathways that link it to the top of the brain.

The hippocampus. This memory center is larger in women than men, and there are more neural pathways from it to emotive centers in women than in men. Have you ever wondered why it seems that women can remember more physical and emotional details than men? Perhaps you've noticed that a woman can often remember the color of the tablecloth, the kind of flowers, and exactly what was eaten at a dinner party six years ago, whereas the man—who was sitting right there at the table—barely remembers a thing. Much of this memory gap between the sexes lies in the male/female hippocampal difference.

Over millions of years, the female brain evolved toward a larger hippocampus, which was more capable of connecting memories, words, and feelings to each other. Probably because women performed intimate care of children and the children's lives depended on a woman's ability to read complex emotive/verbal cues, the female brain evolved this way. Males didn't have to remember these cues while hunting or building, nor make as many connections between memories, words, and feelings. The hippocampal difference, like all the other brain differences covered briefly here, will be more deeply explored in later chapters.

Brains at rest. Women's brains don't rest (zone out, take a break from stress) the way men's brains do. While doing brain scans at the University of Pennsylvania, Ruben Gur discovered that women's brains are constantly working, whereas the male brain "zones out," for instance, in front of the television. Men take "mental naps" more than women do. They stare at the TV screen in front of them, but often they are not actually engaged. The female brain takes fewer mental naps. There is simply more neural activity in general in the female brain at any given time. In fact, there is 15 percent more blood flow in the female brain than in the male, with more brain centers lit up in the female brain at a given moment than in the male.

The cingulate gyrus. When the female brain does rest, more of its neurotransmission stays lodged in the cingulate gyrus, a very important feeling-and-emotion center of the limbic system, than does a male's. The male brain, on the other hand, shows greater neurotransmission in the fight-or-flight brain stem when it naps. In the pictures on television of firemen and policemen running into the World Trade Center during the 9/11 terrorist attacks, we saw a graphic illustration of greater activity in the brain stem of the male brain. Males spend less time than women thinking out their feelings. Especially when the danger signal is triggered, the fight-or-flight mechanism kicks in quicker. Females gain a social advantage by thinking more about their feelings but are also less inclined to rush into danger.

Are Male and Female Brain Differences Lessening or Getting Stronger?

In exploring basic qualities of the male brain in a brief, introductory way, we've only begun our journey into a man's mind. Even in these few pages, you have probably gotten a general picture of a male brain and how it has evolved over millions of years. You might be wondering: Since human life has changed a great deal over the last few thousand years, isn't it reasonable to wonder if the male brain is evolving differently now than it was, say, a few hundred years ago? It is important to answer this question very early in our exploration of the male brain because there is an unspoken question behind it: Can male brains be changed?

Differences and similarities between the male and female brain are both increasing and decreasing today, depending on where you focus. While many men are learning emotional and family life skills their fathers did not have, studies show that, for the most part, the differences in the male and female brain still remain clear. As most of us have learned intuitively in our relationships with the other sex, the maleness or femaleness of the brain is not as changeable as many people might wish.

One key reason is the length of time it took for the brain to form. Until about ten thousand years ago, when the agricultural age began, human beings were hunter/gatherers. In order for our species to survive, we needed to divide labor. Since females carried the organs and hormones for gestating children internally, they were not as well suited for hunting activities. Gathering activities—looking for hidden roots and tubers—as well as child raising, elder care, and intratribal social arrangements were dominated by women. Hunting and large building activities, along with tribal protection, were dominated by men, who were physically, emotionally, and mentally freer to wander and roam, and also more dispensable from a social point of view.

During the agricultural age, which lasted until a few hundred years ago when the industrial age took over, our brains continued this development. As populations grew, and there was more competition for resources, more warfare occurred, larger buildings needed building, larger civilizations needed organizing. Many people moved from nomadic to sedentary life.

In cities, males became physically bigger than they were a hundred thousand years before. They increased muscle mass. Over hundreds of thousands of years, females increased fat-to-muscle ratios. Skeletons got bigger. The male and the female brain continued to develop as male and female, with the spectrum of brain activity growing to meet social technologies. As life got more complex, the brain got more stressed and continued adapting along the lines of the tried-and-true mental division of labor that had helped it survive over millions of years.

The world's population continues to grow, and so we are involved today in heightened competition stress. The more people there are on earth, the more each brain system experiences competition over physical, social, and mental resources. Economic challenges for families are more complex than ever before. As rules for mating and marriage break down, competition for mates becomes more complex. As nuclear and extended family systems break down, individual children are competing for the affections of trusted, bonded adults. We are under significantly increased neural stress from social technologies and direct neural encounters with media, like TV, film, and computers.

It is accurate to say that we are closing gaps between the male and female brain in some areas. For example, since we emphasize verbal skills in our schools (reading, writing, complex thought-to-word ratios), we are forcing boys as a group to do better than they might have thousands of years ago in verbal skills, reading, writing, and complex speech. We are compelling more neural pathways in the male brain to go to work in search of verbal acuity.

Since the marital and other relationships men are involved in rely more on words now than they did when men were hunting millennia ago, their increased verbal skills are adaptive and can serve them well.

Despite these small changes, however, the brain difference in verbals between males and females is still very great. The children who get their language skills later in life (on average, one year later) are boys; the children most likely to fail in verbals and find themselves in Special Education are boys; the children and adults who use fewer words are mainly male; and men are much less likely to read a book than women are. Even beyond these comparisons, some brain researchers believe the gap in word use between men and women may actually be increasing as more women gain more social power and, quite simply, talk more in social settings.

Other male-female difference gaps are also increasing rather than decreasing. The male muscle mass and female fat-to-muscle ratio differences are increasing. We are producing men with larger muscle mass than even a hundred years ago (think of the seven-foot-tall basketball players), and we are producing women with more fat than a hundred years ago. Nutritional, social, and other factors—all of which affect our bodies and brains as men and women—are not only closing male/female gaps but also increasing them.

When we think about men and women, we think about them as large groups, and in this perspective we can certainly say that male/female difference is not at all evolving out of the human condition—it is still very prevalent. Yet when we think of individual men and compare them, for instance, to their own fathers, we can see some very big differences. The beauty of the individual brain is its ability to adapt. All brains develop on a wide spectrum, and they always have. What we can probably say most truthfully now about human brain development is that its spectrum of development is getting wider with every generation. Thus the sheer variety of possibility for male-brain development is widening. Let's take a look at just how wide this spectrum is.

Some Men You Know

On one end of the spectrum is the most male brain we can imagine—low serotonin, low oxytocin, small corpus callosum, small language center. This brain is called *highly masculinized*. It is defined by testosterone surges in the womb.

On the other end of the spectrum is the most female brain we can imagine—high serotonin, high oxytocin, large corpus callosum, many language centers. This brain is defined by lack of testosterone surges in the womb. In a woman, this brain might be called, in popular language, "very feminine." In males, we would call it a bridge brain.

To think about the very masculinized brain system, think of action heroes in movies. These men are singularly task focused. There isn't much cross talk between hemispheres. They like things that are loud and that blow up—they possess less aural neurons, so loud noises don't bother them. These men do not rely much on word production. In *The Terminator,* Arnold Schwarzenegger's character speaks perhaps thirty words in all.

These men emphasize aggression rather than direct empathy, possessing an enlarged amygdala with less neural signals to the frontal lobes; and they have high testosterone. Schwarzenegger's typical male character is relatively emotionless, though he is certainly compassionate with those to whom he has bonded. Possessing a smaller hippocampus, with low-range neural pathways to emotive centers, he does not rely heavily on personal memories or sensory detail.

He is very spatial and mechanical—he relies on objects moving in space with mechanical design—cars, trucks, guns, bullets, his own fists—enjoying more right-hemisphere cortical use, less left.

Action heroes give us an illustration of the very polar end of masculinization on the brain spectrum. Schwarzenegger is playing a stereotype, of course. Stereotypes generally tend to be the polar ends of spectrums because they are simplistic, and simplistic characters tend to be good ones on which to hinge simple, entertaining tales. Yet even as stereotypes, they are recognizable as the most "masculine" end of the brain spectrum.

On the other end of the spectrum—the most neurally female end—we can picture the most talk-oriented, nonspatial woman. She would love soft things. She would have a hard time getting a basketball into a basket or trying to hit a softball with a bat. As a little child, she'll want to hold and care for dolls as much as possible, cooing to them and talking to them. She won't like loud noises, since she hears very well. She'll have a better-than-average sense of smell and taste. She'll probably love to read. Even as an adult, she won't be able to tell us how tall a building is by looking at it, but she'll have an acute color sense.

You might say, "He's stereotyping women now." I am, indeed, painting an extreme portrait of a polar end on the brain spectrum. I am describing women with almost no testosterone at all. These women are generally born without ovaries, thus their bodies produce very little testosterone. Since they had no ovaries, very little testosterone was secreted during gestation by their developing brains and bodies. Thus they have a very "female" brain, nearly untouched by the masculinization of testosterone.

Their spatial and mechanical design functions in the right hemisphere tend to be underdeveloped, so they don't rely on these as much as other women might. Many of these women even find driving a car more difficult. Their brains generally have more highly developed cortical areas for verbals, sensual, and tactile experience. With little testosterone, they have better than average hearing, making loud noises painful. They see a broader spectrum of color than even the average girl or woman. Galvanic skin-response tests show their under-the-skin nerves to be immensely sensitive. They have low pain tolerance.

With the highest testosterone male and the female who can't produce testosterone, we have illustrations at the extremes of the brain spectrum, useful, not to define us as human beings, but to help us see the outer boundaries of masculine and feminine brain development. In order to help you see where a specific man in your life falls on the spectrum, I have created a questionnaire, written to the male point of view. If you are a woman, you can certainly answer it for a man you know well. I'll refer to a man's companion in this survey as "wife," but please substitute another appellation—e.g., girlfriend or partner, as is appropriate in your life. If you take this test "for" your spouse, you might check the answers with him. You might be right on most of them but wrong on a few. Discussion of this test can make for fun and fruitful conversation.

THE MALE-BRAIN QUESTIONNAIRE

On another sheet of paper, list "A" "B" and "C." Pick one answer for each item, making for ten answers in total. Give each A answer 3 points, each B answer 2 points, and each C answer I point. At the end, figure the total points.

1. When you are in the car talking to your wife about a party you've both just gone to, she says something like, "Did you notice Judith and Tony seemed to be having marital problems?"

    A.   Judith and Tony's relationship is not something you want to talk about.
    B.   Now that you think back on it, maybe there's something to what your wife is saying, but you didn't notice anything between Judith and Tony at the party.
    C.   You noticed trouble between Judith and Tony during the party.

2. When you and your wife sit together to "channel surf' in front of the TV, possession of the remote control is very important to your enjoyment of the experience.

    A.   You will become anxious if you do not have control of it; she will want to watch programs that bore you or make you agitated.

   B.   You will not enjoy yourself if you do not have control of the remote control, but it's okay with you if she controls it a small percentage of the time.

   C.   It really doesn't matter to you what channels she or you channel surf to during the time together in front of the TV.

3. When you and your wife talk about things that happened many years ago, she remembers how everything looked, what was said by whom, and other exact sensory and feeling details.

   A.   You rarely remember these experiences with as much detail.

   B.   You often remember these experiences with as much detail.

   C.   You have as good a memory as she does for these sorts of sensual details.

4. Your wife complains that you don't hear her or that you don't listen to her.

   A.   A lot of the time.

   B.   Some of the time.

   C.   Never or almost never.

5. When you are looking into your computer or doing another task of concentration, you have difficulty (and even become impatient or irritable) when your wife interrupts you to talk or to ask questions.

   A.   A lot of the time.

   B.   Some of the time.

   C.   Rarely.

6. When your wife has had a hard day or is obviously hurting about something and wants to talk to you about it:

    A.   You feel anxiety.

    B.   You listen briefly then try to help her solve the problem she faces.

    C.   You are excited by the opportunity to connect with her and explore her feelings with her.

7. When you see a bunch of kids playing a physical game and a boy falls down:

    A.   You immediately say, "You're fine. Get up and get back in there."

    B.   You observe passively for a while to see if he's okay, and if you think he is, you challenge him to get back up and into the game.

    C.   You move, physically, toward him and bend down to him to see if he's okay and help him up.

8. In a utopian world where you are king and can spend your free time as you choose, you would prefer to do which of the following:

    A.   To exercise and/or play something physical and athletic or to play a nonphysical competitive game (like chess or poker) or to work on a project or hobby that involves building or repairing something with your hands.

    B.   To relax and read a book during a beautiful sunset or call a friend and chat.

    C.   To shop, preferably with someone who enjoys that activity as much as you do.

9. When you go on a drive or family trip, it's important to you to
    know where north, south, east, and west are.

    A. More often than your spouse.
    B. About the same as your spouse.
    C. Less often than your spouse.

10. While you and your wife are studying some written material,
    the radio playing in the background changes from one song to
    another.

    A. You are less likely than your wife to hear it quickly and
        comment on it.
    B. You and she apprehend and express the change in sound
        and song with the same frequency.
    C. You are more likely than your wife to hear this and
        comment on it.

The Score

The highest possible score on this test is thirty, the lowest is ten. All
scores, even the extremes of thirty and ten, are within the range of
normal, so there is no "bad" score. To say that one score is better than
another would be like saying that an assertive personality is better
than a shy personality. Obviously, one's personality is simply one's
psychosocial ground of being; it is not something to be judged.

This test and the score received is only one measure of where a
man fits on the brain spectrum and ought to be used for entertainment and interest only.

If the man scores between twenty and thirty, his brain system
probably leans toward the more male end of the brain spectrum. If
he scores below twenty, his brain system leans more toward the

female end of the spectrum, and he may be a bridge brain. There is no way to know beyond a doubt from this survey, but each of us probably has an intuitive sense of who is a bridge brain. A PET scan is a good tool for exact knowledge of bridge brains, but this technology is presently too expensive for common use.

BRIDGE BRAINS

On the questionnaire, I score a twenty-four. In trying to help people understand the men in their lives, I try to share freely who I am. Given my personal understanding of the life I've lived, what the people close to me tell me about myself, my male-brain questionnaire results, and other medical studies, like endocrinological studies on my testosterone levels, I think that on the brain spectrum mine is about 60 percent "male" and about 40 percent "female."

Given all the markers I've been able to gather, as well as my questionnaire results (I scored three on six answers, two on three answers, and one on one answer), I wouldn't call myself a bridge brain. In specific areas, however, I have bridge-brain qualities: for instance, in my enjoyment of discussing my feelings. I answered C on this one (question 6), and as Gail will attest, sometimes I go on and on about what I'm feeling! This result might make me think I'm a bridge brain; yet I don't think that's true. My emotive expression is an example of a brain quality that can appear to be at the female end of the spectrum but also can be quite masculinized. When I'm in emotive crisis, I do not rely much on words; rather, I tend to look for quick tension release or take a long hard run, or go inward and silent, or delay my reactions (see chapter 3 for more details on how the male brain tends to prefer to handle emotions). So though I enjoy listening to Gail discuss her feelings and experiences, and I enjoy talking about my own if I'm not in an agitated state, I am still pretty "male" in my responses to my own feelings when I'm very stressed or upset.

What I would call a true bridge-brain male will answer 1 to question 6, and would also probably rely on words to express his own feelings more than he does on physical action, quick tension release, or problem solving. He might well have a worse sense of direction than his spouse. He might not really enjoy sports or games as much as sensual activities like shopping, and he might be drawn to provide hands-on nurturing for people in need. He would probably have lower ambition than many people around him (he's not lazy, just not too driven to conquer the world). He has a job and does well at it but tacitly cares more about his relationships with the people he meets there than about furthering the product. He would probably not be effective in a high-power sales position because it requires high degrees of social aggression. When he channel surfs in front of the TV, he might enjoy dramas and shows with a lot of emotional conversation and romantic tension. He may well not be as driven by the need for sexual variety as are some of the men he knows. This bridge-brain male might be experiencing slightly higher estrogen/progesterone levels than the average male and lower testosterone. This would be wired into his hypothalamus and will probably have begun during gestation.

Frank is most probably a bridge-brain male. Here's what he wrote me:

I am a first grade teacher. When I was a boy, I liked being with the girls more than the boys. I'm heterosexual, so this wasn't about being gay. It was more about that I thought like girls rather than boys. It caused my parents a lot of consternation. They thought I just wouldn't make it in the world. My mother tried to change me more subtly than my dad did, but both of them were very worried about me. I liked jewelry, girls-clothes, dress up. There were a lot of tomboys who were more boy-like than me.

It was worse in school and then during Vietnam. In school, I was pretty bad at all sports, and I wasn't very competitive at all. I got beat up, harassed. I signed up for the Selective Service, but I couldn't imagine having to kill anyone. It wasn't about religion for me. It was more about who I was—I just wasn't going to go kill. Luckily, my number wasn't called.

I heard you speak the other night about bridge brains and that's what I think I am. I have two children now and ironically, my son is very male. I joke with my wife that he takes after her more than me. It's so interesting to have a son like this—I think this is the son my parents were hoping they would get.

I later met Frank and learned through our conversations that he had suffered far more than his E-mail described. He was a bridge-brain male who had grown up with a brain system that was, especially during his boyhood, out of sync with social expectations for men.

How Many Bridge-Brain Males Are There in the World?

There is probably no way to know for sure how many actual bridge-brain males there are in the world. In the future, perhaps we'll be able to PET scan everyone. For now, we can only estimate. While all of us have at least one bridge-brain quality, I would estimate that about 25 percent of males worldwide are actual bridge brains. That is a significant number.

As we said earlier, every male is somewhat of a bridge because every man has some estrogen/progesterone in him. And if we approach humans on a spiritual level, we must certainly say that we all combine the masculine and feminine. However, the statistical probability is that a woman reading this book will be in an intimate relationship, not with a bridge-brain male, but with a man who possesses more masculine than feminine neural qualities. This can present a problem because the bridge-brain male has become idealized by many women during the last four decades. Many women wish there were a lot more bridge-brain males out there since it seems, at least in theory, that it would be easier for women to relate to these guys because they're more female in their thinking.

Throughout this book, I'll develop different aspects of how this idealization of bridge brains is one of the reasons our relationships struggle so much today. When women idealize the bridge-brain male

and feel betrayed that most men—quite often the ones they love—
are just not that kind of man, they have unconsciously bought into
the idea that to be in love we must be emotionally alike and relationally immersed in each other. Luckily, this is simply not true.

THE THEORY OF INTIMATE SEPARATENESS

Throughout our understanding of brain research, we come face to
face with modes of relationship. To study the human brain is to
study how human beings love and are loved. When I first began
researching information about the human brain, I didn't realize this.
I was merely curious. I wanted to increase my professional knowledge and, if possible, know myself better. As my interest grew, I
wanted to be a better therapist, father, and community member. I
could not see what I see now: Once we come to the center of our
understanding of each other's minds and hearts, we discover a key to
long-lasting relationship: the theory of intimate separateness. What
we learn about the nature of the male and the female brain takes us
face-to-face with a very important theoretical and practical framework for long-lasting love, relationship, and marriage.

There are many theories in social philosophy and self-help fields
on how to have happy and long-lasting intimate relationships. Many,
if not all, carry a kernel of truth. As family therapists, Gail and I
have taught and lived many of them, but none has been as powerful
for us as the theory of intimate separateness. If the two words juxta-
posed, "intimate" and "separateness," feel paradoxical to you, there is
good reason. It seems that nature has set us up to love each other
through paradox, setting human love relationships to be a union of
contradictions, who hinge their own and their children's future on
creating understanding and compassion by means of both intimacy
and separateness. When people say "s/he is the opposite sex," or
"opposites attract," their intuition is borne out by brain research. The
male and female brain are not only inherently different, but those
biological differences are expanded by the pressures of intimacy.

Throughout the book I intend to show that intimate separateness is essential to human brain functioning and can bring happiness and success to your relationships. Each chapter will develop a different aspect of the theory of intimate separateness. In the next few pages, let me set the foundation of the theory.

The most basic way to explain it is this: Brain growth seems to indicate the necessity for a rhythmic pattern of attachment *and* detachment between human beings. If we get too close to each other, the brain feels stress. If we get too far away from each other, the brain feels stress. The brain is looking for a balance of closeness and separateness. This is especially obvious in two primordial dyads or pairs:

1. Parent-child pairs throughout the child's maturation process.

2. Married couples or partners in a long-term relationship.

I am emphasizing long-term relationships in talking about this theory because, as we'll explore in chapter 4, during the six months or so of initial sexual romance, or during one-night stands and other quick love relationships, separateness is not essential; brain and body want intimacy. It is generally subsequent to the early romance stage of love relationships that intimate separateness becomes essential.

There appear to be natural rhythms in human nature for attachment and detachment that begin in infancy and continue throughout life. The metaphor of ocean tides is often used to describe these. We come toward our child or lover, then move away, toward and away, like the tide moving in, then out.

As babies, we are attached to caregivers, yet we also detach from them to observe the world. As we grow, we gradually separate from them, though continuing to love them. Separation means we become increasingly independent in the psychological sense: Our brains grow toward self-reliance. In adolescence, we make an almost traumatic separation from our parents. Males tend to make a more defined separation from parents than females do.

During the last decade, we've been able to see, with brain-

imaging equipment, how the brain works when it attaches and sepa-
rates. We can move beyond the metaphor of tides to watch the
rhythm of intimacy and separateness in the brain. With equipment
that measures cortisol (stress hormone) levels, we can actually measure the rhythm in brain chemistry. For instance, when a person
moves across a room toward the person she or he needs at that
moment, stress hormones decrease; when she or he walks away, they
increase. But if a person moves toward a person he or she does not
need at that moment, stress hormones increase; when he or she
moves away from this person, they decrease. The human brain is
sending signals through stress hormone levels about attachment and
separation at given moments during the day and during a lifetime.

Before brain research, an unconscious belief existed that human
stress was always decreased and human love increased by intimacy.
Brain research shows us that our own internal nature has relational
intelligence wired into it. This intelligence seeks to manage the natural need for ebb and flow of attachment and separation. This relational intelligence doesn't just seek to ensure more intimacy; it also
seeks *less* intimacy at given times of the day, week, month, year, or
lifetime. As we'll discuss further in chapters 3, 4, and 5, this is especially true the further along the masculine end of the spectrum the
man or woman is. To the more male brain, forced and constant intimacy is often too much—it feels like enmeshment, imprisonment.
Everyone needs privacy and separateness during a relationship;
many men need it more than we've realized.

While the theory of intimate separateness grows most clearly from
the study of the male brain, it is of immense value to the female
brain as well. Women tend to present to their relationship partners a
malleable self. Higher oxytocin levels are one primary reason. In
search of bonds, attachments, and intimacy, they will often "give
themselves up" to a relationship, then—years later—feel utterly
trapped. Among men, the feeling of being trapped tends to enter a
relationship much earlier. Men tend to be less malleable than
women, leaning more toward greater independence. Higher testosterone levels are a primary reason. In the male/female dynamic, the
separateness that the male yearns for and the intimacy that the

female yearns for create competing ebb and flow. If they are not managed by the partners, that competing ebb and flow can destroy the relationship. If men and women better understand the practice of intimate separateness, it is possible to create a middle ground for long-term partnerships that benefits both women and men. As we discuss intimate separateness throughout this book, we will help relationships and marriages gain immense strength. Gail and I have experienced this new relationship strength. We've found the intimate separateness we need. As you'll see in case studies I'll share throughout the rest of this book, everyone can practice intimate separateness. It is often a simple and clear adaptation of destructive behaviors in a relationship or marriage.

THE POWER OF *NATURAL IDENTITY* IN OUR RELATIONSHIPS

After centuries of having a relatively limited view of the variety in human natural identity, our twentieth-century humanity experimented with the idea that human nature was only a small part of human life and love. This led to innovations in social technologies and to the expansion of male and female social roles. At the same time, these innovations led to a neglect of the natural identities of men and women. We swung the pendulum of human thinking very far away from our knowledge of biological identity, so that most people now try to carry on relationships without a deep appreciation of the minds and hearts of their own partners. This has transpired as we neglected millions of years of natural history. There is always a consequence to that! As the old TV commercial put it, "It's not nice to fool Mother Nature."

In each of the following chapters, I will conclude my exploration of the male brain with evidence of the intimate power relationships gain when the brain system is fully understood. When we remove our cultural blindness to human nature, we gain healthy power. In my books *The Wonder of Boys* and *The Wonder of Girls*, I explored how thinking about boys' and girls' natural identities can positively and permanently alter our ability to fully love our children. Ultimately, the work we do to understand the natural identity of boys and girls and women and men affects, not only individual people and relationships, but also our whole society. Through this work, we can move humanity into new successes at all levels. Fortunately, the new sciences are now showing us the unlimited potential of human nature. These sciences are not taking us back into old roles. In fact, quite the opposite. They liberate us to discover who and what a person really is. They free us to make love convincingly, to love compassionately, to honor the human soul, to notice human courage, to make marriages work again, and to care for others as human beings yearn to do.

Understanding the men in your life is a path to power: power in your home, in your workplace, in your family, and on the street. To delve more deeply into this power, let's now ask the fundamental question, "What is a man?" and answer it as only nature can.

2

How Nature Answers the Question, What Is a Man?

Why does he do what he does? He's so driven, but by what?

—Anne, thirty-six, married, mother of two, economist

"Being a man" is so important to boys and men!
It's just so built into them.

—Tracy, thirty-three, single, school counselor

Steven Spielberg's World War II film *Saving Private Ryan* ends with two of the most moving scenes in American cinema. In the first scene, Captain Miller, played by Tom Hanks, is dying on a stone bridge in a French village. His right hand shakes and his eyes are glassy as Private Ryan, played by Matt Damon, bends down to hear his last words. Captain Miller whispers, "Earn this."

Private Ryan stares at him, watching him die. The camera shows us Matt Damon's face as he tries to comprehend what Miller means. We then see a match cut to Private Ryan's face decades later, when he's in his seventies. Ryan's face as a young man becomes, cinematically, his face as an old man and now he is standing with his family at Captain Miller's grave. Tears rise in his eyes as he remembers the profound words spoken to him by Captain Miller years before.

"Earn this." A man must earn his life.

Like all men, Captain Miller knew this primal truth: that a man's place in the world and his worth as a man is rarely, if ever, given to him. Miller was a mentor during the war to young men like Ryan who needed to understand what it meant to be a man. And Ryan was, in the French village long ago, not only every man, but also an individual young man with a heavy weight on his shoulders: His three brothers had been killed. Captain Miller and his crew had been sent in to save Ryan, to help him get home, as he was now the only child left to help work the family farm in Iowa. When Captain Miller murmured, "Earn this," he was not only saying, "You are a man who must earn his way in the world," he was also saying, "Many people have died so that you could live. You, James Ryan, need to make something of yourself."

Looking up from Captain Miller's grave and from his memories, his eyes brimming with tears, the elderly Private Ryan turns to his wife and asks, "Have I done it? Have I led a good life? Have I been a good man?"

His wife, touched by his emotion, even though she doesn't fully understand its primal importance in this man's life, assures him, "Yes, you have."

The camera pulls back and we see James Ryan, his wife, his children and grandchildren, and the graves of thousands of men who have died so that he could earn a life.

In the whispery command uttered by the dying young captain, "Earn this," is one of the core truths of male nature. In the question, uttered by an old man, "Have I been a good man?" is the hope that the core truth has been lived.

In this chapter I hope to show you that the life of a man—various, complex, irreducible—begins in the male brain's drive to prove worth against all wounding, all hardship, all challenge.

I hope to show you that boys and men make a lifelong, nature-based search for self-worth, and that their search, while similar in its humanity, is very different from a girl's or a woman's.

THE DESPAIR OF MEN AND THE CORE OF MANHOOD

Born in the "baby boom" generation, many men you know grew up in a time that took "man" out of the human dialogue and replaced it with "gender roles." "Becoming a man" lost its meaning. For a few men, this seemed to work well; but for most men, this became an invisible despair that first attacks adolescent males, touching their lives with confusion and, at times, the urge to destroy their communities and their society. Research over a twenty-year period has shown us that most men of the baby boom generation, and therefore the women who love them, face despair at some point. Books like Susan Faludi's *Stiffed*, Robert Bly's *The Sibling Society*, Christina Hoff Sommers's *The War Against Boys*, my own *A Fine Young Man*, *Angry Young Men*, by Aaron Kipnis, Warren Farrell's *The Myth of Male Power*, Sam Osherson's *Finding Our Fathers*, and David Blankenhorn's *Fatherless America* have hoped to show the despair of men and boys who try to live without a clear sense of male identity.

The despair of inadequate identity development can come to anyone in this circumstance—male or female. For men particularly, it is not only the despair of not knowing how to value the nature of maleness but also the despair of being ashamed of being male. According to recent research, if a man does not learn who he is, he will tend to experience the devaluing of self and the despair in one or more of these ways:

- By wandering in search of something in life and relationships that he never finds and ultimately punishing others for withholding it from him.
- By becoming a workaholic who only provides material goods for his family, not the love they need.
- By seeking power over women.
- By stretching ethical standards beyond the breaking point and lacking compassion when others are harmed (for instance, corporate and other business ethics violations).
- By physically or socially attempting to destroy others

who appear to hold identity and territorial authority (for instance, gang violence or terrorism).

In very human terms, the hidden despair many men feel was put to me in a letter from Sandoval, forty-seven, a father of two and a psychologist:

When I was young, in my teens and twenties, I wanted to know what it meant to be a man. I couldn't really get answers, and this led to a lot of pain for me and for other people. Two decades of my life were really about experimenting on other people to figure out who I was. I wasn't a bad person, I didn't want to hurt people, especially women I loved; but I didn't want some group, depending on their politics or religion, telling me what they thought a man *should* be. I wanted to know what a man actually is. I wanted to find some sort of core of manhood. Even in my early thirties, I still felt bad about being male and still didn't know who I was.

Sandoval's identity crisis has become a great problem in contemporary society—so many men wandering and never finding, obsessed by work at all costs, seeking power over women, hurting or dominating other people in order to make themselves feel worthy. Fortunately, our culture is awakening to the despair of boys and men. I will not focus on it, for that focus would repeat work that has already been done by myself and other researchers. Instead, I will present what I think is the core of manhood from a neurobiological perspective. What is it that Sandoval and, to a great extent, all men are trying to find? What is this identity they seek?

I hope to show you in these next pages that at the biological core of manhood is the drive and will to prove self-worth, not just as a person, but as a male. This core of manhood represents maleness at its best—self-sacrificing, devoted to service, loving, wise and powerful, and at its worst—brutal, shaming, destructive, dangerous.

As with every point made in this book, I will be asserting what a man *could* be thinking. I do not presume to understand everything about what a particular man *is* thinking. This list is only a list.

THE BIOLOGY OF MALE IDENTITY

Have you noticed these things?

- Men will tend to put their pursuit of self-worth and personal power first, intimacy second. It's much more difficult to get a man to put the hands-on care of his family before work at the office that needs to be finished.
- Men tend to relate to others with greater degrees of personal independence than women do. Men tend to expect more independent behavior from children than women do.
- Men tend to search out ways to become wounded, show off their wounds, live by their swords, make games out of giving and getting wounds. They test themselves. They push themselves into physical pain as much as possible, such as playing a sport even when they are injured or avoiding the doctor when they really should go.
- Men do not tend to be as satisfied as their wives often seem to be with making a nest and exploring the relationships within it; they tend to need to leave the nest, even project distant abstract goals through which to experience their own sense of power and worth.
- Men tend to berate each other, cut each other down, negate each other, and generally treat each other in ways women find nasty and mean. Yet the men laugh, jostle, jest, motivate, and seem to feel helped, supported, and loved in the process.
- Men yearn to show bravery and courage, to sacrifice themselves toward the highest possible standards of

worth and power, against all odds, seeking the power and status that come from battling the impossible and making it possible. During the Vietnam War, when men sacrificed themselves and lost rather than gained status, they sensed that collective manhood had been betrayed.

Many of these tendencies have been identified in our culture and studied from a social or psychological perspective. Let us deepen our understanding of men by adding the biological perspective. As we understand the core of manhood by means of biological trends, we will be exploring the effect of these elements of biology on male life:

- **Testosterone, the dominant male hormone, associated with sex and aggression, the search for social power, ambition, and independence.**
- **Vasopressin, a brain chemical males have more of than females, associated with territoriality, hierarchy, competition, and persistence.**
- **Oxytocin, a brain chemical more dominant in females, associated with maternal nurturance, verbal-emotive connection, and empathic bonding.**
- **Differences between men and women in the way their brains gather sensory and sensual information.**
- **The male brain's greater development of cortical areas for spatial thinking and abstract systems.**
- **The role of female hormones, including estrogen and progesterone.**
- **Biopsychological drives to discover and express potency that are hardwired into male reproductive processes.**

The Performance Imperative

Understanding the core of manhood begins in noticing the performance imperative in most men. Most of us have observed men doing, doing, doing:

- The workaholic man.
- The man competing constantly.
- The man racing his car through the stoplight just to show that he can.
- The man pushing his child to be his or her best.
- The man who sacrifices his life for others based on a supreme principle he believes in.
- The man who believes he is worthless unless he feeds his family.
- The man who sits watching a sunset, but only for a moment, then moves back to his job.

Both women and men can have these experiences, but there is a biological tendency in men to seek self-worth through personal, independent performance; in women, there is a greater tendency to experience worth through relationships and intimacy. This difference, while certainly socialized in all cultures, finds its origins in human biology.

Given the higher levels of the bonding chemical, oxytocin, in the female bloodstream and brain system, as well as higher degrees of estrogen and progesterone that enhance similar kinds of bonding, and given that men are driven by testosterone, an aggression hormone, a biological foundation is laid, in women, for the development of identity through what I have called an intimacy imperative. In men, the biological foundation is laid for a performance imperative.

Against All Odds, and Even in Pain

Testosterone propels men toward taking greater risks, pushing their own and others' limits, acting independently or in clear hierarchies toward goals, even if it means getting hurt. The male neural web itself is another key to this imperative, especially brain activity in the very top of the brain—the cerebral cortex (sometimes called the "neocortex" for short).

Men don't hear as much as women do nor take in as much from the other senses. Galvanic skin-response tests show that male skin is less sensitive than a female's—a woman's skin is ten times more sensitive to touch than a man's. Male skin takes in less physical pain, and brain scans show less neocortical activity in pain responses. Men and women, in short, experience physical pain differently. Less sensitive to pain, men don't tend naturally to shy away from it. Even more than that, men seem to seek out pain.

Nature-based theory suggests that men may unconsciously spend their lives trying to experience as much pain as women come by naturally through menstruation and childbirth. I don't know how one would prove scientifically this theory of biological motivation for the male pain and self-testing process, but there is no doubt that it is a biological trend for males in not one or many but in all cultures to seek out more self-testing and physical pain than women do. No matter the culture, the male search for potency often overwhelms other concerns, and the male brain helps this happen. When we say, "Wow, that man is driven!" or, "My son just won't quit!" we are seeing, among other things, male testosterone at work, and we're seeing fewer pain centers in the male, thus less resistance to the demands testosterone makes on the body and brain system.

AGGRESSION NURTURANCE

Men tend to relate to others through aggression nurturance more than women, who tend biologically toward empathy nurturance. This one difference—born of hormones, reproductive systems, and the brain system differences—creates constant confusion between women and men. Women often think men are insensitive—even immoral—because they seem to have less natural empathy than women. Men often think women are "soft" or "weak" because they lack the aggression responses of men. Couples often see this in conflicting parenting styles. A man wrote me: "My wife thinks I don't care about the kids as much as she does because I push them so hard. I think I do. We fight about this a lot." He went on to describe a conflict over how he helps his children with homework. He calls his style "hard-nosed," but she calls it "insensitive." When I wrote him back, asking him how the children were doing, he said they were flourishing—except for his and his wife's fights. When I asked his wife to write her side of this, she agreed that she thinks his style is harmful, yet she agreed that the two children were doing well in the most important aspects of their school work and relationships.

This couple, like so many of us, were in conflict over naturally different nurturing styles. Both women and men are very nurturing, but they often nurture others—including mates and offspring—in a fundamentally different way. The male biological trend is to nurture the self-esteem of another person by challenging that person to create a neural bypass around a traumatic event and return to the pre-set goal. Men tend to see the goal as the high priority and need to be convinced that a person, even a child, is really incapacitated. This is aggression nurturance, though it can be painful for a child or friend.

When a man walks by a child playing basketball who has just fallen down, he is far more likely to say, "Get up, get back in there," than is a woman, even if the child's knee is skinned. For the man, this is the best way to protect the child's journey toward potency, self-esteem, and self-worth. The female biological trend is to nurture the self-esteem of another person by encouraging the emotional processing of a traumatic event. Since her brain system includes far more emotion-based pathways than the man's, she tends to project her emotion-based thinking onto the world. She would want someone to bend down and ask how she was doing. Getting the ball in the basket can wait—it's just a bunch of metal and netting! Since she would want someone to be empathic if she were hurt, she gives to the world what she'd want back. The man is also doing this in his own way.

The female style of nurturance has become the norm for nurturance in the last decades. Immediate empathy, combined with emotional processing, has become the social ideal. For people relating to males, this can be confusing because the biological trend among males remains to be who they are: Men who tend to be less sensitive to others' emotional needs and more inclined to push others toward personal repression of feeling and expression of self through goal setting and risk taking.

If we resist prejudging the male nurturance style and, instead, consider that nature has evolved this behavior in our lives for a reason, we come to see it in a different light. Direct empathy in the face of life's little traumas is a crucial and useful female biological skill but not a superior style. It emphasizes bonding and emotional literacy at the expense of goal setting and independence. Male nurturance is an essential element, too, even in the interaction between child and adult. The self-esteem of all humans is as much aided by goal setting and independent self-reliance as by direct empathy and emotional processing.

A hundred years ago, our defining political structures—like our religions—overemphasized the male style; in the last decades our popular psychological and sociological literature has overemphasized the female style. When we see these nurturance styles as biological trends rather than religious or sociological constructs, we respect both styles. Both are crucial to the nature of the developing human.

Where He Gets His Sense of Significance, Power, and Self-Worth

Men certainly can get a great deal of their sense of significance and self-worth from their children. That is a given. In women, there is a biological urge, encouraged by society, to make their children, especially their very young children, the center of their lives. Women have neural and hormonal pathways for attachment to children that are different from men's. When they become pregnant, for instance, progesterone and oxytocin levels rise exponentially in comparison to similar male increases of these bonding chemicals. During the stage of a woman's life that involves raising children, we generally find a larger part of her self-worth defined by her children than we do a man's. Women are, thus, neurochemically attached to children. In all cultures, males tend to need to rely on emotional and social attachment to children in order to develop commensurate bonds with infants and toddlers that women get directly from hormones and brain chemicals.

It is natural to begin a discussion of how a parent gains power and self-worth by mentioning the children because we know that all parents gain a great deal of power and self-worth from procreation. Given the differences in male/female bonding biology, the drive to gain certain degrees of power and self-worth outside of parenting is, for men, stronger than for women who are raising their children.

Many people do not need brain science to lead them to this understanding. Many people have intuitively noticed that a man's self-worth is often more directly defined by his actions in the larger social and work world than by his actions as a father. A client once told me, "Men seem to be trying for the 'big' things in life, and women seem to get more out of the 'small' things in life." My client explained herself. Whether it's tidying the house or arranging the flowers on her desk at work or wiping her child's nose, women seem to get more significance from fulfilling these sensual things. Men, she felt, have their eyes elsewhere.

My client was describing the biological trend, set in the male and female brain, which often gets amplified by cultural socialization. The male brain, more spatially oriented, focuses on abstractions more than the female brain, which is more sensually oriented. The male brain does seem, more often, to need abstractions—principles, companies, hierarchies, sports—through which to attach and find meaning.

The Cambridge University sociobiologist Simon Baron-Cohen has recently elaborated this point in *The Essential Difference*, a new scholarly work on male and female biology, which presents a body of biological evidence to show that men have a tendency to analyze and construct *systems* while women are inclined to empathize. Where a woman's brain will tend automatically to empathize with the individual involved in a life situation, the male brain will tend automatically to fit that individual (including the self) into an abstract system of principles and hierarchies.

UCLA psychology professor Shelley Taylor, in *The Tending Instinct*, has argued, "A woman is biologically hard-wired to nurture, provide comfort and seek social support in times of stress. Our hormones, brain chemistry and response to the world around us all reflect this natural inclination. Men have (the tend-and-befriend) instinct too, but to a lesser degree because of hormone differences and personal choices."

The female brain seems to get more meaning from what it touches, smells, who she listens to, who confides in her. For women, especially mothers of young children, oxytocin and other hormone levels are high, contributing to the common tendency to give up full-time, ambition-track, hierarchical jobs. A woman's brain chemicals drive her to care for the child and gain meaning therein. Unlike the brain chemistry formatted by testosterone, women at this stage of life do not appear as much to need large hierarchies in which to find personal power and meaning.

Testosterone is the male hormone that gets the most attention when it comes to motivation of the male drive toward hierarchical self-expression. But another powerful brain chemical, vasopressin, also plays a part. It is initially found, like oxytocin, in the hypothalamus. It regulates sexual persistence, aggression, hierarchical displays, and territorial marking. It does this not only in humans but in other higher mammals. Not surprisingly, vasopressin, like testosterone, is found in larger quantities in males. It is another reason that the care of infants is not and never will be dominated by men. Nor will first-grade classrooms ever be taught by more men than women. Those classrooms need higher levels of oxytocin, not vasopressin. High school classrooms are more likely to have more male teachers because adolescents are already more independent and thus may now need the kinds of aggression challenges that males bring to them.

"Men will sit around arguing about things like sports," a woman, thirty-six, E-mailed: "They think who has the best team or the best pitcher is important, but a lot of it seems boring to me. I try not to be judgmental."

"Once I had my daughter," a mom wrote, "I couldn't wait to give up working. My job just didn't seem as important to me as it did before I had Chloe."

"I had my son and looked into his eyes and knew why I was put on this earth," a mom wrote. She enjoys working outside the home but has cut it back to half time.

"I watch the 'men' and don't understand a lot of their priorities," a woman, twenty-one, in college, wrote. "They're going in a very different direction than me. I think they're still boys, but I'm already a woman."

Each of these comments reveals a biological distinction between vasopressin and oxytocin, testosterone and estrogen/progesterone. It can liberate our thinking to focus on brain chemistry as the foundation of our being. While some of those college males may very well be immature, many may simply be men driven by hormones that seem contradictory to a young woman who has not yet fully understood how different her own oxytocin base is from a testosterone base. By the same token, if a young mother is assumed by a man to be inferior to him because she has turned away from a product-oriented, hierarchically driven workplace to enjoy more direct bonding with infants, the man has misunderstood her nature and missed the full beauty of human life.

As young mothers look into the eyes of their children, their oxytocin levels rise higher than the oxytocin levels of men who look into their children's eyes. For these women, it feels good to touch this beautiful small child. It feels better than good. Her core self, her core identity, is greatly fulfilled. A man's great love for his child is fulfilled, too, as he holds his child and looks into the child's eyes, but he may well look out the window, too, into far-away worlds, feeling the call of vasopressin and testosterone and a hundred other signals of exploration and high risk in his brain and blood. This man does not love his children less than does the woman, but he will probably express that love in ways she does not fully understand (ways we will explore further in chapter 8).

MEN SEEK A CALLING

A sense of calling, exhibited in the image of the man looking out the window, is a biological characteristic in men, one we gain by exploring in depth. It is a hormone and brain-based compulsion to create a singular focus to their journey of potency and development of self-worth. People often notice how men seem to hear a call when they are young, and try to focus on it in order to guide their adult lives toward high standards of meaning. Men can be very concerned about the legacy they will leave. The notion of legacy is wired into men. As more men live longer, we see that different callings—different paths to worth and legacy—can dominate different stages of male life. Perhaps the key to understanding the difference between the male and female biological trends in this regard is to recall what a girl is born with and a boy is not: A girl is born with an inherent, directly natural path to self-worth. Nature has provided her with a natural calling and intimately biological legacy: the future gestation and then biochemical attachment to her offspring. She is born with an inherent path to personal meaning. She may choose never to have a child (about 15 percent of women choose not to), yet she is still born with this inherent worth.

A boy is not. He must, as we've noted, earn his meaning. Boys know this from very early on, turning their eyes outward into the world, seeking new experiences and challenges through which they experience their hidden potencies, earn a sense of self-worth, and gain importance. During this process, they gather together fragments of a proven self and bring those fragments back to those who love them. They ask, "Have I done it? Have I lived a good life?" They look in the mirror and ask, "Am I worth anything yet? Have I proven myself? What is my status? Have I answered one of life's big questions yet? Does my father think I've made it yet? Does my mother think I've earned a place in the world yet?" They look at their children and wonder, "Must I push my children harder, especially my sons, to be better selves so that they do not have to feel what I feel—that they have not found their calling, have not made it yet, have not earned their place?"

A woman in her fifties wrote:

> When I heard you speak last night about this desire for a calling in
> men, I had a big "ah ha" moment about my husband. I felt a huge relief,

because I realized that when he seems to reject what I want and just keep pursuing his career, it's not about me. I want to go on vacation. I want to buy a home on Kauai; we have the money. I'm ready. But he just wants to keep working, investing, and pushing himself. I took it as rejection of me, but now I see that it's not. I've raised two kids from my previous marriage. I've accomplished a lot in my work. I'm satisfied. He's still trying to find himself.

Women and men both feel, throughout their lives, the despairs of inferiority, inadequacy, and low self-esteem. Every human being can feel the ontological insecurity of not having fully "arrived," having accomplished, having created stability, wealth, honor, and personal power. Many women have spoken the inner soliloquy of calling to themselves and about their lives. Yet each of us knows there is a difference for women and men. We have noticed how the men are so very driven, and though they won't admit it, very fragile. Oddly, at least on the surface, it seems that men won't ever cope with their fragility—they just keep pushing themselves toward developing and showing potency, toward acquiring and utilizing social and hierarchical power, even as it kills them eight years younger than women and often takes them away from other human values.

Human biology provides the key not only to male drive but also to male fragility. From an early age, boys are constantly pursuing, projecting big goals, dissing others in order to feel tough, caring for others close to home as needed, then exploring out in the world again. They know they are different from girls; and though they rarely admit it, they feel a little envious of the inherent path to self-worth girls are born with.

At puberty, the difference in inherent worth is even clearer to adolescent males and females. By late adolescence, boys understand that they lack inherent meaning in comparison to girls and must go out and find it. By late adolescence, most males begin a course of attaching personal meaning to some sort of calling. They will go so far as to risk losing their lives in war in hopes of finding meaning.

The male willingness to risk injury and death in a quest for self-meaning is often easiest to see in population groups whose social structures tend to crush the individual human spirit. In societies where poverty, lack of a homeland, lack of economic opportunity, or racial or social oppression dominate, the inherent male sense of meaninglessness is amplified, as is the male's drive to earn his meaning through the highest personal risk. In these populations—especially if the males are emboldened to do so by misinterpretations of religion, as in the case of Islamic fundamentalism—young males will so attach their adolescent and adult psychology to gaining meaning through "big goals" that they may even become suicide bombers. Their calling—the route by which they gain worth in the social world—becomes physical self-annihilation for the sake of God, nation, homeland, or family.

What could a man be thinking? In much more of his life than we realize, he could be thinking about his calling. He could be thinking about how he will forge worth, power, and meaning from his life—test it, modify it, lose it, and gain it again, show it off even while hoping to be humble in it, bring this worth to his God for confirmation, and to himself, to his children, and to his mother or wife.

Do Men Make Careers Holy to Them?

There is an old German adage; "If you take the cause out of a man, there is no reason for the man."

The Zen master Deshimaru wrote, "You must concentrate on your work every day as though a fire were raging in your hair."

Eric Gill, the English author, wrote these words in his book *The Holy Tradition of Working*:

> To labor is to pray. Work is the discipline by means of which body holds its noise and leaves Soul free a little. Recreation is for the sake of work. Leisure time is for the sake of re-creation—in order that the laborer may the better return to work. Leisure is secular, work is

sacred. Holidays are the active life, the working life is the contempla-
tive life. The object of leisure is work. The object of work is holiness.

These words, written for anyone, male or female, who labors and
focuses on a cause, were written, not surprisingly, by men. These
quotes deepen our understanding of how men find their calling in
their work. Because work is a clear pathway toward potency, power,
and a feeling of fulfilling a calling, men often make their work into a
"holy" enterprise. This can be very frustrating for their mates and
children.

"I'm most proud of passing on the family business to my daughters," a man in a nursing home wrote me.

"Since I didn't get an education," a man in his eighties told a
newspaper reporter, on the day he retired from being a janitor in the
local school system, "I decided that by hook or by crook I was going
to get my kids an education. My kids are all doing well now."

While more and more women have entered the industrial and
information age workplace, men as a group still work more hours
than women. Even given the important progress that has been made
for gender parity in the workplace and increased opportunities for
women, women still more often choose to work fewer hours, to
work part time, and, if possible, to work in the home rather than in
a social corporate career.

In Western economies, where work statistics are measurable, nine
out of ten men work full time, while only five out of ten women do.
When men and women who work full time outside the home are
compared, men on average spend more time at work per week than
do women. Men also spend more time getting to their workplaces—
they travel twice as far as women, on average. A recent study on gender and transportation further showed that women use slower
modes of transportation to get to work in order to utilize travel time
to shop and take children to their schools. For men, the most direct
route to the workplace, and the most efficient journey to the place
of career, is most important.

While both women and men are capable of making their career

into the frame for personal calling—the "holy enterprise"—statistics indicate that men are more likely than women to do so. (Not surprisingly, by the way, bridge-brain women—often these are women with high-octane careers like criminal lawyers or CEOs of a large company—have higher than average female testosterone, and girls born without ovaries—thus without any testosterone—do not generally pursue high-powered careers. Not only in men but in some women as well, there is a direct association between the male hormone and the career track). Men feel for their careers what most of their male ancestors felt in the hunt and conquest—that career is a sacred way of developing inherent worth and of belonging in society and the greater world.

The biological trend to amplify the inherent worth of career becomes even more amplified when a woman becomes pregnant. The vasopressin/oxytocin and testosterone/progesterone differences shine through even further at this time. Women often love their careers, but when their biochemistry changes to accommodate childbirth, their sense of the relative importance of their career may change. Men, whose biochemistry does not change as significantly when they have children, continue to steadily regard their work as an equal or greater marker of success. Except for bridge-brain males, who sometimes seek to leave careers in order to care for children, men continue to seek the challenges of the world that lie outside the home.

Men, Testing Grounds, and Families

It is crucial to put together in our minds these threads of male experience—the need to earn a self, to pursue a calling, to express potency and power, to explore life from vantage points outside the home. Men love wives and children and gain a sense of holy enterprise in their families, but families and love relationships are often not primary testing grounds for male development in the way that a career might be. And though this can frustrate women—for men spend lots of time away from home and family—it can actually be a very good thing for women and children. Though we must explore strategies for bringing women and men together in their homes and families (we will do so very practically and specifically in chapters 7 and 8), it is crucial to base our exploration in admiration, rather than fear, of a man's tendency to make the career and the search for self in the outer world his primary test of potency. Intimacy between men and women, especially intimacy that builds home and family, is meant to be inherently safe. One way it remains safe is by power struggle remaining something men engage in outside the home. It is natural and thus quite useful for men to go away from family, into work, career, and sports in order to rise and fall with the tide of their own biological pursuit of potency and self-worth. It protects their families. Among our ancestors, men experienced the testing grounds for personal power in their hunting; later, in agriculture and soldiering. Now they do it in work and career.

While it is important that we help men to balance work and family better than many of them do, it is also important that we nurture men further toward keeping their testing grounds out of the home. This is a biological necessity that has become especially confused in two-family circumstances:in grossly male-dominant homes, where men exact obedience and subservience from wives in the home; and in the divorce culture, where the home and family becomes the most difficult kind of power struggle. In both these cases, the biological necessity of males to involve themselves in dominance activities and the human tendency (both male and female) to struggle over emotional power encroaches on family safety. The feminist philosophy has helped many families that were involved in male dominance to rethink male/female roles. As yet, the divorce culture has not found a powerful social movement by which to curb the destruction of family cohesion. Given the necessity in some families for divorce—especially in cases of danger to a spouse or child—curbing our new predilection for power struggle within family systems may be a more complex task than our present laws and philosophies can yet measure.

In nature-based theory, however, there is help. If we understand the necessity of men to seek areas of dominance (rather than think-ing this kind of seeking is "immature" or "unnecessary"), we have a natural base for rethinking our lives with men. We find that we have to pause somewhat when we hear ourselves saying, "My family life would be better if my husband was home with me, doing the things and being the man I and the children want him to be." While to some extent we might be wise in saying this, to some extent we might be setting up our families for the very power struggle that can crash our families. In much of the social philosophy espoused over the last four decades, women have been coached to see male interests in external callings and testing grounds as interests that robbed women of opportunity and love. Male nature—without our realizing we were thinking this—has been thought of as a threat to women. In the face of the threat, two primary power strategies have been provided to women: (1) that women take over external career callings as much as possible from men, and (2) that men on their own curtail these callings, bringing their focus of power away from external pursuits and directly to providing for women's emotional and romantic needs.

A nature-based approach looks at all this a little differently. As it has been throughout history, men must be coached to care for their families in intimate and hands-on ways, but especially with high-testosterone men and with men who test out to the middle or higher ends of the male-brain questionnaire, women can bring sta-bility to relationships and family by using the knowledge of male nature to help manage their relationships in three distinct areas (to be covered in depth in this book): the romance stage, the marriage-selection process, and the marriage (long-term partnership) itself. Chapters 4, 5, and 6 will specifically detail these areas of relation-ship and provide very practical advice for managing the ebb and flow of male-female biology in each. We will especially look at how to manage and fulfill both male and female needs without a power struggle in the home and family.

As women understand the role of the male brain and male hor-mones on the male's search for testing grounds, they can put into effect a practical philosophy that relieves the home of being a testing ground for power, while helping the man to remain deeply attached to women and children. The creation of this balance between testing grounds and intimacy has been one of the primary drivers in social systems throughout human biological history. We are called, now, to improve on these rather than throw them out in the present, for through "masculinity socialization" we can use human nature to help us make boys into the loving, wise, and powerful men each of us wants them to be, and each boy feels called to be, by his own trem- blings of nature.

THE MAKING OF A MAN, FROM THE INSIDE OUT

The anthropologist Margaret Mead said, "Women are created at their birth; men are created by their culture." Girls, she argued, become women because their bodies, particularly their hormonal systems and brain changes during and after puberty, force them to mature into women. Boys, on the other hand, must be "raised" and "matured" externally to a greater extent than girls. In all societies, boys naturally mature later than girls, sometimes many years later. Worldwide research over the last thirty years has shown that paying attention to the kind of maturation needed by male biology leads to more mature men, especially men who remain stable in their rela- tionships with women and children.

Mead is not saying that all girls mature to perfection without cul- tural help, nor that they do not suffer the pains of maturing during their adolescence. She knew that while boys will certainly become male adults in physique and hormonal surges, they won't become men unless they are led by their civilization and society toward maturity in a communal system of male upbringing she called *mas- culinization*. Girls need to be formed into women, but they also have a biological advantage over boys. Boys need to be masculinized (by "masculine," of course, Mead is referring to the term in its biological sense, not as a cultural stereotype). By studying cultures around the world, Mead learned that boys must be led to manhood in a masculine system of human development that presupposes that the tribe or society will provide:

1. High expectations of the masculine system and the males— usually these expectations include self-sacrifice, service, and selflessness.

2. Planned activities and groups in the local community that help boys reach goals of masculinization, including a series of rites of passages, committed to over a period of years during male adolescence.

3. Daily nurturing in masculinization by a specific few people in a boy's life—mother, father, grandmother, grandfather, mentors, etc, with fathers, grandfathers, and and other mentorial men taking on a primary role during testosterone-charged adolescence.

4. Wisdom in the civilization, community, and family about the *stages* of male development—from infancy to old age—and the people and personnel needed in each stage.

Margaret Mead learned in her research that civilizations, communities, and loved ones must care about boys not only as "children" but as boys, not only as "adolescents" but as young men, not only as male adults but as *men*. Boys will always be boys unless they are made into men by a journey of manhood led by the three social systems: civilization as a whole (nation, country, ethnic history, culture), local community (including school, church, and storytellers—in our age, the media), and family. In this journey, boys will be guided toward their callings. Many people will help them—by unconditional support and sometimes seemingly brutal provocation—to discover who they need to be as men.

In my decades of helping parents raise children, I've yet to meet a family or community that did not intuitively understand Margaret

Mead's wisdom. Our popular and academic cultures may argue over words like "masculine" or "men," but no matter the politics, everyone raising boys has confronted the "how to" questions of raising them into adult men. How do I do this? What does he need? Who does he need? It is not only parents of boys who are moved by Mead's intuition and mourn when they have not fulfilled it, but also parents of girls who may very well one day marry boys who are confused about their identity. Girls don't want to marry men who are still adolescent boys suffering despair in nether worlds between "boy," "male adult," and "man."

In my work to help parents and others raise boys into men, I've suggested, especially in *The Wonder of Boys* and *A Fine Young Man*, that our whole society—one family at a time—spend more energy making sure we help boys make their individual search for self-worth. In those books, I've presented practical ways to incorporate healthy masculinization for boys from birth to adulthood, with a primary focus on the three stages of male adolescence (these begin at nine and end at about twenty-one). A boy may appear to want to find his calling on his own—he may appear for years at a time to be a lonely boy—but simultaneously he yearns for his mother, father, mentors, teachers, friends, and even foes to team up with him to help him find his calling. This urge does not leave him when he becomes a man. The calling is the part of male identity with which he wrestles all his life. Even when he retires from "work" and "career," a man wonders, "Have I made it?" "Have I lived a good life?" "Have I been a good man?"

In this latter question is one of the secrets of male identity development: Men are driven biologically to attach more personal identity to pride in their own integrity than they do to their feelings at any given moment.

MALE IDENTITY AND CHARACTER DEVELOPMENT

When anthropologists study the masculinization of men in all cultures, they find that at the top of the list of "things that are naturally encouraged in adolescent boys" is moral identity. It was at the core of what Captain Miller wanted to inspire in James Ryan, and it was at the core of Ryan's life-defining questions at Miller's grave. Captain Miller and James Ryan understood the push in the male brain and hormones toward attaching identity to abstract systems rather than moment-to-moment emotions. All around us, we see examples of a man's inner struggle with moral identity and his own biology.

- Male territoriality informs male morality—males will often not back down (e.g., when cut in front of in a grocery line), perhaps actually picking a verbal fight with the offender. This "I won't back down" is based in brainstem territorial instincts. The verbal fight also provides opportunities to show prowess, to protect. Just a small thing like being cut in front of can become an identity testing ground in a man's mind.
- Men often pick a principle or system to follow and base their moral identity on adherence to it. They may even appear to value the abstract principle more than human lives, including their own. When we look at recent historical events, including suicide bombings, we can see that though there are a few female suicide bombers, it is mainly men who can be led to attach their whole identity—including their lives—to a singular, nationalistic moral principle.
- Men often do not see aggression as the same moral issue women do. Men can watch violent shows and feel very little. They can forgive more aggression among children than women might.

A family friend, Carly, provided an interesting illustration of this. She said:

Jack and I rented the Brad Pitt movie *The Fight Club*. [In this movie, young men whose lives are meaningless episodes of work and one-night stands decide to find meaning and masculine stimulation by fighting other young men in back street "fight clubs."] I understood the point of the movie—that young men lack meaning in their lives today—but I thought their response to their situation was immoral. I have two grown sons, and I don't want my sons acting this way!

But Jack said, "Fighting isn't a moral issue in this movie. The men all agreed to fight each other. No one was a victim. Only if the men hurt someone who wasn't in the game could it be a moral issue."

I said, "It's wrong to just brawl on the streets. It's against the law, for God's sake!"

Jack said, "The men set up the game and kept each other inspired and did not hurt anyone. The fighting isn't the moral issue. If there is one, it's how young men are raised today in our society and how meaningless their lives are, how little identity they get from society."

Carly ended her story by saying, "I agreed with him about the deeper social issue, but there's certainly no way we could agree on the fighting."

- Men also take risks that lead them to step out of moral boundaries more often than women, from breaking the law, to brutalizing other people they feel have broken the law. In a workshop I asked the question, "Are women more moral than men?"

A mother of two, married, a real estate agent, Janine said, "Absolutely. Women think more about the consequences of their actions than men do. They're more moral."

"Definitely," Grace, twenty-nine, said. "Women can be mean, even vicious, but women basically want people to feel good, so we try harder to do the right thing by people."

Cenis, fifty-one, said, "If by moral you mean, will

women follow the rules better than men, yes, I think
they do. They don't take as many risks. Men like rules,
but they like to break them, too. Women like to keep
everything going smoothly."

Throughout human history, human stories and
intuitions have noted a "male" approach to moral identity development but without being able to peer into
the brain. Now things have changed. We can look into a
man's mind. We can see in it all the exceptions to the
generalizations we just made, and we can see why those
generalizations so often fit our lives with men who seek
a calling, and an identity, through the biology of character development and moral life.

Male Morality: Biological Factors

Here are key neural and hormonal factors in male moral and ethical
development that set up and interact with a man's environment to
create a "male mode of morality"—a "male" way of being moral and
thinking about morality and personal identity. The women in the
workshop intuited the primary difference between the male and
female neurobiological modes of moral thinking: Women tend to base
moral thinking more on their empathic responses to others and their
environments, while men tend to base moral thinking on their adherence to abstract systems. Here are some key neural reasons for this:

Fewer limbic pathways. The male brain possesses fewer neural pathways to and from emotion centers in the limbic system. In issues of
identity and morality, they will tend to rely more on set standards
for character than on individual case-by-case explorations of personal feelings.

Fewer verbal-emotive applications. Males process less of their
moral and identity development through their verbal functions in
the left hemisphere than women. Instead, males select other parts of

the brain to do this work, making their moral identity less a matter of verbal self-reflection than of action.

Greater brain-stem emphasis. Males rely more heavily during their interactions on the older brain-stem section of the neural web than women do. This increases their likelihood of being more physically active than women in their moral and identity development.

Slower frontal and prefrontal lobe brain development. Males have slower frontal and prefrontal lobe development than females. Throughout the first twenty years of life, girls develop these "thinking-things-out" and "impulse control" centers of the brain more quickly than boys. One reason males have to be taught character development more constantly than females is this brain difference. Smart societies train males—especially during puberty—in self-control of physical impulse and abstract moral systems of character.

Less gray and more white matter in the brain. Women have more gray matter in the brain, where information processing is done, and less white matter, long fibers that transmit electrical impulses from brain to body. The male brain, by contrast, is white-matter dominant, meaning more physical action. This is yet another reason males are trained to and try to rely on character development systems—like martial arts—for a sense of personal identity and self-control.

More spinal fluid. The male brain has a greater volume of spinal fluid than the female. Spinal fluid moves physical impulses from the brain to the body. The more of it you have, the more quickly physical impulses will move to the body. Here, again, is a root of male impulsivity and an internal drive to try to manage that impulsivity effectively through character development systems and principles.

When these brain differences are added to higher levels of aggression chemicals, testosterone and vasopressin, with lower levels of calming-down chemicals like serotonin and empathy chemicals like oxytocin, the male moral system becomes somewhat clear, as well as the need for males to attach a lot of identity and self-worth to both the abstract character systems they are trained in and the high-risk proposition of constantly testing those systems.

With fewer neural pathways to the emotive centers in the limbic system and less verbal routing for data, as well as slower frontal and prefrontal lobe development, the male brain does not process moral stimulation through the same routes the female might choose. She is more likely than he is to process the data with emotion-laden responses, increasing that processing with the use of verbal responses and connecting those emotional responses to the decision-making functions at the top of the brain. Thus, he is more likely to "not back down" when he's standing in a grocery line and someone cuts in front of him, or when he's driving down the road and someone cuts him off. He will probably have a greater brain-stem territorial response and is more prone to impulsively do something unempathic, even immoral.

Were males to rely less than females on frontal lobe thinking, emotional response, and aggression and impulse control without having a compensating neural moral factor, we would live in a very dangerous world. But there is a powerful compensator in male neurobiology: the cortical areas used for abstraction and systematic thinking. The male brain takes a lot of the same data that females make verbal/emotive and makes it spatial/abstract. Males rely on constructing abstract systems in the mind and adhering to the principles, rules, traditions, symbols of those systems. As the biology of masculinity is trained by societies, character development is considered absolutely key, for without it the male mind is not able to do what it does best: develop a moral identity. A male brain that does not develop this kind of identity ends up hurting others terribly. Sometimes a male does this by killing, raping, and physically destroying. More often, he does it from within a competitive or hierarchical system: perhaps corruptly and greedily altering stock and accounting reports to pretend his company is making a profit—leaving millions of shareholders at a loss when the company fails—or stealing, cheating, and lying in some way in order to amass personal worth at the expense of all others.

Despite this reprehensible downside to male moral biology, if males were as immediately and directly empathic as females, our civilization would not exist today in its present form. The natural environments we live in are inherently dangerous, as is the human custom of civilization building. Sometimes a mind that specifically does not empathize with an individual but instead lives and dies by an abstract group principle—or even by the self-interest of a particular group—is the mind that can save us. At its highest and loftiest, it is the mind that will, unthinkingly, sacrifice its very life to save a country or a people.

Though it's possible to say, "If everyone were empathic like women and less adherent to physical/impulsive responses and systemic/abstract thinking, we wouldn't have war." That statement in itself is an abstract ideal. In the reality in which we live, the male biological tendency to function in abstract systems more than in individual empathy responses seems so deeply integrated into human consciousness that we are foolhardy to think it will dissipate anytime soon. It is not only a part of male identity and self-worth development, but also human nature. It is part of how nature answers the question: What is a man?

BRINGING IT ALL TOGETHER: MEN ARE ON A QUEST

Men can be quite confusing—following the rules in some ways, breaking them in others; giving up their lives to save their country, but paying little attention to their own families; searching for self-worth in the long-term accomplishment of goals, but giving up self-worth that they could gain by being more empathic every day. What puzzles men are!

Yet given what we've learned about the nature of a man, there is one thing about men that is not puzzling: Almost every man you know is on a quest. This quest—the outward manifestation of his mental and emotional interaction with his external environment—brings together elements of calling, work, family, identity, emotional life (to be covered in greater detail in the next chapter), and moral character. How he makes his quest is the man's ultimate marker of self-worth in the world.

Have you noticed how boys already prepare for their quest from early on in life: testing themselves and each other; looking for new ways of being and thinking; inventing, building, climbing into the world? Have you noticed that human societies all share one primary way of framing and nurturing male development: through the encouragement of the hero's journey? Much of the history of male literature involves heroic quest. Even the video games that companies produce for boys to play are nearly all heroic quests.

Not surprisingly, during the time between puberty and middle age, when testosterone is high, males experiment with heroism, trying on many different masks and costumes of the quest. Always the boy, as he joins the world of men, is looking to fulfill the duties and dreams of his quest for something ever greater. Boys are more likely than girls to pursue life as a heroic quest. Throughout life, men are more likely to test themselves constantly on the quest, seek status and worth in hierarchies and competition. Entrepreneurs of business motivation sell the logic, love, and language of the heroic quest in our competitive business world. "You can be anything you want to be!" "You can make a million dollars by the time you're thirty!" "You hold the keys to your own kingdom—use them!"

When men begin to move through male menopause—which is biologically caused by the drop of testosterone in the brain and bloodstream—they become gradually less interested in constantly testing themselves. But until late middle age (and for some men, not even then), the experience of the heroic quest is central to the male journey. Women want to be heroes, certainly. They are on a quest as well. But even they seem to want men to be heroes. Studies all over the world indicate that women between puberty and middle age select, for romantic relationships and marriage, the men who are on a quest toward achievement and status. Women want men who aspire to be kings, (even if only at a local level), warriors (protectors who make them feel safe), magicians (men who have, even if in a love of gadgets, some magical power that leads to success), lovers (men who make women part of their quest). Women don't want stereotype heroes—cardboard video-game action figures; they want loving, wise, and powerful heroes—men. As nature seems to have planned things, women's heroic expectations not only drive men but can actually add to male fragility, especially to the sense of fragility felt by men who lack physical or mental prowess.

Sigmund Freud, Carl Jung, and the many psychologists studying the human mind in the past acknowledged the archetypal hero's existence and the hero's quest in our psyches but did not have the scientific proof that we now have for this statement: The hero is biologically wired into men's minds. Testosterone, vasopressin, greater spinal fluid in the brain, less serotonin, less oxytocin, and the way the male-brain system projects life onto an abstract and spatial universe, leads men to see the world in terms of action, heroes, warriors, even lovers who must negotiate landscapes of challenge.

If you are a woman, you may have noticed that your boyfriend or husband may talk in the evening about his accomplishments or inventions or the way he vanquished a business opponent. He is involved in realigning his sense of self-worth with what happened that day along the lines of the heroic intentions that he (or perhaps even you) projected for himself. You may notice it gives him pleasure and pride to review his accomplishments and potentials, whereas you may feel less of a need to review your own with your friends or even with him. As he provides you with details of his potency—his accomplishment and potential—a beautiful and mysterious thing is going on: he is bonding with you through the presentation of himself to you.

If he has done nothing heroic on a given day—or in a given week—he may well feel like a failure, and he might try to overcome this feeling by living vicariously through the accomplishments of his favorite sports star. When a man has a less than heroic job, he may leave the grind behind and seek an activity outside his work or family to achieve transcendence of the mediocre. It will generally involve some kind of competition. Even if he does this in a poker game or by outdrinking a friend, he'll probably feel better, feel that he has, after all, overcome a challenge—acted heroically, with freedom and power.

Perhaps one of the most primal ways men experience their internal wiring for a heroic journey lies in the mainly unspoken envy that men have for warriors—soldiers, policeman, firefighters. It is more obvious in men's love of fantasy landscapes, knights, TV cops, detectives. Men want to fight the good fight. They use these landscapes as imaginative mirrors of their own quest. Boys start from a very young age with the quest and the search for the duties, loyalties, honors, and challenges it will entail. Adolescent boys are initiated into the adult world of male life by healthy family and mentoring systems, and they initiate themselves toward manhood in sports, on the streets, chess matches, debate tournaments, or any number of other external challenge experiences.

The male impulse to be heroic; to be the best; to be conspicuous even if only in one key area of life; to be the one who saves the family, neighborhood, community; to win the girl's attentions; or to conquer the workforce is the impulse not merely to live everyday life but to project himself onto the faces of the heroes and success makers of past and present, thus making life into a risk-filled, success/ failure, win/lose quest for worth and power.

A number of "proofs" of the biology of the male exploration quest exist right before our eyes. These proofs have been tracked by the neural sciences over the last two decades, as these sciences have tracked the differences between boys and girls.

- Boys begin their exploration outward, away from safety and toward external performance, at an even earlier age than girls. Toddler boys, for instance, explore farther away from their parents than toddler girls do.

- Boys not only take more risks, but even experience less emotional and physical fear in new situations than girls and women do. Male heart and pulse rates rise slower than female in risky situations, and remain lower. This difference begins in infancy and continues throughout childhood and adult life.

- When girls and boys six months old have something they like taken away from them—such as an action figure or a stuffed animal—girls are more likely to cry more quickly, utilizing a strategy of sympathy in hopes of gaining the object back; boys are more likely to push, pull, grab, and otherwise stubbornly seek to gain the object back themselves. They are already showing their wiring toward independent heroics, and competition for resources.

- In later age, men who find no heroism in their lives are more likely than women to becomes suicidally depressed—e.g., when they lose their job. The trauma to the male brain of the loss of outward quest and calling is more profound on average than it is in the female brain.

Still another, and very interesting, way of acknowledging the male quest biologically is to notice its link with testosterone, then to notice that women with higher testosterone levels resemble this "quest profile" more than women with lower testosterone. Levels of testosterone have a direct impact on how outwardly the person lives out the quest profile, and how much the person organizes his or her verbalizations around the topics of accomplishment and tasks of potency.

THE FUTURE OF THE MALE QUEST: THE FUTURE OF TESTOSTERONE

Driven by hormones, brain systems, culture, and developing self, men often know they are on a quest even though they don't talk about it. Driven by an aggression hormone that seeks outlets in the world, and imbues those outlets with a moral, identity-driven sense of the heroic task, men learn to provide their own biology with a sense of direction. A man, forty-two, a pediatrician, wrote me: "I admire my wife, who can take ten years off work and just focus on raising children. Even I, who love kids and have devoted myself to them, can't see myself separating my job from my life. If I didn't have my work, my family would not have a reason to love me. I know that sounds strange, but that's the way I feel. I need to be doing something to make them proud of me." In this honest self-assessment is biology. This man is verbalizing the drives of his brain system and his testosterone. He has created potency in a job and service framework in which his internal biological life finds success and comfort. It is very appropriate that he brings those drives to the framework—his pediatrician's office—in which he lives out his quest. His home is not and ought not be the primary frame for his aggression hormone. Certainly testosterone is needed in the home, especially to keep adolescent boys in line, but it needs more than the home—it needs a hierarchy, a structure, a planned life, a goal to be attained, others to pit the self against, others to team up with, a quest to be made. It needs an external journey in which the hormone leads the self toward plumage, posture, material rewards, power, and status. These rewards of the quest are then brought home as gifts to family and friends.

Women who are struggling to find common ground with men might ask, "Can't we just have a world where men don't need this whole quest thing, this power, this status. Let's get rid of testosterone." Finding the behavior of men to be baffling, they may fantasize, or even begin to believe, that masculinity (and its associated behaviors of aggressiveness, competitiveness, and focus on career) is a purely social or artificial construct that can be undone and reshaped at will.

I hope in this chapter, you've seen the difficulty in this position. To think this is to disregard fundamental truths about human behavior. From a biological perspective, it is important to know how deep is a man's sense of dissociation with himself—sometimes evidenced in a deep sense of shame—when he cannot fulfill his calling, his drive, his ambition in a heroic way. This biology is not something a woman is responsible for—it is her husband's journey. It is not something that she needs to take personally (unless he strays too far from her and the children). In later chapters, we will explore how to put this knowledge of his driving biology to practical use in our relationships—presenting practical suggestions and solutions.

As I work in the field of male development, I hear some people say, "When will we all grow out of the heroic quest?" as if the biological quest, this base of male experience, is a matter of maturity or immaturity. The psychiatrist Allen Chinen wrote a book called *Beyond the Hero* in which he explores how men in older age, when testosterone declines, become "elders" who move into a mentoring role, and out of a warrior role. This move is a very important step in the life of a man and for society as a whole, for all cultures need elders who can look back at their lives with wisdom and then share that wisdom with the next generation, telling stories, listening, reflecting, giving permission to others to become who they must. Yet, even in this "beyond the hero" stage of life the elder is still fulfilling the call of the quest, shaping now the younger people he loves toward their greatest success in finding their quest, and meeting their callings head-on.

BRIDGE BRAINS: EXCEPTIONS TO THE RULE

Having explored the hardwiring of the core of manhood as it appears in most men's lives, it is crucial to take time to explore the men who are exceptions to the rule:

- These men may take fewer physical risks.
- They may appear to have less motivation to show potency.
- They may avoid competitive work and careers.
- They may have a lower rather than higher sex drive.
- They may choose empathy nurturance as a dominant relational strategy rather than aggression nurturance.
- They may not care about any of the trappings or stories of the heroic quest.

- They may have no interest in any aggressive sport or video game.
- They may prefer sensuality to principles and abstractions.

Men with three or more of these qualities may be bridge brains, men whose brain systems are lower on the testosterone/vasopressin scale and favor development of cortical areas in ways that lean toward the more female end of the brain spectrum. There will probably be some area in life where the heroic quest still comes into play, for the quest biology is basic to male hormones; but for the bridge brain male the quest biology may only exist in his love of sci-fi novels or watching karate movies, not in his daily active life.

Watching the world's reception of these lower-testosterone and bridge-brain men is often painful. The heroic quest is so instinctual to us when we relate to, and as, men that many people look with disdain on the man who is the exception. Fortunately, the last thirty years have been the most welcoming for bridge-brain males.

Women have more control over how we feel about bridge-brain males than they may realize. Men have always and will always make their heroic quest in part to be impressive to women. In chapters 4 and 5, we will explore in more detail how this sexual selection works. The drive for heterosexual men to be sexually selected by women is so powerful that men are, in large numbers today, trying to become not only more heroic every day but also better bridge brains (or bridge-brain imitators). Men are trying to fine-tune male/female emotional conversation. They are trying to name and share their feelings. They are trying to be better listeners to women. Men are generally not doing this because men feel they can't personally live without these skills; rather, they want to impress women and have noticed that increasing numbers of women are selecting more emotionally sensitive males. Women have power!

Yet we should not think that the new experimentation with "sensitive men" has created a world in which bridge-brain males are now dominant. Interestingly, even women who claim to want a bridge-brain man often find themselves conflicted about their own desire. While they may enjoy his sensitivity, they may also miss the career drive and emotional strength of a questing male.

"I feel safe because he's so strong," a woman said of her husband at a couples workshop. "I like that he is becoming a better listener, but I don't want him to become too soft."

"When I'm really being honest," a woman wrote in an E-mail, "what I like most about my husband is that when I'm with him I feel like I'll never be hurt by anyone or anything."

The first line of a contemporary romance novel reads: "The strength in his eyes mesmerized her soul." Since romance novels comprise one-third of the entire book publishing business, these stories of women loved by high-testosterone men speak eloquently of the deeply held, primal need that women have for the feelings a high-performing man inspires in them.

Romance literature is a powerful example of how conflicted we all are about the bridge-brain males among us. Though women may hypothetically yearn for a gentler, more sensitive man, they also continue to crave the heroic standard of the potent, powerful hero in whom bridge-brain qualities are secondary.

The trend toward accommodating bridge-brain males is going to get stronger as humans evolve, especially as male careers become more sedentary (more time in front of computers, more time reading and writing, less physical competition time). Dominant male biology—millions of years old and the basic male trend—still inspires higher testosterone levels for males, but there is more room for bridge brains or near-bridge brains—the kind of men who perhaps as boys were made fun of by dominant male and female groups while growing up, but who have learned to see even that distressing and painful circumstance as a personal heroic test of the self. These men have risen above the shaming to play their best part in natural society.

PRACTICING INTIMATE SEPARATENESS

Just as I began this chapter with reference to Steven Spielberg's *Saving Private Ryan*, let me end it with reference to *The Rookie*. While showing a man's core search for self-worth, as well as the elements of maleness we've already begun to explore, this Disney movie very effectively shows how a man's female partner can gain immense power by practicing the intimate separateness that can make a marriage strong. Both movies are archetypal stories that advance our ability to understand male biology.

In *The Rookie*, Jimmy Morris, played by Dennis Quaid, is a high school science teacher and the coach of the high school's losing baseball team. He lives in Big Lake, Texas, with his wife, played by Rachel Griffiths, the high school counselor. They have three children.

Jimmy is an avid baseball player and fan. He pitched semiprofessionally in his youth, but his arm gave out. Four surgeries later, he decided to quit pitching and create a good life with wife and family. He has become a moral identity teacher to young women and men, especially the boys on his baseball team. He feels some fulfillment. He likes his life. But in the evenings, as his eight-year-old son sleeps or watches from the cab of the family pickup, he goes out to an abandoned oil rig and just pitches the ball till he's exhausted.

Jimmy Morris has a dream, a deep inward sense of an unfulfilled heroic calling. He knows it, and so do others in the town. His wife knows it. The boys on the baseball team he coaches know it. Jimmy Morris wants to return to the major leagues.

One day, while he's trying to motivate the boys to play better, they offer him a deal.

"If we win district, you go try out for the majors again."

Thinking nothing will come of this, he takes the deal. To his surprise, the boys do win district, motivated in large part by their deal with him. He now has to try out for the minor leagues, which can lead to a tryout for the majors. He goes to a tryout and throws the ball ninety-eight miles an hour. This speed, even at his advanced age, gets him noticed.

That night he is offered a pitching job in the minor leagues. When his wife finds out, she is conflicted at first. She's perturbed that he didn't tell her he was trying out, and she is scared for him. She has watched the pain of his surgeries and knows how terrible it can be when dreams fail. She worries for herself and her family for they need his income from the school, and the minor leagues barely pay. She knows it might be a long wait before he hits the majors, if he ever does. Does he really need to pursue this dream, this calling? At first, she hopes not.

She says, "You can't eat dreams." Jimmy, a man who loves his wife and family, at first gives in to the reality that she sees. He hears her concerns and decides to turn down the minor-league job. But that night, as she watches their eight-year-old son sleeping, she sees beyond her worries and fears to the core of manhood and the heart of men. She tells her husband that she understands what must happen. "We have an eight-year-old boy in there," she says. "He loves baseball the way his dad does. You need to go do this, not only for yourself, but for him."

This life partner has made a decision between discouraging the core of manhood and practicing intimate separateness in her marriage. She has the power to give him permission to stretch toward his calling, and she chooses to give it. Now he becomes worried about money and how overwhelmed she'll be as a single parent. In a perfect cinematic expression of intimate separateness, she replies, "I'm a Texas woman: I don't need the help of a man to keep things running."

She not only gives him permission to stretch toward the heroic in his life but shows that she, too, is independent. She assures him, in this way, that she is as capable as he is of the intimate separateness required for his heroic calling to be fulfilled, and her own needs to be met.

Jimmy Morris goes off to the minor leagues to play. Ultimately, after hardship for him and his family, he is drafted by the Tampa Bay Devil Rays. He pitches for two years in the majors, then retires back to Big Lake, Texas, a happy man, living in a happy family. No one could be prouder of him than his wife and family. As she watches her husband pitch against the Texas Rangers, Rachel Griffith's face shines with a deep understanding of his core self, his search for self-worth, his pride of calling, and his core drive to prove his inherent worth to the highest standard to which he as an individual man, is capable. She knows that he could have neglected this dream, but he would not have reached his highest standard—that lack of reach would haunt him, her, and the children. She knows that in order to integrate a man's core search for self-worth into a happy family life, a spouse must often stretch her mind and heart toward his impossible dream.

PART II

What Could He *Really* Be Thinking?

———

It's like the story of the prodigal son. All my life I've heard it told and then one day I really got what it meant. On that day, so many things fell into place. Figuring out what my husband was really thinking . . . this was one of those experiences, too. It was like I finally got what was going on in his life-story.

—Jan, thirty-nine, remarried, two children, one stepchild, grocery store manager

Being a physician, I enjoy science. But I hadn't applied brain science to myself. Actually, we didn't learn about the male brain and female brain in medical school. We just studied the brain. In the last year, though, as I've begun to explore the differences between the male and female brain, I've gotten a lot from it. Truthfully, I was a skeptic about it, even though as a physician I should be the last person to doubt the use of science, but now I'm convinced there's something here that can move our human relationships forward.

—Richard, forty-eight, married, four children, family physician

3

What Could He *Really* Be Thinking . . . About Feelings and Emotions?

For one human being to love another, that is the work for which all other work is but preparation.

—Rainer Maria Rilke, German poet

We know when we raise kids that they have to have their own feelings and thoughts. We know it's our job to help them learn how to feel and think for themselves. But when it comes to our marriages, we don't even treat our partner with the respect we know we should give a child. We think we know what our lover is thinking or feeling. We think we should know. We think it's our job to tell our lover what to think and feel. We think he should know what we're thinking and feeling. What a mess! Both men and women do it with each other. Stopping the cycle has to start somewhere. I've decided to stop it with me.

—Hillie, thirty-four, married, one child, physical therapist

The couple, in their thirties, walked into my office together. Henry was a large man in a white shirt, tie, and black slacks. Judith was a small woman in a tank top and jeans. They had been married for eight years. He had a daughter from a previous marriage, who was twelve, and they had a son together, age six. They were both lawyers. Judith had told me on the phone that they needed marital counseling. They were arguing so much their marriage was in trouble. They'd be coming in during her vacation time, she said. He hadn't wanted to take a vacation this year. Their previous therapist had told him he needed to get better at expressing his real feelings. He had disliked this therapist, and so now they were coming to see me.

"Henry heard that you really understand men," she told me on the phone. "Maybe he'll trust you, and you can help us. I really want things to get better between us."

During the course of eight months, the therapy Henry and Judith underwent covered many issues—their own childhoods, his previous marriage, work crises, how they raised their children, even why vacations always seemed to become battles. Throughout it all, Henry and Judith each spoke a constantly recurring theme:

Judith: "He won't share with me how he feels."

Henry: "She hasn't got a clue."

In therapy, everyone has a set of refrains. All of us circle back to the same key grievances, the same key issues, the same key memories. The refrain is like a plea for help. If in a marriage, it isn't heard, the refrain can be like the words written on a tombstone. Years later, after a divorce, we might look back and say, "My ex just wouldn't share how he feels," or, "My ex just didn't have a clue," speaking the words to a new lover, and the cycle starts again.

After two months of meeting with Henry and Judith, I pointed out their refrains to them, asking if they'd noticed.

"Yeah," Judith said, "you're right. We do keep saying the same thing."

Henry nodded silently, then said, "I guess."

This began a deepening spiral of communication between them and me. As in most cases of marital therapy, I learned that neither person was physically dangerous to the other. This was a marriage that would end with him pulling away into work, television, the Internet the more she tried to bond with him. This was a marriage that would end with her feeling unfulfilled, for as years passed, he would become emotionally unavailable, making her efforts at attachment and bonding empty. After great conflict, probably during the divorce process, he would end up feeling that she never really wanted to be married to him in the first place, so she never should have agreed to it eight years before.

Was this ending inevitable? Judith and Henry had come to me hoping it was not. In addition to pointing out their refrains, I asked them to dig deeper into their dynamic.

I did a simple exercise I've done many times in marital therapy. I asked them to switch chairs. After they had done this, I asked Henry to say, "She won't share with me how she feels," and I asked Judith to say, "He hasn't got a clue." They each spoke these words that had been their lover's refrain about themselves.

Then I asked Judith, "Do the words fit? Is it true that he hasn't got a clue about you?" She said yes, it was true. He didn't understand her, what she needed, or who she really was. And worst of all, it didn't seem as if he even tried anymore.

I asked Henry, "Do the words fit? Is it true from your perspective that she doesn't share with you how she feels?"

He nodded. "She thinks she does, but she doesn't. She only shares certain feelings, usually about what she doesn't like."

Judith said in exasperation, "All I do is tell him how I feel!"

I pursued this. "But does your husband learn from you how you feel mainly when you're dissatisfied with him?"

Judith looked me in the eye, her teeth grinding behind her cheeks. "How could I do any more for him? Shouldn't I tell him how I feel when I don't like what he does? I don't like what he does. It's how I feel!"

We left our session there. I asked Judith and Henry to think for the next week about the other person being the speaker of their own complaint. Just as an exercise, I asked them to relate to each other during the next week as if they were living in the other person's heart. Judith would try to see herself as a person who didn't share feelings in ways that Henry could enjoy. Henry would try to see himself as a person who did not understand the woman he loved.

As we began the therapy process, I hoped that Judith and Henry would prepare themselves to walk through a doorway into a more advanced kind of relationship. As we met together over the next weeks, we focused on what lies behind the door: the commonality of human experiences—that couples in a long-term relationship grow so close together that when one of them voices a marital problem, he or she is actually speaking for both. This commonality can reignite the possibility of friendship again for it shows the partners that they are both suffering the same pain. From this place of commonality comes the ability to use one of the best tools for marital recovery: knowledge of how similar men and women are in their emotional pain, but how different they are in their emotional *method*. In my experience, most marriages break up during a time when both people have lost their compassion for the other's pain and come to the end of their own knowledge of the other's nature.

Within three months of marital therapy, the commonality of the pain was established, and Judith and Henry were ready to move into their profound differences as men and women, which showed up nowhere better than in the different visions Judith and Henry had of how feelings worked or did not work in the marriage.

Over the course of a number of sessions, we learned:

1. Judith trusted feelings; Henry trusted reason and facts.

2. Judith put her feelings at the top of her list of "things I can't do without." Henry did not.

3. Henry wanted the processing of feelings to end quicker than Judith did.

4. Henry felt things by doing things; he didn't spend much time discussing his feelings. He did like to talk about what he *did*. Judith discussed her feelings frequently.

5. Judith spent a lot of time talking about the feelings and emotions of her friends, children, husband, and others. Henry did not.

6. Judith experienced herself as someone who did not withhold feelings. Henry experienced her as someone who talked about lots of feelings but withheld her feelings of love for him.

7. Henry experienced himself as someone who was honest about the love he felt toward her and the children; Judith experienced him as someone who withheld his love and was, therefore, dishonest.

8. Henry wanted Judith to show her feelings more in what she did (actions), like having more sex with him, trying different sexual acts, and caring better for their home; Judith wanted Henry to tell her how he loved her and show her, more frequently and more clearly, with flowers, vacations, and other romantic gestures.

These two people had come together in love but now experienced their daily feelings quite differently. This difference at times enraged each of them, and at times made each despair. They were self-controlled people and so did not act out their rage in violence toward each other. Rather, they let the rage leak out in their everyday life, with fights, little rejections of each other, negative judgments. They were not, by genetic disposition, depressives, so they did not walk around in despair. Instead, they pulled away from each other—she into criticism, he into work.

With hard work, Henry and Judith saw themselves and their relationship more clearly. They identified specific issues of marital rage and despair. They understood their similar pain but dissimilar emotional methods. Throughout this process, they came to understand just how differently their brains and bodies approached the very experience that united them, the experience of being a human being who feels love and the passion for life, family, and mate. Human nature, which was, in a sense, breaking them apart, became the key to putting the marriage back together. The last few months of their therapy were spent in restructuring the marital relationship to accommodate the difference between the biology of female emotion and the biology of male emotion.

When I saw Henry and Judith at a workshop two years later, they were still together.

Judith said to me, "I'll never look at any man the same way I did before I came to see you. Henry and I are doing fine. We still have some bad days, but we love each other for who we are."

I gave her a hug.

Henry shook my hand and said, "Thanks for helping out when you did."

I said, "You bet," and then we all turned away, back to our lives.

THE BIOLOGY OF MALE EMOTION

From a biological perspective, is there a "male mode of feeling?" Do men experience their feelings and emotions differently from women? An excellent answer comes from the pen of a child. Brittany, sixteen, E-mailed me: "Can you please tell me how men and women are supposed to get along? Guys are just wired differently than girls. It drives me nuts."

Let's delve more deeply into what nearly destroyed Judith's and Henry's marriage, the same thing that drives teenagers crazy.

The popular word "wired" is a good place to start. Brain research has borrowed it as a companion word to "circuitry," i.e., "brain circuitry is wired in the following way. . . ." As I use this language, I hope you won't feel that brain research is reducing feelings to mechanical wiring. They are more than that, rife with metaphor and mystery. The joy of feeling and emotion grows as much from the mystery as it does from understanding the mechanics. But understanding the mechanics can save us all a lot of trouble in many walks of life—from computers, to cars, to family dynamics, to the health of relationships.

What's happening in the wiring of the brain when we feel emotions? Even more important to us in this chapter: What's happening in the male and female brain?

In general, emotional stimuli—sad faces, emotional criticism, a baby's cry, a kiss, a sunset or sunrise, the laughter of a friend, the weeping of an elderly parent—all these and a million other sensory stimuli move through a person's senses to the limbic system. The nerve endings of fingers, visual cortex, the eardrum, taste buds, and nostrils apprehend light, color, touch, movement, sound, and fragrance, sending signals to and through the limbic system. If the signal sparks a lot of emotion, that emotional content is first handled in the limbic system then parsed out to the upper and lower brain. If a friend is weeping, the limbic system will look on a PET scan as if it's on fire. Because so much emotion is attached, it will look different than if a person, on a lazy afternoon, just bent down by a river to pick up a stone and toss it in.

This, then, is a picture of the emotional brain in a general sense. If we PET scan the brains of men and women, we find that throughout this sensory/emotive process, they look and feel very different. Even when two people sit in a therapist's office and come to understand that their marital despair is very similar, their brains look and feel differently. Here are some of the areas of the brain that ensure this:

1. **The hippocampus (memory storage and emotive processing in the limbic system).**

2. **The amygdala (emotive processing, aggression impulses in the limbic system).**

3. **The cerebellum (connector neurons for complex tasking, including emotive tasking, throughout the brain).**

4. **Neural pathways (connecting the limbic system to the cerebral cortex).**

5. **The brain stem (basic functions and fight-or-flight responses).**

6. **Hormones (driving body and brain to act on feelings and emotions).**

7. **The corpus callosum (connecting right and left hemispheres of the brain).**

8. Brain chemicals (carrying emotional responses in their composition).

9. The cingulate gyrus (key emotion center in the limbic system).

10. The cerebral cortex (generally transforming emotion into
    thought).

While men and women can come to the same conclusions, see
the same sunsets, hear the same baby's cries, and listen to similar
words of love or rejection, their brains are fulfilling these functions
with a different end result for daily relationship in mind. Women
want something from emotional life that the male brain, quite often,
makes difficult to impossible.

The hippocampus. With a smaller hippocampus in the limbic system, males remember less of their emotional experiences than
females do. When men talk, they have less stored emotive experience to converse about, thus their conversation is not as feeling
laden as women might wish.

The amygdala. With a larger amygdala, males are more likely than
females to choose a physically aggressive response to a situation.
They are, thus, less likely to pick a more tender feeling or conversation response to a situation.

The cerebellum. With stronger connection pathways in the female
brain between the cerebellum and both verbal and tasking centers,
women tend to rely more on talk when faced with emotional stimuli, and their brains tend toward more multitasking, which favors
emotion/feeling talk. Emotion/feeling conversation is inherently a
multitask from the brain's point of view—more than is, for example,
a conversation about how to repair a joist. Men often gravitate away
from multitask conversations involving emotion.

Neural pathways. The female brain generates more neural pathways, not only from the cerebellum to other brain centers, but gen-

erally throughout the brain. The female brain is, in general, a more active brain than the male, allowing for more emotive tasking. Emotional experience consists of some of the most complex experiences a brain will need to handle in its lifetime. The female brain possesses more pathways to and from emotive centers of the brain, making it better suited not only to handle emotive complexity, but to seek it out.

The brain stem. The male brain relies more heavily on brain-stem activity than does the female brain, especially during emotive experience. When, for example, a crisis situation appears, the male brain tends to process less of the crisis in the emotive centers of the brain and more in the fight-or-flight brain stem. He'll tend to act first, think and feel later. This creates delayed emotional responses.

Hormones. The fluctuation of female hormones during a monthly cycle directly affect a woman's emotive processing because female hormones are mood regulators—they are directly connected to brain chemicals and limbic system emotive activity. While the dominant male hormone, testosterone, can certainly affect mood, it is not a "mood regulator" because it does not catalyze emotive brain chemicals as directly as estrogen and progesterone do. Because its dominant hormone does not connect as directly to mood and emotion as do the dominant female hormones, the male brain spends less time relying on emotional processing than the female brain does.

The corpus callosum. This bundle of nerves connecting the right and left hemisphere of the brain is about 25 percent smaller in the male brain than in the female. Emotions, and thoughts that grow from emotions, cross talk between hemispheres in the female brain quicker and more fully than in the male. This is crucial to emotional expression because the male brain relies on hemispheric cross talk in order to make emotions into words (the male brain makes language out of emotion mainly on the left side of the brain, so it needs the thoughts to cross talk feeling neurons over to the left). With a smaller corpus callosum, the male brain doesn't move as many feeling-thoughts to the left and thus communicates fewer of them.

Brain chemicals. Norepenephrine, dopamine, serotonin, oxytocin, and other brain chemicals help the brain process feeling in the same way water conducts electricity. The female brain, in this analogy, has more water by which to conduct emotive electricity. For instance, the female brain secretes more oxytocin, a bonding chemical that catalyzes emotional bonding strategies, giving the female brain greater reliance on emotional intimacy.

The cingulate gyrus. Emotional intimacy strategies may be "conducted" by brain chemicals, but they can be said to be *"overseen"* by the cingulate gyrus, a very powerful emotion-processing element of the limbic system. The female brain processes more life experience through the cingulate gyrus than does the male. With more neural pathways to and from this gyrus in the female brain than in the male, the female brain is more emotion laden.

The cerebral cortex (neocortex). The four lobes at the top of the brain function differently in men than in women. One clear case involves verbal and spatial strategies. With more cortical areas in the male brain used for spatial experience (moving objects in physical space, such as throwing a ball), males tend to turn their life experience into physical spatial responses. With more cortical areas in the female brain used for verbal experience (talking, writing, reading), females inherently tend to turn experience into emotive verbal responses. Because the female brain does language in about seven brain centers, whereas the male brain does it in only one or two, there is a greater tendency in the female brain to process all of its experience, including emotive experiences, by using words.

Given just these few brain differences that affect emotion and feeling, we can better understand this crucial fact in male/female relationships: The male brain does not tend to pick emotive processing as a dominant strategy, whereas the female brain does. This fact, as profoundly as any other, affects the future of a male/female relationship. Henry and Judith, like so many couples, rejuvenated their relationship by coming to grips with this fact. And like so many couples, each went through a stage of feeling that males or females are superior. Judith reported feeling that her greater emotional-processing ability created greater emotional strength and courage, thus the female brain was superior in a marriage. Henry reported feeling the opposite: that less emotional processing leads to less distraction and more efficiency in relationships, thus his way of loving was superior. "I process emotions better," Judith said. "I have more access to feelings and intuitions. I'm more emotionally literate and empathic." Unconsciously, she was saying, "Our marriage would work if Henry did as I do."

Henry said, "I don't spend as much time and energy running emotions and thoughts about emotions through my head." Unconsciously, he was saying, "Judith should do like I do. Be efficient. Cut to the chase. Don't read so much into things."

You have probably heard this debate go even further in your own relationships or among friends. A woman might say, "Men are scared of feelings and emotions. He might have more physical muscles than I do, but I have more emotional muscles."

A man might say, "She's running through so many emotions so much of the time, always ready to cry about this or that. She's the weaker sex."

Men and women are often very brutal with each other when they notice the fact, now supported by brain science, that women and men handle emotions differently. Men and women make unfortunate biological judgments of each other. More liberating is to see two equally valuable brain types, essential to human survival, self-fulfillment, and ongoing love.

THE MALE MODE OF FEELING

The less emotional male brain is good for love? Really? Much of this book is about answering this with a resounding Yes! Let's set another piece of foundation for this positive answer by exploring more deeply the male biological trends in emotional life. These male trends are just as valuable as the female. After exploring characteristics of this "male mode of feeling," we'll look at bridge-brain males—men who are exceptions to this mode.

Men tend to delay emotional reactions. A grandmother provided me with an example of this very male strategy. "When I wanted Bill to think about something important to me, I'd tell him about it before he went to work and then talk to him when he got home. I'd give him at least a day."

Recent studies have shown that men can take up to seven hours longer than women to process complex emotive data. New neural studies corroborate the fact that given the circuitry and wiring of the male brain, we can expect "delayed reaction" to be part of the male mode of feeling. Certainly women can delay their emotional reactions, and men can have very quick emotional reactions. But on the whole, we can expect the following to be true:

- Men more than women will not know what they feel at the moment of feeling and will take longer to figure it out.
- Men more than women may not be able to put their feelings into words in the moment and will tend to take longer to express feelings in words than women do——if they choose a verbal strategy at all.

Men tend to favor *physical* **emotion over verbal.** "Women talk, men do." This is a cliché, but one that often can be true. Women want to sit down and talk; men want to go shoot hoops. Certainly some men sometimes want to talk about emotions but not for as long as a woman might. The higher the testosterone level in the male (or female), the more spatial and physical will be the emotional-processing strategies he relies on. The higher the estrogen/progesterone in his brain system (the more he leans toward being a bridge brain), the more verbal-emotive processors he'll build, and thus the more likely he'll be to talk. With more circuitry in the male brain for physical processing of emotional stimuli—especially the male brain's tendency to retain processing in the amygdala or move more emotive signals to the brain stem—he is more likely to respond physically to a feeling. This can manifest itself in the following ways:

- If he feels hurt, he's more likely to hit something than she is.
- If he feels tense, he's more likely to try to get physical exercise than she.

Oxytocin drives a woman to find someone to talk to because her brain circuitry knows that if she has a chance to talk about what's bothering her, her oxytocin level will increase and calm her tension. But what many women don't realize is that talking about one's troubles can actually have the opposite effect on the male brain: It often creates as much stress as it relieves. Knowing this from a lifetime of neural experience, a man will often resist emotion out of self-protection.

Since a man isn't likely to tell his wife or partner, "Hey, you're oxytocin's firing up right now as we talk about this and you're feeling better, but all I'm feeling is worse," a woman might have to learn how to identify his signals. For example, while talking, a man might become physically fidgety, or his eye contact might drift. He might interrupt, he might try to problem solve, or he might try to get out of the conversation so that he can go do something else, such as "zoning out" in front of the TV or working on a project.

When it comes to feeling and emotions, the male brain not only thinks differently from the female but at times in contradiction to the female. What is so comforting to her can be uncomfortable for him. Her ability to accept this and to recognize his signals of discomfort can help guard the couple against additional stress.

While processing feelings, men put on masks. A woman's ability to read men's "masking signals" is a case in point.

Given male-brain circuitry, it is more difficult for men to name feelings than for women.

With a smaller corpus callosum, men don't cross-talk feelings through the language centers of the brain in the same way women do. A man may feel something and the signal of the feeling may start out in the limbic system to move upward to the neocortex. It may well move up to the right hemisphere. But then it may well get stopped, disappearing into neural oblivion because the signal found no access to a receptor in a language center in the left side of the brain. With a 25 percent smaller corpus callosum, the male brain is less likely to find a crosstalk pathway than the female is, and since the female brain has six or seven language centers throughout the right and left hemispheres and the male may only have one or two in the left hemisphere, her brain often doesn't even need hemisphere crosstalk in order to name a feeling and then express it verbally. All in all, her brain is better set up to take a feeling as it comes, process it, and verbalize it. The male brain isn't as good at this and has adapted. Delayed reaction is one adaptation, masking another.

The male brain has adapted to its lack of emotive-processing speed with more reliance on masking feelings than females use. It takes the male brain longer to process the feeling than his life circumstances may allow. If he is living with a woman, he may not yet have processed the feelings she senses are in him. The male brain will often mask the original feeling with a less painful feeling or an avoidance of feeling. Everyone masks feelings at some point; men simply employ the strategy much more than women.

For example, a man's boss has demeaned a man in front of others at work. The man's brain circuitry registers the hurt. When he comes walking through the front door after work, the hippocampus and other brain centers might still be aflame with the sensory/feeling stimulants, but he does not show the hurt directly in his words. Instead, he might be wearing a self-protective "leave-me-alone" mask:

Woman: "How was your day?"

Man: "Fine. Call me when the kids get home." He walks down to the family room and turns on the television.

Or he may put on a "let's fight" mask.

Woman: "Are you okay?"

Man: "You always ask me that. I hate it."

Some men do come home and immediately talk about what happened to them that day. But many men need to find another way out of the stress they feel. Their sense of self has been hurt and needs recovery so that neural balance can be rediscovered. In the two cases we described, the "leave-me-alone" mask allows the man to retreat in order to lower stress and recover his emotional stability. The "let's-fight" mask allows him to create a conflict with someone he can try to dominate—in this case, his wife. This dominance helps him reposition himself higher on his internalized sense of hierarchy and thus feel better. When he wears this mask of dominance, he is generally not conscious of the fragility of his ego. He is also not generally being malicious to his wife (though his dominance strategy can be very uncomfortable).

A third common mask men wear is the "nothing-to-worry-about" mask.

Woman: "How come you seem so down?"

Man: "I don't know. Just a hard day, I guess." This mask helps a man regain neural comfort and protects others from his internal distress. His neural circuitry is working through the emotional stimulation of the day, but he does not express the feelings to others—probably because expression will create greater neural stress for himself and burden others directly with his own stress. He protects his spouse and children.

Relationship experts, and perhaps every couple, can argue for years about whether male masks are good or bad for a marriage. From a neural point of view, they are neither. Male masking is a biological reality. It is a strategy of human adaptation. It is natural for women to try to reduce male masking in favor of a more direct verbal expression of feelings, yet it is vital to understand that masking is an important, protective part of male life. Not surprisingly, as couples mature in their marriages, they often develop the intimate separateness to allow masking to occur in a marriage without recrimination. Not understanding the importance of masking can cause conflict that becomes dangerous to a marriage. Our popular culture—through self-help books and television programs—trains men to use less masking and more verbal cues in relations with women. We must augment this training with equally powerful coaching for women to understand why it is vital that men be allowed to protect themselves emotionally.

As we develop this kind of coaching, we will aid women to understand how they react to masking. They will see how they themselves participate biologically in it. Given female brain chemistry, which is so driven toward immediate and constant verbal-bonding strategies, male emotional masks often feel to women like rejection and abandonment of the female self. Women often react to male feeling masks as if they themselves have been abandoned by the man who wears the mask. They miss the fact that, for the most part, his mask is a biological necessity to manage stress and even to protect relationships. Focusing unconsciously on their own feelings of abandonment, they are drawn into a bitter drama.

That both the man and woman are drawn into this drama of male emotional withdrawal and female feelings of abandonment is logical. In any of the three scenarios we described above, we can easily interpret the realities as the male rejecting the woman's preferred brain strategy.

- The words he uses when he speaks through the "let's fight" mask lead, probably, to a hurtful argument that pushes his wife or partner away.
- The words he uses when he wears the "leave-me-alone" mask rejects her ability to help him feel better.
- The words he uses when he wears the "nothing-to-worry-about" mask shut her out.

In these situations, a woman's self-talk might be:

- Why is he taking it out on me? (Doesn't he love me?)
- Why won't he share himself with me? (Am I worthless to him?)
- Why does he try to make me into the bad guy? (Am I the cause of our problems?)

Sometimes I hear men say, "She's crazy. Sure I love her." This, too, is a mask men wear: the mask of incomprehension.

A woman is hardly crazy to feel the way she does. Her feelings reflect her neural experience. From her point of view, her partner has emotionally rejected her.

Yet, in all this, she has a choice. She has control over what internal logic she will apply when he wears masks and tries to pick an argument or to pull away from her for a while or to proceed as if everything's fine. She can choose whether to resent his lack of emotional contact, or she can look to him with compassion.

Women like to express feelings, while men like to *release* them. While women tend toward expressing feelings, men lean toward masking them or doing something physical. In this male/female difference is another hidden difference: Men try to release or expel feelings, rather than store or express them. What do we mean by this rather fine distinction?

With a smaller hippocampus than women, men tend to store less emotional and sensory experience in their brains. Fewer active neural pathways to the hippocampus contribute to the male brain's tendency to rely less on an emotion-storage strategy than women do. With more emphasis on amygdalic and brain-stem responses to emotions, men tend not to store feelings for gradual expression but to activate emotions toward quick release. Less of the male brain is devoted to the processing of feelings than in the female, so he will tend to store less feeling memory, finding the releasing of feelings more functional. "If I can get these feelings out of the way quickly," his brain is saying, "I can get back to what I'm working on." What he's working on is usually a task or job.

A woman, on the other hand, might continually *increase* her storage of feeling memory. She may remember something that happened a year or ten years ago, reflect on it, and even talk about it, then store this new reflection along with the original emotional experience. She might say to her partner or husband, "Do you remember on that day in February when we were at that wonderful seafood restaurant, you were wearing your blue suit, and you said to me . . ." She might remember the incident with a lot of emotion. She and her husband might discuss it (he is less likely to remember it than she and far less likely to remember details), and he might say, "I do remember that, but I guess I don't have feelings about it anymore" (a comment that can get him in trouble!). She might store this conversation along with the memory. Two years from now she may well come to her partner or husband saying, "Do you remember . . ."

The man involved in this may have released whatever happened in the restaurant from his emotional web long ago. He may not have stored it in the hippocampus. If he does remember it, he may remember it but without much emotion attached. It can be difficult for male/female relationships when the female brain wants to extend the life of a feeling, but the male mode of feeling wants to release the feeling quickly.

The couples communication movement that has developed during the last two decades, by which men are taught to paraphrase what women say back to them, is immensely valuable for couples; the more men can learn to say to women, "So you're saying . . ." Similarly, the more a woman can learn to notice when a man has already released a feeling experience, and the less she tries to press him to feel what she feels, the easier life will be in a long-term partnership.

To men, emotions are often design problems to be solved, rather than feelings to be enjoyed. The notion that "women like to talk about feelings, men like to problem solve" is quite accurate from the point of view of neural circuitry. As we noticed earlier, emotions are often less enjoyable for the male brain than the female. In addition, the male brain system tends to move thinking processes into a focus on abstract design more quickly than the female. The male brain often does this at the very time that the female brain is still experiencing the concreteness or sensuality of the emotional experience.

A decade of tests around the world using PET scans have confirmed the male brain's tendency. When male and female college students are put on PET scans and asked to figure out what emotion is expressed on a face shown to them in a picture, the women score better than the men, and PET scans reflect how much more of the female brain is being used to process the emotional signal. When, on the other hand, the men and women are asked to perform a spatial or abstract puzzle, the men tend to outperform the women. Cortical areas and neuroprocessing in the brain that women use for emotive processing, men use for spatial and abstract functions.

When, in everyday life, women notice men trying to problem solve emotional experiences as quickly as possible, they are noticing the male tendency toward mental abstraction. Higher oxytocin levels in the female brain drive that brain system to keep the emotions sensual and immersed in feeling so that the empathy of the person a woman is talking to will get stimulated, and thus there will be even more emotion between the two people who are talking. More emotion, in this case, increases oxytocin, which decreases female stress. For males, it is mental abstraction that decreases stress.

Hormones play a role here. Male testosterone and vasopressin tend males toward a problem-solving response. Testosterone and vasopressin are dominance and aggression chemicals, and problem solving is a dominance strategy—the solving of the problem is an aggressive way of ending a problematic situation. Both the male brain and male biochemicals move the man to avoid the extension of the life of the feeling but instead to transform the emotion into an idea that can be managed safely. If a man thinks an emotion is causing even minimal danger, he is likely to try to move it quickly toward dominance and transformation.

While it is crucial that men learn to see the world through a woman's experience, helping her to express herself as she needs to, and while many men today would enhance relationships if they would simply 'be engaged' more patiently, it is equally important that women understand the primal nature of a man's mode of feeling and his style of relating. Nothing less than her safety and the health of her relationship and family may depend on her developing oxytocin-based relationships with other women (and bridge-brain males) with whom she can more fully develop her own emotional world and thus depressurize her emotional relationship with her partner.

Among our ancestors, this kind of extended family approach to a marriage was assumed. The contemporary study of human biology asks us to take it to a new level, as we'll deal with even more practically in a moment.

A BOTTOM LINE: WOMEN TRUST FEELINGS MORE THAN MEN

Let's end our understanding of the male mode of feeling with a crucial "bottom line." Given the different brain structures of men and women, it will come as no surprise that men inherently distrust feelings, and women inherently trust them. Certainly this is a generalization, yet your personal experience has probably confirmed it.

If you think of the men in your life, you'll probably notice that the majority of them don't tend to think of their own feelings as the final comment on an experience. Men don't tend to think it possible that just "feeling" the experience is actually enough. Feelings are often seen by men as something other people experience.

A man and a woman try to decide what movie to go to. Which movie does he tend to choose? The action movie, the one that will lead to *less* feeling. She tends toward the emotional drama or love story—the movie that will lead to more feeling.

Another example might be the activity of buying a house. The woman is more likely to trust the feelings she gets when she walks into its closets, touches its drapes, stands silently in its kitchen, waiting for invisible signals to touch her emotions. The man is more likely to wonder over the price and to stand waiting for his performance imperative to be satisfied—such as the moment of negotiation with the realtor or contractor. He is more likely to see the buying of the house as part of his life's journey; she is more likely to see it as part of her heart's journey.

This is not to negate that a part of a man will wait silently to feel good in the house, nor that a part of a woman wants to negotiate and perform; it is simply to demonstrate what we've experienced in our own daily lives: A woman inherently trusts the very experience of feeling that a man inherently distrusts. Feelings aren't very logical, and he needs logic. Logic isn't very emotional, but her brain, her heart, her senses awaken in ways his do not.

Martin Buber, the twentieth-century philosopher, wrote this in his classic philosophical text, *The I-Thou Relationship:* "True community does not come into being because people have feelings for each other. . . . A living reciprocal relationship includes feelings but is not derived from them."

"How male!" a woman in a couples workshop exclaimed when I used Buber's passages as part of my teaching. "I mean, really, what is he talking about?" the woman said. "Of course community comes from feelings!" Not surprisingly, to most of the men in the workshop, Buber's comment made absolute sense. Feelings are illusions when compared to reason and logic. As one man put it, "Communities are built on logic and laws. It's feelings that get them in trouble."

I'm using this illustration not to say that all men prefer logic to feelings or all women prefer feelings to logic. In fact, in our daily flow of life, feelings and logic blend and merge so that it is artificial to make a distinction between them. And yet . . . it is still fair to say that women trust feelings more inherently than men. As this chapter has shown, our brain sciences reveal the reasons why. When we hear people say, "Boys shouldn't cry," our brain sciences guide us to look very closely at the person saying it and at the boy or man who accepts that credo as a natural part of his life.

Feelings and Stress

In the recent karate film, *Iron Monkey*, there is a scene between a father and son. The movie, set in ancient China, depicts a battle of good and evil, in which three warriors—two men and one woman—fight oppressive regimes. In a scene between one of the warriors and his ten-year-old son, the warrior Wong instructs him: "A strong man sheds blood before he sheds tear." The son—whose mother has died and who will fight huge physical battles—does, at one point, shed tears. Wong is not abusive, but he criticizes his son's tears and forces his son to stop their flow. The tears, in his mind, are not to be trusted.

Scenes like this—whether in movies set in the ancient world or on playgrounds between men and boys today—provide an illustration of a tendency in men to tell boys to repress their feelings. Many people—especially fathers and other male mentors—have intuitively understood that for many boys certain feelings increase stress rather than decrease it. In order to protect the boys from the stress, these adult caregivers try to compel boys to repress their feelings. This practice is controversial because some psychologists say that it hurts boys. Sometimes, especially when the "Don't cry!" is abusively employed, it is dangerous to boys (and all children), as well as to men and women.

Yet contrary to popular belief, neural science shows us that most of the time, it is not a "good" or "bad" thing nor is it "right" or "wrong." It is simply a part of a male's mode of feeling. Males don't have access to tears the way females do. By the time of puberty, females have up to 60 percent more prolactin in their bloodstream. Prolactin is the hormone that controls breast-milk and tear-gland production. Most women have larger tear glands than men and thus will process more feeling through crying and tears. Men will tend toward other ways of processing or toward repression, lacking commensurate access to tear mechanisms and glands. Many caregivers of boys and friends of men know this intuitively. Yet many do not.

A phrase proffered by a psychologist on talk shows became popular for a time after the Columbine school shooting: "If boys don't cry tears, they'll cry bullets." It was reflective of the popular tendency to believe that boys become violent because they are taught to repress their feelings—especially their tears. This kind of thinking has affected marriages, too. A woman in my therapy practice put it simply: "I think if my husband cried more, our marriage would be better." Similarly, it is popular to say that marriages fail because men have learned, through an oppressive culture, to repress not only their tears but their discussion of feelings. Our popular culture seems to say, without tears and feeling talk, a man can't love a woman adequately.

From a neurobiological standpoint, the idea that "if boys don't cry tears, they'll cry bullets" is well-meaning but not scientific proof. In fact, one can just as well prove that the fewer tears boys shed, the more peaceful the neighborhood or community will be. In Japan, for instance, boys are raised to repress tears and to repress feeling talk. It is considered "shame" for a male to cry, and there is far less emotional conversation between mothers and sons and husbands and wives than in the United States. Yet Japan has one of the lowest violence rates in the world—exponentially lower than the violence rate among males in the United States. The situation in China, the home of *Iron Monkey*, is very much the same.

The United States, in contrast, is one of the most emotionally active cultures on earth. Both our males and females talk about their feelings and cry more than in most cultures, yet our male-violence rates, within and without marriage, are among the highest in the world.

If we look at the scene from *Iron Monkey* in a different way— feeling sympathy for the boy whose feelings are forcibly repressed but also looking with depth at why, biologically, the father may have tried to teach the lesson he taught—we gain insight into a male biological trend: the tendency for males to seek safety, not in direct expression of feeling in tears and words—which might cause stress and overstimulation—but in other strategies that cause calm and focus. From this perspective, we're seeing a father who understands his son. Wong understands that if the male brain does not practice emotional self-restraint, it becomes overstimulated. Wong knows himself in his son, for he is male—he knows that feelings confuse him and values self-control rather than confusion.

While it is crucial that all cultures help males cry and talk about feelings, it is also crucial to the future of long-term relationships and family life that we look at the repression of male emotion from a nature-based point of view. For many boys and men, it is intuitive and functional to try to relieve the stress that complex feeling, talking, and crying have both on the male brain itself and, potentially, on the situation the brain is trying to manage. This can seem counterintuitive to women, yet a new study conducted in Germany might shed light on the wisdom of the male approach to feelings. This study showed that supportive conversation and sympathetic talk about feelings, can actually increase stress in both women and men. While women do tend to relieve more stress through feeling talk than men, even their neural stress levels can be affected by the very strategy they rely on!

As we relate to men, it is important that we acknowledge how differently they ascribe meaning to emotional experience and how the very feelings that a woman might enjoy having run through her neural web will stress a man's brain. For about thirty years, it has been wonderful to see parents encouraging little boys to express feelings in words. Many males have been led to discover parts of themselves previously forced underground. Marriages have been helped by our improvement of emotional literacy. At the same time, it is problematic to hinge human institutions as important as love relationships and marriages on the idea that a man can one day communicate his feelings to a woman to the extent she believes is ideal, or that he should experience and communicate feeling as if his brain worked like hers. It is crucial that we don't hinge the health of marriages on a man's emotional literacy or an adolescent male's ability to cry. In my work with couples, I've asked them to use a "10 percent rule" when it comes to talking about feelings in the relationship. I encourage couples to discover an amount of feeling talk that fits the actual nature of the man, then add 10 percent. So, for instance, if a man is average-to-high testosterone and more masculine on the male-brain questionnaire (and couples can add other factors into this equation, especially how the man was raised by his parents and ethnic culture), he will probably trust feeling talk about 20 percent of the time for emotional processing. The 10 percent rule requires him to add another 10 percent to that, making it his responsibility to apply feeling talk about 30 percent of the time. This is a way of compromising with his wife or partner's approach to feelings.

Once I taught this strategy and a woman very logically pointed out, "But 30 percent isn't meeting a partner "halfway." And yet, for that male's brain system, it may be. Not surprisingly, this system seemed inherently more satisfying to the men at the workshop than the women. And yet, by the end of the workshop, most of the women understood what I was getting at. As one woman put it, "If I can get him to talk about his feelings 30 percent of the time, I'll be lucky. Now getting him to cry, that's another matter."

As a student of human nature, I worry little or not at all if a man does not cry tears. I do not worry that a man who doesn't cry will necessarily hurt, demean, or inadequately love his spouse. I am one of those men who has small tear glands and cries tears very little. I know of other ways to cry—in solitude, when I watch my children give a recital and my throat catches, when I hear about something that upset my wife and my heart misses a beat. I know that I lean more toward the bridge-brain end of the brain spectrum rather than the high-testosterone end, and I just don't cry tears. This is who I am. Yet I know how to love. Most men, whether they cry or not, and whether they talk about feelings 50 percent of the time or do not perform this high a share of verbal life, know how to love. They just do it in a very male way.

I hope, by the end of this book, you'll agree with that. Even more, I hope that in understanding that there is actually a lot of good in not trusting "feelings" all of the time, you will find whole new worlds open up to you and to your relationship.

BRIDGE BRAINS: EXCEPTIONS TO THE RULE

"Are you kidding?" Thomas, forty-four, asked me during a lecture. "Kay, my wife, won't open up about herself at all. It's me who's the emotional one in the couple. It's frustrating how little Kay talks about her feelings. I must be one of your bridge brains."

We've spent this whole chapter establishing that there are biological trends that make women rely more on emotional life than men, and yet we all know men care deeply about emotions and that some men are even more feeling-talk oriented than women.

All of us have probably met at least one true bridge brain—a male who outdoes any woman in emotional processing. A man like Thomas may have a larger corpus callosurn than even his female partner, so his brain allows more cross talk in the brain, which in turn allows him to make more words out of his emotions than many other people can. Knowing that Thomas may be a bridge brain—at least in the area of emotive processing—doesn't reflect negatively on Kay. Bridge brains are everywhere, and they teach all of us constantly that human nature is widely varied. Kay might well be a bridge-brain female.

Sometimes I will talk about bridge brains with people, and a woman will say angrily, "Are you saying that since I'm more spatial, my brain's more like a man's?" Or a man will say, "Are you saying that since I'm more emotional, my brain's more like a woman's?" In fact, that's what we're saying from a neurobiological standpoint, not from the standpoint of stereotype or judgment. In emotional processing, my brain will appear, on an MRI, to look a little more like a woman's in certain ways than would, perhaps, my next-door neighbor's brain.

In the next decades, the ideas we've developed about each other's gender will doubtless become less like gender war and gender fear and more like mutual appreciation. We'll learn to appreciate the variety, even as we respect the male and female biological trends. When we accomplish this feat, we'll find ourselves healthy practitioners of intimate separateness.

PRACTICING INTIMATE SEPARATENESS: FINDING POWER IN THE *NATURE* OF EMOTIONAL LIFE

Marcus Aurelius, the Roman poet, said, "Waste no more time talking about great souls and how they should be. Become one yourself."

Both women and men can practice this as they decide to enjoy the nature of emotional life, especially the biological trends that tend to make men act in love relationships in ways women don't.

Men often forget Aurelius's wisdom, demanding their wives live in a rigid image of "wife." Women often forget Aurelius's wisdom, projecting onto their husband or boyfriend the idea that "he will be a great soul when he learns to feel the way I'd like him to."

Encouraging a man to expand his expression of feeling is worthwhile, but for women who are called, by life and intimate relationship, to enjoy the male brain, there is an even greater opportunity to become a great soul by adapting oneself to a relationship with a man (especially a higher testosterone, more masculinized male). This journey can seem lonely for a woman because her partner may actually not be equipped to satisfy her emotionally. It may also be lonely if she does not let go of the belief that it is his job to do so. If she buys into the idea that he must make her emotionally whole and healthy, she gives him ultimate power over her emotional life; she tacitly buys into the idea that he, her "soul mate," is her only true mirror. This is a lonely journey if a woman has brought to her relationships significant issues regarding her own father. It will be hard for her to see beyond her emotional demands on her husband if her father did not provide her with emotional warmth during girlhood.

If a man—a boyfriend, a husband, a "soul mate"—is, by personality and character, incapable of loyalty and fidelity, then a woman has less control over the outcome of her relationship than I am hinting here. To become a "great soul" in relationship to this kind of man, she will require an almost saintly spiritual journey through life. People may even say to her, "To stay with him, you must be a saint." And if the man is abusive to her, becoming a great soul may well mean leaving him.

But given that most men are, by nature, good and healthy for women (something women clearly intuit in their longings for male love), a woman's journey is the least lonely the more greatly she understands it. The woman who understands how the male brain processes emotions will be able to decrease her unreasonable idealization of her husband's emotions and her desire for his emotional structure to match hers. Intuitively, she might find herself utilizing these practical strategies:

- She'll ask him to think about something before he goes to work and thus give him time to process it.
- She'll spend time noticing how he does process his feelings—the games and sports he plays, the way he talks, how he stands silently, how he zones out in front of the TV, how he problem solves.
- She'll come to enjoy all the "ah ha's" she experiences as she sees a different brain system at work. These revelations will bring her joy, for she'll realize the immense variety of human experience.
- She'll alter her expectations of his feeling life, his communication techniques, and of the marriage itself.
- She'll emphasize emotional life in her friendships outside her marriage more than she did, especially with women friends and some male friends who are not an emotional or sexual threat to her life partnership.
- She'll take better personal care of herself—exercising, gaining personal time, caring for her health and well-being, so that her own emotional web is in balance.
- She'll express clear and reasonable emotional expectations to her husband. She'll not assume that he knows what she's feeling, even though, sometimes, he will.

These strategies are the tip of the iceberg. Many more will evolve as we go further in this book and its subject areas. By the end of *What Could He Be Thinking?* a whole system for intimate separateness will emerge, one that I hope will not only help your relationship or marriage, but will help you to feel you are making the journey of a great soul.

Each of us, woman or man, deserves to make that journey. In the end, it is the journey that most men want to help the women in their lives to make. Men love women and want women to be happy. It reflects painfully on a man's self-worth to know that his girlfriend or wife is living in loneliness, in a lack of love. Men want to bridge gaps with women. Men are not built to know a woman's heart the way many women might wish, nor are they built to experience life in a way that immediately transfers to words and feelings; but they feel one thing very clearly: that the women in their lives deserve the great journey. As the practice of intimate separateness is revealed, I hope you'll notice men journeying in it with you from the very beginning, the very first days of romantic love.

4

What Could He *Really* Be Thinking . . . About Sex and Romance?

> No matter what dull clay we seemed to be before, we are every one of us a poet when we are in love.
>
> **—Plato**

The candles light up the room, their light emanating from the mantle of the fireplace, along the windowsill, in the center of the small dinner table. Two plates, two glasses, two knives, two forks, everything is in twos, as if all of life, on this romantic evening, has coalesced to the moment in which two can become one. The woman, in her twenties, spent time in the shower, in front of the mirror, in contemplation of how she should look, and then in a gradual creation of that look for the self. She did her hair a certain way. Her clothes are set on her curves just right. She has known the man for a month. They've had six dates. Tonight is the night they'll have sex. She loves this man, loves the way he smells, the way he walks. His eyes hold both fierceness and tenderness. He could be the one, the one she's been looking for since she was a girl. She has the candles just right and the table just right and the aromas of the food she has cooked carry with them memories of evenings he and she went out to restaurants, walked in the park. Something wonderful is going to happen tonight, and she feels ready, her skin tingling with life.

He can see the candles from the sidewalk as he looks up at her apartment window. He has twelve roses in one hand and a bottle of wine in the other. Though a man in his late twenties, he feels like a young boy, nervous, excited, as if this were his first date. This woman has changed his life, his whole way of thinking and feeling. He's never been in love like this. She just accepts him for who he is. She's told him everything about herself, and he's shared everything about himself, and she found nothing to dislike, and he found everything to like. Fears he had in the past that he'd never find anyone have been allayed by the feeling he has that in her he has found everything he'll ever want. Tonight the kissing and petting they've done will turn to sex. He senses this with senses he never knew he had. He's ready. He's ready for anything she wants or needs. He's glad he's learned everything he's learned from previous sexual partners. He'll be the best partner she's ever had. As he enters her vestibule, he hears Dave Matthews playing on a disc player upstairs. It's coming from her apartment. Dave Matthews is his favorite. He smells aromas of food in the hallway. He smells her perfume. As if he were lit up by an eternal sun, he feels warm, tingly, as his hand reaches for the door.

There is a special feeling reserved for young lovers. The mixture of sex and romance on which human continuity hinges so much of its future seems nowhere better displayed than in the evening date toward which a couple has been moving in their first weeks or months of relationship—the evening that will bring a meeting of their sexual and romantic passions. As they approach it, transfixed by the aromas and perfumes, the flowers and fantasies, they do not think that in this date might be the end of their relationship; they only think that with each date comes new beginnings. Two people in love and lust, they feel as if they have stumbled, after decades of searching, into the drama of companionship for which they were born.

Indeed, they may have done so. They may end up being with this partner for years, decades, a lifetime. Or they may not. Their brain biology will make that determination.

THE BIOLOGY OF SEX AND ROMANCE

There are few areas of life in which the differences in male and female neurochemistry show up as well as in the romance and sex that dominate the early stages of a love relationship. PET scans, MRIs, endocrinological studies, and galvanic skin-response tests now show us how the brains of men and women function when they explore the mysteries of lust and love. Every hope and dream we bring to a candlelit dinner is touched by our nature—our hormones, brain chemicals, and key parts of the brain.

The Link Between Sex and Aggression

For two primary biochemical reasons, sex and aggression are intricately linked in male sexual biology. This is much less the case in females. Three biochemical elements make sure of this.

1. *Testosterone.* This dominant hormone in men is the human sex and aggression hormone. The higher its levels are in a man, the higher his sex drive and the more aggressive he is. Remember, aggression does not necessarily mean violence. Aggression is a complex activity formed by the whole brain and can mean a hundred kinds of task-focused activities like climbing a corporate ladder or being the best car salesman on the lot. While testosterone is a dominant male hormone, it is the hormone that provides a sexual and aggression/assertiveness baseline for all humans. Higher testosterone levels in women mean higher sex drive and aggression in women, too. When female androgenic hormone (testosterone) levels are cyclically higher near ovulation, women feel a surge of sexual desire; when women are injected, artificially, with testosterone, they become more sexually aggressive, as well as more assertive in the workplace.

2. Vasopressin. Without this brain chemical, sexual activity is very difficult for a man. Like testosterone, the study of vasopressin shows us how greatly sexual activity in men is, at its baseline, an aggression activity. Vasopressin is an aggression chemical found in the amygdala, one of the emotion-aggression centers of the brain and the anterior hypothalamus, the hormone regulator in the limbic system. Vasopressin is predominantly involved in territorial marking and sexual aggression. During foreplay, this chemical is secreted in males. Interestingly, higher vasopressin levels do not increase the courtship functions in females but instead curtail them. The higher the vasopressin, the more the man wants the woman, but the less the woman wants the man. If during foreplay, the man secretes vasopressin and the woman also does, he'll want her a lot, and she'll want to pull away from him. Like testosterone, vasopressin levels in the brain are partially determined by the testes: if a man is castrated, his testosterone and vasopressin levels both decrease considerably.

3. Dopamine. This neurochemical, which plays a crucial part in the general health of the brain, also plays a key part in male sexual aggression. When dopamine is removed from male brain activity, the male loses sexual desire. He will stop searching for females. When, on the other hand, dopamine is removed from female brain activity, her sexual interest is not affected.

In looking at testosterone, vasopressin, and dopamine, and in noticing the primary link between sex and aggression in men, it's important to remember that the patterns of their activity are not "learned behavior." A boy does not learn how to increase his testosterone levels so that he'll want to pursue mates. He does not learn, from Mom and Dad or society, how to link his vasopressin or dopamine to sexual desire. Nor do girls and women learn to delete the link in their brain systems, that vasopressin provides males. Rather, these brain patterns are set in the womb by the secretion of testosterone levels in the developing male and female brains. We will learn subtle arts concerning our sexuality, but the sexuality is inborn.

It is important for a woman to remember this when she feels frustration with a man who seems far more bent on sexual pursuit and conquest than on long-term romance. Especially in his youth, his brain is wired for sex (foreplay, intercourse, ejaculation) more than for romance (cuddling, exclusive commitment to one mate). Much of his brain activity ends once ejaculation occurs. His brain has been working toward a goal. It is not necessarily the same goal a woman is working toward. For him, romance is generally a means to a sexual end. To her, sex is more likely a means to a beginning.

Sex and Bonding

Female hormones make the woman's brain better wired for long-term romantic activity than the man's. Nowhere do we see this more clearly than in oxytocin activity in the hypothalamus. Male oxytocin (bonding chemical) levels are lower than in females. In many men, they can be ten times lower. Just as testosterone levels are much higher in males, oxytocin levels are generally higher in females.

However, there is one time of the day when the male oxytocin levels approach the normal female levels—during sexual orgasm. When a man ejaculates, his oxytocin level shoots up to the levels that females experience during other times of the day. When a man ejaculates, he bonds utterly with her.

Soon his oxytocin level will go back down to its normal level, and when the woman does not receive a phone call from him the next day—despite the fact that he said he loved her and would call her—she is experiencing his postsexual drop in oxytocin. During orgasm, the female-dominant chemical became his dominant chemical. Testosterone and vasopressin, which got him to the point where he could successfully achieve coitus, receded in dominance—their job complete—and oxytocin, the bonding chemical, took over. But then testosterone and vasopressin begin their journey back to dominance, while oxytocin recedes.

One of the primary reasons that men want sex more than

women (on average) is because it feels so good to them to have the high oxytocin—it feels great to feel so bonded with someone. All humans get an explosion of joyful brain chemistry—oxytocin being a major player—when we achieve bonding. In male biochemistry, sex is the quickest way for a man to bond with a woman. Even though the chemical bond is transitory, nature appears to hope that the transitory bond will turn more permanent—oxytocin receding, but perhaps the man feeling closer and closer to the woman so that, over a period of time, he bonds with her with the more complex brain involvement we call love.

Nature has given females a different way of approaching sex and bonding. Where the young man might feel completed at the point of climax—utterly bonded for the moment—the young woman feels that bonding is a process that has only just begun. For him, chemical bonding will be paramount during the sex act; for her, bonding will go on at a biochemical level throughout the days of courtship and during her preparation for romantic evenings. It will be quite heightened during sex, but her oxytocin levels are so much higher so much of the time that the sex act is better integrated, for her, in the long-term bonding process. She will not tend to emphasize sex as the ultimate activity; it is only a momentary surge in oxytocin. She will emphasize the hundreds of activities, thoughts, phone calls, gifts, candles, feelings that accentuate, every moment of every day, her developing bond with the male.

In presenting this scenario, we are presenting something that can feel like a tragic love story. Perhaps there is no worse pain than wanting something romantic or sexual from someone who is unwilling or unable to give it. Women can spend months, even years, trying to romance romance out of men. Men can spend months, even years, trying to romance sex out of women. Sometimes we succeed, and sometimes we fail. All the while, our biochemistry is omnipresent.

And this is only one small part of this picture.

Male Reproductive Biology and the Sex Difference

As an adolescent, a male generally reaches a point of coital desire—the surging need to ejaculate—earlier than the girls around him feel the need to achieve orgasm. From the beginning of his internal sexual experience—played out mainly in sexual fantasy that involves little or no romance—he hopes, earlier in life, for more sex than girls and women do. In his lifetime, the average man will have more sexual partners than the average woman.

People have often thought this occurred because males have more testosterone. While testosterone is one reason (higher testosterone females have more sex than lower testosterone females, too), testosterone is not the whole picture. For males, another key reason for the male emphasis on sex and sexual fantasy lies in the connection of the male brain with male reproductive biology, specifically: Male testes, under guidance from the hypothalamus and pituitary gland, generate trillions of fertile sperm in a lifetime. This creates the reproductive compulsion to ejaculate a great deal in search of sexual partners who are potentially reproductive.

Male reproductive biology is set up on speculation, i.e., any nubile female is potentially fertile at any time, so let's go to it! The male brain, through the hypothalamus, makes sure that testosterone and vasopressin constantly surge in the male, making him ready to accept sexual-bonding opportunities in an instant and making him capable of competing for and pursuing sexual opportunities (or, if he's very shy by personality, fantasizing these opportunities more than he pursues them).

Female reproductive biology is not based in the creation of constant fertility but, just the opposite, in the limiting of fertility opportunities. Women generate about three hundred fertile eggs in a lifetime. Compared to trillions of sperm, a fertile egg is rare. It specifically does not need the female hypothalamus and pituitary gland to link it to constantly flowing sex-drive testosterone. Instead, it needs links to female hormones, estrogen and progesterone. Testosterone does come into play especially at time of ovulation, when female androgenic hormones rise, increasing sex drive. This surging lasts about forty hours, not all month. Women, as opposed to men, are not constantly at the ready, in this biological sense, constantly living in hope of coitus.

Sexual promiscuity is not as much in female nature as in males primarily because female reproductive and brain biology mitigate against it. Creating only three hundred fertility opportunities in a lifetime, a woman will more likely view sexual intercourse more carefully than many, if not most, of the men around her, her limited number of eggs echoing through her brain. The fact that the male has an infinite number echoes through his. For a few years during the 1970s, it was argued that sexual behavior such as masturbation, promiscuity, sexual fantasies were "learned behavior," and that women and men were the same in these areas. It was considered immature or unliberated of women to not be like men in their sexual lives. This was an interesting experiment, but not very long lasting. While many women are now enjoying more access to these activities, women do not, on average, masturbate as much, discover as many sexual partners, or engage in as many sexual fantasies as men because they do not have as strong a biological compulsion to do so.

In popular culture we often hear people joke about "men thinking with their penises." Biologically, to a greater extent than we realize, this is quite true. It is also one of the primary reasons human beings dominate the natural ecosystem. If sex is taken away from a man for whatever reason—for instance, erectile dysfunction that results from prostate cancer—the devastating effect on his sense of self cannot be overestimated. One of his primary sources of self-worth is gone, the natural link between brain and testes broken by illness.

Sperm Competition: Male Sexuality and Self-Worth

Part of male sexuality is the issue of worth and prowess. It is as if the brain and body are saying, "If I can just get laid, I will finally be of worth." This is not just true of adolescent boys, who are beginning their development of self-worth, exploring all possible avenues toward it. Many middle-aged males still acquire a great deal of self-worth from sexual conquest.

That the male does not associate as much self-worth to romance as to coitus should not surprise us. Romance fantasies are a greater domain for females, sexual fantasies a greater domain for males. His self-worth is linked, to a great extent, to how often and how well he engages in the sex act, while hers is, to a great extent, associated with nonsexual gains made in her romantic alliance: personal security, hierarchical advancement through her association with a male, potential stability for the future care of her children.

The greater need that males have, on average, to explore, conquer, and perform in order to acquire their worth reflects the inherent path to worth in female biology and the lack of an inherent path in male biology. The individual sperm of the male is not inherently worthwhile. A male spills billions of sperm on himself, into towels, onto floors, and many other places as he masturbates. He knows that his individual sperm are worthless in themselves. He knows that the worth of his sexual action comes from the sperm competition: the ability of a sperm to compete with other sperm (his own and, if a woman has multiple partners, other men's) toward the moment of fertile impact with an egg.

Female sexual biology works in a different way. Females certainly compete for male attention, (just as males certainly work hard to develop their romantic abilities), but females do not compete in order to have sexual orgasm. They compete in order to select the mate who is potentially most useful and loving to them in the long term. Females are less likely than males to judge a man ill-suited just because he looks geeky or is otherwise physically unattractive. If he is successful or shows success potential (intelligence), he is more likely to be selected by a female. If he can mirror her emotionally, which most men can now do in the early stages of romance, he will also more likely be selected by the female. If he is good in bed, that's a plus for her; but it is rarely the primary reason for selection or rejection.

Men, on the other hand, are more likely to reject a partner if she becomes physically unattractive or remains sexually inept. This one biological fact can seriously affect long-term relationships today, as we'll see in chapter 6, because many women do not realize the full impact their changing bodies have on male-brain biology over the period of years.

How the Rest of the Brain Helps Work with Sexual and Romantic Chemistry

We've discussed hormones, brain chemicals, and sexual organs. In doing so, we've looked at the brain's participation in sex and romance. Let's now examine even more closely the parts of the brain and how they help men and women come together for sexual and romantic unions.

Sexual fantasy. According to recent brain studies, males have 400 percent more visual sexual fantasies per day than women. The higher incidence of male sexual fantasies crosses cultures: Whatever the continent or country, male sexual fantasizing is, on average, more prevalent than female.

Fantasy is a projection of imagery that grows from imagination. Imagination gains its imagistic quality in the cerebral cortex. Its emotional motivation generally links to the limbic system. Fantasy life in males and females share similarities and differences based, at a biochemical level, on the interplay of oxytocin, vasopressin, testosterone, and the other hormones and chemicals on the neurotransmitters for imagination. The chemicals themselves are regulated internally, by genetically and fetally coded brain systems. Your testosterone and oxytocin, for example, will flow as coded by your DNA and by testosterone surges that helped form the brain in the womb; also, by stimulation in the biological environment—the home, the media, the streets, what we hear, what we see, what is said to us. By the time sexual fantasies begin in the imagination—around ten years old—those fantasies represent neurochemistry of the most complex kind. Like all of what the brain does throughout its life, those fantasies exist in the brain for reasons of adaptation.

Sperm competition is such a powerful biological reality in males, so utterly affecting male life, that males rely on sexual fantasy, not only for entertainment, but for base sexual performance. This is the adaptive quality of sexual fantasy.

Some people object to the idea of male sexual fantasy. To traditional moralists, for example, sexual fantasies are sins. Feminists point out that sexual fantasies represent the objectification of women, which may lead to oppression. From a religious or ideological point of view, these may be valid arguments—and pornography can be a very dangerous thing—but sexual fantasy, if studied from the point of view of brain biology, serves a crucially important function in the lives of male/female relationships.

Male biology, compelled toward intercourse and ejaculation, often needs to project sexual fantasies onto women in order to create variety in their selection process and in order to make the sex act possible even when they have selected someone whom they do not find too sexually attractive at a given moment. The male brain, especially with its greater emphasis on brain stem and lower limbic involvement, can instantaneously create a sexual fantasy in order to make sex possible. The fantasies a male uses to masturbate are practice for the fantasies he may well need in order to make love to a female at every possible opportunity.

Women often do not realize how many times in a year a man must include fantasies in the sex act. A woman might want sex at a given moment but might smell bad to the man, might look unattractive, might catch the man when he's tired or preoccupied. But especially in the first decade of his sexual life, he will try his best to have sex, compelled biologically to do so, hoping to give and receive pleasure. The fantasies he uses to help him achieve erection and then orgasm in turn make bonding more possible.

Studies show that the male brain projects a sexual fantasy every few minutes—some argue that it is every few seconds—whether the man is at work or at home, tinkering in the garage or making love to his partner. The male visual cortex will turn, in an instant, to assess the sexual and fantasy value of the body of a nubile female walking near him. This can be frustrating and threatening for women, who pick up on the attention the other woman is receiving. While it is never completely comfortable for either men or women to see that a spouse is exhibiting sexual interest in another person, it can help women to keep in mind that his interest is almost always temporary, rooted in brain biology; it's not a threat to his primary romantic relationship, and at a biological level, it's part of why some of the sexual bonding in the romantic relationship is possible.

Moral codes that have remained blind to nature do not last long. Moral codes that include knowledge of human nature generally survive the test of time. If a woman condemns sexual fantasies but does not realize their use, she may have trouble with long-term relationships with men. If a woman values the long-term friendship with her mate but shames him for letting his eyes stray toward a beautiful young female, she will probably put a strain on that friendship. If a woman values friendship but refuses all sexual experimentation with her mate, she may well lose that mate. It is crucial to get help for men who are sex addicted and unhealthy, yet most men who fantasize are simply normal.

And just as male sexual fantasy confounds women, it is useful to notice that women's romantic fantasies often confound men. Women, it seems, must have flowers, cards, sweet letters in order to be happy. To men it seems that women want constant phone calls, constant reassurance. Women seem to want men to be whatever they want at a given romantic whim. This morning he should talk a lot about his feelings. Tonight he should silently hold her. At five o'clock in the morning, when his testosterone peaks and he is very horny, he should value her by letting her sleep. While the male imagination spends more of its time projecting sexual fantasies, the female imagination constructs a picture of the man who will be her romantic ideal. It is a picture of a man who *will evolve and change* as she wants him to. This is an almost tragic difference between women and men. His sexual fantasy will specifically *not* include much change. He wants variety of accoutrement from her but not permanent change of attractive appearance. He wants her to remain as nubile as possible.

Women have rebelled against the "cult of youth" that males project onto them, pointing out that men yearn for women to remain young and nubile so that women can meet male sexual fantasies. Men as a group dislike woman's projections of romantic fantasies and point out that women buy into the cult of youth, not only to be attractive to males, but to avoid the feeling of getting older.

Our society is presently struggling over these issues and, to a great extent, wasting time blaming the other sex. Human love works when confusion becomes compromise. The couple who sit at the candlelight dinner will face these issues as they get older, in later stages of relationship. Luckily, for now, these issues are in the background. Pheromones are one of the reasons they remain there, for a time.

Pheromones. Pheromones are wonderful brain chemicals that allow males and females to feel, during the courtship and romance phases of life, that they can "read each other's minds." Pheromones are, in fact, telepathic brain waves that work through the nostrils and the olfactory system (our ability to smell), making us able to smell each other's neurosexual biology and alter our brain system accordingly. Males can smell when females are estrous (ovulating) and will often be able to provide very romantic gestures and feelings during this time, which in turn may make females more sexually receptive.

For instance, the "I love you" that males speak, making females feel good, go up in frequency when pheromones alert the male brain that the female might be more receptive now, just a little more ready. Female pheromones also become alert along with male biology. Without pheromones, human love, in the first few months of a relationship, would be very different indeed.

The cingulate gyrus. We have mentioned this part of the brain before, a very important emotion center in the limbic system. While pheromones can alert a brain to loving behavior, PET scans of couples who are deeply in love show that the cingulate gyrus carries that love and makes it real for the man or woman. If two young people who think they are in love could get PET and MRI scans, the technicians could tell them if they actually *are* in love or if one or both partners are simply projecting romantic and sexual fantasies onto the other without the deep love that leads to long-term partnership. Yet, unfortunately, in the phase of life we call romance, which lasts sometimes only until sexual conquest is achieved, and often for about six months to a year, the cingulate gyrus can deceive us. It can light up as if in love; but then, after the romance phase is over—perhaps after we've gotten married but now realize we were not suited for each other—it will show less activity, and we'll know we were never in love the way we thought.

People will say, "We fell out of love." The same person might later say, "I fell in love again." This can be quite accurate from a neural viewpoint. Our brains, including the cingulate gyrus, are wired for serial relationships because they are wired for serial sexual activity. Though many of us prefer monogamy and have larger or more active cingulate gyri that better support monogamy, not all human brains are coded for the cingulate gyrus to "fall in love" only once. In the next chapter, we will talk about how to help work toward monogamous marriage, but monogamy is never assured in human beings, in large part because everyone's cingulate gyrus is somewhat different. Not surprisingly, on average, the cingulate gyrus in men is smaller than in women.

Many of the biological factors we have discussed here are gradually becoming a part of our cultural dialogue. Our scientific technologies are enabling us to investigate who we really are as men and women hoping to love each other. When I hear people talking about issues of biological difference, I feel great optimism. Soon, I believe, the almost tragic gap between what men and women want and need from sex and romance will get closed by our new understanding.

Recently I overheard a woman in a restaurant say to her female friend, "You know, I just heard that men glance at a woman's eyes then settle visually on her body, but women glance at a man's body then settle visually on his eyes. That makes sense, doesn't it?" Fragments of biological knowledge seem to be penetrating our culture. It is important that the bits and pieces available become a whole new nature-based vision for human living. That is certainly the intention of *What Could He Be Thinking?* For women to carry on relationships with men in a state of ignorance of male biology is tantamount to a woman giving herself over to a stranger.

HOW ROMANTIC IDEALIZATION CAN MAKE AND BREAK LOVERS' HEARTS

In all the biological and relational material we've explored in this chapter, there is a hidden theme: the theme of idealization, both sexual and romantic. Women tend to spend more time in romantically idealizing men and men in sexually idealizing women. This has been the case for millions of years, yet there are two profound differences between the far past and the present:

1. In the past, human social sanctions that protected marriages were paramount. Idealizations didn't matter much because religions and social sanctions made sure men and women stayed married no matter how they idealized each other. In the present, these sanctions have dissipated, but our idealization of romantic alliances has risen exponentially.

2. In the past, marriages were considered inferior if they did not last. In the present, male-female partnerships are considered inferior if they are not based on ongoing *romance*. How long they last is now less important than the quality of romance they possess during the partnership.

Until recently, both sex and romance were considered less than critical elements in male-female alliances.

Sex was important but could be done as "duty." Women intuited that men bond through sex and so tried to accommodate male sexual needs in marriage. Sex could also be pursued "behind closed doors" by men with other partners besides a wife. Generally, marriages were not broken because they were devoid of sex or a man was not monogamous.

Romance, too, was an optional part of ongoing male/female alliances. Since marriage was a practical matter, couples were brought together by arrangement and found romance later, by the habit of living together and caring for young, or often they did not find it at all.

Presently, we are involved in a human experiment. With marriage seemingly an optional choice rather than a necessity of survival, we are putting romance higher up in our personal and cultural hierarchies of needs. Human civilization now has the freedom to seek the complete immersion of brain and body in the sensations and activities of uninhibited pleasure, sex, and romance. The women's movement has been central in raising the bar. Especially over the last century, women very powerfully noticed that sexual and romantic alliances, including marriages, were generally run from the male point of view. Women might be getting their financial needs met by men but not their romantic needs. Women may be the ones who select mates for sex, forcing males to compete for that selection, but that is often not enough to fulfill a human heart.

As we come to the candlelight dinner in the new millennium, both male and female ideals of sex and romance are being projected on the other. Men and women link in pheromones, brain chemicals, emotions and passions toward the continual immersion of themselves in each other, sexually and romantically. But beginning at the moment the dinner candles die out and the sexual flames consume, the ascendance of the female vision of romance occurs. If the man has only been after sex, he will not call back the next day, and the affair will end. But if he is in love with this woman, he will now begin a process of immersion in *her* romantic idealizations in order to sustain the relationship. Within a few weeks, he will probably begin to hear her wondering why he doesn't talk to her as much as he did in the first few weeks, why he doesn't call her in the morning and in the evening, why he doesn't want to go dancing, why he doesn't comment on her clothes as much. Within a few months, he may begin to feel an overwhelming pressure from female romantic idealization.

He was a complete mirror of her in the first few weeks, able to show to her, via his mirroring, her hidden self. He had seen in her the real woman no other man had seen. But six months to a year later, he no longer does this as much. Where did that King of Romance go?

Many emotionally pleasurable things happen between this man and woman, and they may well marry and stay together for fifty years, but first they must make it through this period, which can be very painful. The heart is tearing a little now, and many romantic partnerships die out within the first year, hearts broken. Two brain chemistries, different at their core but temporarily masking their differences through immersion of hormones, neurotransmitters, and sexual and romantic fantasies, make love possible at first, then they may make it seem that the great romantic love of just a few months ago was a lie.

For a woman who is seeking to learn how to help sustain a romantic union and avoid the pain of a broken heart, a vital step is to understand and acknowledge the extent to which she may carry (often unconsciously) romantic idealizations of men. Having done that, she must then understand and accept that most men—even the most well intentioned—will not be able to live up to those expectations after a year or two.

The most obvious romantic idealization prevalent today is the desire for men to "talk about their feelings." As we hinted earlier, women hold as one of their highest criteria a man's ability to express innermost feelings (especially the feeling of a woman's attractiveness). With that in mind, we must now answer the question, "Why are men so good at talking about their feelings and making a woman feel so special in the first six months or year of a relationship, then they return to just being like any other guy?"

The biological base for a man's ability to accomplish this extended romantic gesture occurs and then reduces in the first months (even year or so) of romance. Pheromones, which naturally peak during this time, allow the male brain instant access to the female mind (and vice versa). The male cortex is catalyzed by signals from the cingulate gyrus and other parts of the limbic system to concentrate on the stimulation of words in the left hemisphere, as well as to make eye-to-eye contact and to focus on listening ability. The brain is, quite literally, taken over by the task of romance.

When a number of months have passed, the brain has accomplished its primary goal: a male-female alliance that will lead to sex, bonding, and companionship. Pheromones decrease, the limbic system returns to concentrate, not just on this romantic partner, but on other things that are equally important in life—such as making a living, then, once children come, on child rearing. The woman may well feel she is loved less because the man expresses his feelings less. Certainly it is possible that she is loved less, but even this will not be caused by his decrease in expression of romantic feeling. And in most cases, she is probably still fantasizing the pheromone-aided, romantic ideal of the man at the candlelight dinner. The man she loves is that same man, but his brain is adapting over the years to the next era of life. Simultaneously, she is the same woman, and her brain is adapting. Perhaps she doesn't want to have sex as much as she did. Perhaps she doesn't want to dress up for him as much. What the couple is experiencing is a natural slip in the relationship, one that must be accommodated by the man's decrease in early sexual projection onto his wife and the woman's decrease in romantic idealization of her husband.

When these changes occur, it helps to keep in mind that the romance stage—in which early sexual and romantic ideals are projected—is only one of twelve stages in human love (we will explore all twelve in chapter 6). When we are challenged by the reality of decreasing pheromones and other brain functions, it is vital we change our expectations of human romance and human sexual alliances. We must realize that a man may never talk about his feelings again as he did at that candlelit dinner, but this does not mean he no longer cares.

WHAT ARE *REASONABLE* ROMANTIC EXPECTATIONS OF ONE ANOTHER?

Until the last hundred years, humanity only had to answer questions of moral and social expectations. Questions of romantic expectations were relatively moot. Now they are paramount in our minds. They are paramount in women's minds because women project the romantic ideal and paramount in men's minds because in order to be sexually selected by women, men need to hone their skills in the area of fulfilling romantic ideals, even if they are only able to do this, to the woman's complete satisfaction, for a few months or a year or two.

Not surprisingly, women's romantic expectations do change as they get older. In a survey done in 2001 by Rutgers University, 94 percent of college women said that when they married, they wanted their spouses to be their soul mates, first and foremost. The young women surveyed said, "It is more important to have a husband who can communicate his deepest feelings than to have a husband who makes a good living." However, when women who have children are questioned, the top priority for women now was not romantic idealization, but a man's ability to support the family. In a recent study, 70 percent of women with children said they wanted a man who could provide well enough for the family so that the woman could spend more time being a mother to the children.

This reflects the fact that female hormonal biology changes when children come, causing female idealizations of men to expand to include more of their own father's provider/protector and-protector modality. Women still hope for the same romantic idealizations of certain functions, like "talking about feelings" throughout marriage, but natural priorities are shifting within them. Many of the women who become the most successful in marriage are the women who shift their romantic expectations of men in a conscious way. Women who hold onto unreasonable romantic expectations for more than a few years—the ones they had at the candlelight dinner—often end up unhappy. It is crucial here to make a distinction between romantic expectations and other expectations, such as moral ones. The women who, once they had children, realized that a man's ability to help them support the children was their highest priority were letting go of many of their early romantic idealizations, but not of their basic values.

The biological study of romance and sex provides us an opportunity to adapt even better than we have in the past to both who we are and who our partner is. Though women alone cannot ensure the success of a romance or a marriage, they can gain immense power by consciously adjusting their own romantic expectations of men and, as they do so, becoming masters of what men are thinking. As women adjust their own expectations during and through the romance phase of a relationship, and as they communicate to the man what they need, women also gain by peering into the man's expectations during the romance phase of life.

Let's explore men's expectations even more deeply now. I hope this exploration will help women who love men to feel less pain and more joy in their romantic partnerships by better understanding what they are up against as they begin the journey of love with a man.

What Men Need: Expectations and Interpretations

Especially in the first months and year of a relationship, men are sending lots of signals to women about their needs and expectations. These don't as often come out in words as do the women's signals to them. What are some of the signals men are sending?

I am fragile. As men get more and more intimate with a woman, they need a great deal of reassurance. Women often miss this because, especially in the romantic phase of a partnership, men are compelled by nature to appear strong. Since women do not generally select men who are weak (if women do, they don't generally stay with weak or unsatisfactory men for a long period of time), men know quite well that women are more likely to stay loyal to a man who performs well, less loyal to a man who does not. Contemporary divorce statistics support basic human nature. Now that social strictures on divorce have loosened, the majority of divorce petitions (65 percent) are filed by women. The most common reason a woman seeks divorce is dissatisfaction with the man. Women's power to select mates has increased exponentially by the availability of divorce. Men know that, not only must they keep performing for women, but that the lack of social strictures increases the pressure.

Even beyond this circumstance, fragility is natural to the male psyche because, pushed by hormones to be aggressive, he is constantly putting himself in the position of being shot down. This fragility is only enhanced in contemporary dating and romance, in which rules of chivalry often no longer exist and men aren't sure how to perform with women. Men make many false starts in their romances today and make many "mistakes," hoping that women will respond with subtle or very overt guidance. This gives women a great deal of power in romance. Men are saying: I am fragile, more fragile than you think; I need your expectations of me to be reasonable, I need you to communicate them to me, and I need you to give me as much reassurance as you can, without being cloying. As a woman meets this need, she will notice that her romantic partner is seeking to meet the same needs in her, for she is very fragile as well. A woman must realize that even in a man's bravado is constant insecurity. If she shames him angrily for not meeting her romantic and emotional expectations in a quick manner, he may well leave her.

I need to be needed. Human males, like males of nearly every species, are wired to make themselves conspicuous during the mating period. Female black-capped chickadees watch and listen as the male chickadees do vocal combat. Their songs give them the chance to mate, for the females choose the black-capped male who wins the song contest.

Human males are songbirds too, and human females are constantly eavesdropping on the male song, ascertaining just how powerful is the song of the male they are leaning toward selecting. Human males keep singing until chosen, then keep singing throughout life, hoping to send signals of self-worth and significance.

His own fragile ego constantly present, a man sings, "Look at me! Look at what I can do," and hidden within that: "You still need me, don't you?" Working twelve hours a day, he needs to be needed. His work, which may be grueling and miserable, takes on some light because it is needed by the person he loves. The sense he gains from his romantic partner that his efforts are needed helps him to make the work into a song.

Women who take an interest in a man's aggression activities (his work, athletics, computer inventions) and understand his need to show off who he is and what he does can play a pivotal role in bolstering the crucial sense that he is truly needed in the world.

Many women have to make greater sacrifices than men in order to achieve the kind of success that men (aided by a history of social chauvinism) do in the workplace. It can be stressful, at the end of a long and difficult day at the office, for a woman to feel she must "turn off" her competitive instincts in order to be loved by her partner. However, she may also know instinctively—as well as from experience—that whatever her own achievements, it is vital to allow the man to shine, or she may not receive all the love from him she desires. It can help her meet this challenge by remembering that his need to shine is based in brain biology. The man does not feel he has inherent worth; he is driven to show his worth constantly. She, in contrast, has inherent worth, in a biological sense.

The wish that some women have to be just as competitive and vocal ("song singing") about their achievements is clearly present for many couples in the romance stage of life. It often dissipates later. The longer a man is involved in a secure marital relationship, the safer he may feel—thus, the less he will operate out of inherent fragility. His need to be conspicuous in the mating dance decreases. A few years into a relationship, males still need to be supported for what they've accomplished, but they generally pay less primal attention to how high their status is in the relationship. In fact, most men, after a few years of marriage, find themselves giving over much of their power to their spouse, discovering that she is very good at managing family and relational power.

Men do not generally relinquish their power during the romance stage, however, even when it seems they have become "puppy dogs," or that, "He'll do anything I ask him," or, "He's perfect; he just lets me ask for what I want and gives it to me." During the mating dance, if the man is unable to feel conspicuous, respected, valued, and powerful, he often chooses not to continue the relationship. Even after his relinquishment of power to a wife in marriage, if she constantly disrespects or shames him or minimizes his accomplishments, he may well seek a way of distancing himself from her—from having affairs to isolating himself in work to leaving her.

I need sex with you. Our knowledge of how testosterone and oxytocin work in men helps us to understand why men put so much emphasis on sex during romance. Since one of the primary ways a man bonds biochemically with his romantic partner is through sex, if the man is truly in love, the overt male signal for "I want sex" hides the hidden signal which is: "I need to have sex with *you*." Women can gain great romantic advantage if they learn to understand the difference between the two signals.

If a man is mainly signaling the overt one, his message is, "I want sex and lots of it; if not with you, I'll keep looking elsewhere." His cingulate gyrus is probably not involved much in this romantic liaison. "I don't really need *you*," he is saying, "but you've made yourself available, and I like you, so let's do it." If he is not displaying the hidden signal—that he deeply needs the sex with this particular woman in order to feel whole, complete, bonded, and filled with life's passions—then the woman is immediately empowered to make a decision about whether to bond with him or simply enjoy the sex and temporary companionship. If the man is indeed signaling, "I need sex with *you*," there is greater likelihood he will be not just a sexual and social companion, but a long-term romantic partner.

It is more difficult for a woman to separate the two signals than for a male because her brain biology is based more on achieving long-term bonds than his is, but it is possible. Many women realize men are not "serious" yet enjoy the short-term relationship. The key for her is to realize what the man is signaling as soon as possible. If he is only sending the overt signal, the woman will have to concentrate—through heightened frontal-lobe (judging process) involvement—on "keeping a distance" from him. She'll likely become clinically depressed (her limbic system immersed in stress hormones) if she is unable to keep her frontal lobes dominant in this relationship. This man may be somewhat dangerous to the mental health of some of the women with whom he seeks to have sex. The danger he poses does not come from his malice but from the different romantic/sexual expectations he and the woman may have.

Given this risk, many women instinctively know that it is better for their emotional well-being to wait until a man is saying, "I need to have sex with *you*." At some point, many women who have tried "casual relationships" give them up, risking loneliness for a time but waiting for true love.

***I need you to trust what I* do.** Especially confounding to many woman is a man's deep-seated need to be trusted for what he *does*, not for everything he does or does not say. During romance, women want a man to say certain things, like "I love you," at just the right moments, with just the right objects—flowers, cards, surprises—mixed in. Men work toward fulfilling this need in females. Yet for men the greater show of love comes in the long term, in what they do, especially to keep their status and perform well for their partner and family.

Especially in today's culture, men are increasingly taking their romantic signals from women, reading women loud and clear who say. "What you say to me matters a lot." For males, wired and trained to do whatever it takes to be selected, adaptation requires them to become skilled at saying what a woman wants to hear. Yet even as they develop the romance skills they did not need generations ago in order to marry, they still unconsciously see the world as a place of performance imperatives. They yearn to be trusted for what they do, not merely what they say.

If a woman only praises her romantic partner for what he says, the man senses he is not trusted for his inherent nature. He will not be able to bond as deeply with the romantic partner. If, on the other hand, a woman says, in words and in nonverbal signals, "I love you for your telling me you love me, but I also love the fact that you are so good at your work, your hobbies, your athletics . . ." the man is more likely to feel that she has a holistic love and trust for him. If the woman says, "I love that you tell me you love me and I love how emotional you are," but more rarely indicates appreciation for his work, hobbies, or athletics, he may quickly surmise that she loves him for the aspects of self she wants to mold or project into the future, not for himself as he is, a man.

BRIDGE BRAINS

Cheryl, a business manager and mother of three, married eleven years, wrote:

> I think my husband must be a bridge brain. When we were court-ing, he was even more romantic than I was. He had everything laid out for sunset dinners. He read me poetry. He wrote songs for me. He was the dream man. After we got married, he gave me cards and love letters. He takes such good care of me and the kids. He's in computers and works out of our home. He's always rearranging furniture. He likes it to look nice. Even after eleven years he knows how to make me feel like I'm the only person in the world who matters. All my women friends envy me. Their husbands hardly ever tell them anything about how they feel.

In this chapter we have emphasized biological trends in the majority of males. Yet as we've mentioned, bridge-brain males don't fit many of these trends.

How does a woman know if she has been courted by a bridge brain? This question is a primal, generally unconscious one for women. A woman might ask, "He's so able to read my mind; I wonder if he'll always stay this way?" or, "I wonder if he'll always love me this way?" A woman might ask, "Is he going to change like other men do?"

The best way to get a clear answer to these questions is with time. If a man's brain is already formatted for greater verbal-emotive functioning, with more cortical areas used for feeling talk, this will be clear after about a year into the relationship. Within a year or two, the hormone-based, romance-inducing brain chemistry will generally have subsided enough for a clear picture of his brain to emerge.

Within a few decades, our culture will experiment with inexpensive PET scans and MRIs that couples will use to peer into each other's brains. During this experimentation, women will be able to see if men have a bridge brain from the day of meeting. They won't need to wait a year. But until this technology is readily available, women won't know if they are coupled with a bridge brain until well into the relationship, perhaps even after the wedding day.

Although bridge brains are definitely idealized by some women today, it is important for all of us to remember that during the romance stage, the prime directive of the brain and hormonal system is to be selected by the mate. For a man, this means doing whatever it takes to make the woman happy (within reason!). It is not unusual for many men to appear, during romance, to fit the profile of bridge brains. Even when the man doesn't, the woman may well be so in love that his lack of bridge-brain qualities may not matter.

For now.

PRACTICING INTIMATE SEPARATENESS

Given the difference between male and female brain systems and chemistries during romance, what should we do? Should women just let the whole process continue as it is, often ending up lonely? Should men stop presenting themselves as bridge brains—emotion talkers, perfect mates—during romance? Should women become more sexually promiscuous? What will work?

Given the power of the biology of romance and sex, nature suggests that one of the most important things a woman can do to make a relationship successful is to practice intimate separateness.

The Power of Sexual Selection

In the biological dance of sex and romance, in which men compete for women, women wield great power in choosing when to have sex and with whom. In our modern culture, sex happens very quickly between couples, so men spend less time performing and competing with each other for women. Quite simply, women have made themselves more readily available to men. The advantages of this new situation are many—including sexual adventure. However, a woman also spends less time ascertaining the worth and long-term compatibility of a man before she has sex. Instead, women spend more time ascertaining the man's worth after sex. This trend is a way for women to try to get men to romance them (sing their songs) without sex as an object of conquest. This is an innovation by which women hope that romantic selection, rather than sexual selection, will become the seat of female power.

This new innovation is definitely of value and will continue to be refined in the human dance. The biological power inherent in the nature of sexual selection—by which women delay sex in order to "check out" the worth of a guy—is also a valuable power that women have surrendered during the last decades. Women should not surrender this power lightly. I hope the nature-based theories and sciences in this book are gradually showing that women can have power in the workplace, in the home, in the media, in romance, and anywhere they seek it without having to give up their power to manage sexual partnerships. All other suggestions on practicing intimate separateness during the romance phase of a relationship are less powerful if this first concept of sexual selection is not utilized by women.

If a woman lets a man court her for many months—even enjoying petting, oral sex, and other sexual fun, but withholding intercourse—this simple show of power can affect not only this particular partnership, but her self-image and sense of self-esteem during her years of sexual and romantic maturation. Not surprisingly, a recent study showed that female pleasure was gained through intercourse, but that self-esteem among young women correlated with the withholding of intercourse. High self-esteem of young males, on the other hand, correlated with the gaining of intercourse. Nature is speaking to us loudly here.

In purely biological terms, for consenting adults, oral sex and other sexual options are useful for women in the romance stage of a relationship. Adults engaging in petting and oral sex can satisfy lovers' oxytocin, vasopressin, and other chemical drives while retaining the sexual-selection power base for females. If an adult female tries to retain her power by refusing any sexual activity at all until the man marries her, she stands a serious risk of losing that man. His biochemical drive to bond through orgasm is very strong, and he does not bond as well with her unless oxytocin levels rise during orgasm. In the modern age, there are so many women available with whom to have sexual contact, it's unlikely he'll wait for this woman.

But if she can say, "We love each other, and I want to be part of your sexual life, but I feel that certain parts of myself are sacred to marriage," and if she does her part to fulfill her own and her romantic partner's needs, she is more likely to get the dual gains inherent in female sexual power—time to assess whether he really is the man for her and a primal gain in her own self-esteem, a gain that will carry through her life, even beyond her relationship with this romantic partner (should they break up): that what is hers is hers and the man has to earn the right to fully have her.

I am not saying that a woman who has sex with a man during romance will necessarily have low self-esteem or will necessarily be hurt by the man. I am speaking honestly about biological *trends*. The trauma many women experience today—having sex with a man after one or two dates and then being quickly or gradually discarded—has been felt by millions of women. In the language of contemporary romance, we use the metaphor, "I keep getting my heart broken." What we mean is that cortisol (stress hormone) levels in the female brain shoot up, placing the brain in trauma, which often induces depression. Countless women are experiencing low- to high-grade depression in their short romantic alliances with males. This depression can be reduced, and female self-esteem increased, if the dance of sexual and romantic love is one that better fits female nature.

It is important to remember that women bring a very malleable self to romance. Female brain chemistry, especially its daily emphasis on oxytocin, is a chemistry that seeks not the withholding of the independent self, but its surrender. Female chemistry is a self-effacing chemistry; and nature, very wisely, provides methods of balance. A woman's sexual selection is a balance to the malleable self if she is wise enough to use it carefully. If her yearning for the feeling of immersion in romantic love leads her to give up everything in the first week or month of union, she could be setting herself up for later depression.

On the other hand, if a woman falls in love and creates a sense of mystery and listens to the man and watches him and sees what kind of man he is; if she learns to like him even for his flaws; if she remains constantly aware of her own romantic idealizations but loves him anyway; if, after many months, she is loved in all these ways by him; and if all this occurs, then the night comes when the candles are lit and both partners prepare for the culmination of the sexual courtship—on that night, she will not only feel anticipation but will know herself as powerful. She will have built her own self through the process of giving nearly everything, but not all; giving of herself, but retaining herself.

Two Nature-Based Strategies

Though a woman's sexual-selection power is the primary biological strategy women can use for self-protection in early relations with men, she can also practice other kinds of intimate separateness. Let me emphasize two kinds: the first is a test of the man's true love; the second is a gift a woman can give that often has good results.

Changing appearance. Male attraction to the female is, as women have always known, deeply affected by first impressions. Women make themselves look nice, not only because it is a feel-good sensory experience for them, but also because they know it is crucial to attracting men.

"You never know," a woman thinks, as she gets ready for work. "Maybe today is the day I'll meet him. I want to look good." Given that more than half of today's marriages involve couples who meet at work, she may well be right.

Her concentration on her appearance does not end once she meets "Mr. Right." Even after she meets him, she wants to keep looking good. She does this in the long term not only because she enjoys it—women inherently like to look good because looking good makes them, at a biochemical level, feel good—but also because, having met the man, she wants him to continue to find her attractive.

Men, for their part, also want to make a good and lasting impression, but they know that how they look doesn't have as much of an effect on a woman's selectivity process. What they do and accomplish, their wit and wisdom, have a greater effect. They don't, on average, spend as much time grooming (vain men are the exception).

In the mating dance, the importance of clothing and appearance should not be underestimated. Appearance is a major player in intimate separateness and, therefore, in healthy female power.

If, after a few weeks into a relationship, a woman is still making herself "look perfect" for a man she's dating, she may be missing a good opportunity to test the loyalty of the man. After one or two months into the mating process, she should not always have to look perfect for the man she's dating. If he really is in love with her, his love will occasionally be able to sustain sloppy clothes or a face without makeup. After a few months of romantic love, she might find it an interesting test to let her standards of appearance slide a little.

In this freer self, with a less "perfect" appearance, she will discover a great deal about how much he loves her—how much his cingulate gyrus is actually intent upon adoring her, how bonded he actually is. If he indicates to her that he only likes to see her naked or dressed a certain way he has requested, he probably loves her in areas of the brain stem and neocortex, even areas of the limbic system, but without that deep love that we identify in the cingulate gyrus. To be a little less scientific, he may well not be in love with *her* but rather with an image in his mind of what he wants her to be: a sexual-social idealization of a woman.

Awareness of aggression. Bridge-brain and shy males often naturally enjoy aggressive women. Often bridge-brain males will prefer women who can go out and conquer, for this male prefers a more sedentary life, a life of caring for children perhaps. For shy males, aggressive women provide a bypass for shyness, giving this male a better chance to enter the realm of romance and sex.

At the same time, most males are not bridge brains, and this includes shy males. Most will be operating out of a male aggression imperative in the dance of sex and romance. Most males will find it difficult to fall in love with and sustain love with a highly aggressive woman. They might not mind at all that she made the first call or was the first to say, "I like you, let's date." This can feel like a wonderful compliment to the man. But if a woman continues to be the aggressive pursuer, she may also notice that men back away from her. They back away in two primary ways:(1) they stop relating to her after they've gotten the sex and companionship they want; or (2) they may stay with her for a number of months but all the while withhold themselves emotionally.

These dynamics can create a number of conflicts in romance.

Every woman is charged with asking herself, "What is in my nature?" If it is in her nature to be the aggressor throughout a courtship, she must follow that destiny. If she discovers that men and women distrust her aggressiveness, then she might be trying to be someone she is not. By the same token, if she finds she is disappointed by romance, she might be too aggressive for most males. She might, perhaps, need to find a very shy man or a bridge brain. Or she might want to reconsider her approach to males.

Men fear "the bitch." It has become acceptable for women to say,

"To hell with everyone, I'll be a bitch if I want to." From social ideologies to pop songs, the word "bitch" has come to be synonymous
with female empowerment. But it has a downside in romance. The
more masculinized (that is, aggressive and domineering) a woman
becomes, the greater the chance that her pool of available males will
shrink. She becomes, perhaps without realizing it, a member of a
group of females whom the males will now tend to target for workplace utility ("She's in a position of power, if I impress her I can get
ahead") or competition/punishment ("I wonder if that bitch is as
powerful as she thinks. I'm gonna do my magic on her and have her
and then leave her") or mockery ("She doesn't realize what other
people think of her") or sexual ostracism ("To hell with her; she's a
whore"). No one enjoys hearing men talk in these ways about
women, but not surprisingly, they tend to talk more about highly
aggressive women in these ways than any others.

Higher testosterone women, like corporate CEOs and female
lawyers, also tend, on the brain spectrums, toward female bridge-
brains. In the workplace, this can be of great use; in romance, this
can be a painful liability. Luckily, just by understanding and
acknowledging this fact, a woman has the ability to change how she
is perceived. And she will discover that, paradoxically, she has more
power in the long term if she values nonaggressiveness when it's
needed. As the old saying goes, "Silk is stronger than steel."

TURNING ROMANCE INTO COMMITMENT AND MARRIAGE

The power of selection, the power of appearance, and the power of
silk over steel—these are three nature-based seats of intimate separateness and female power. If a woman's goal is to empower herself
during romance, these are useful in the romantic partnership between
women and men. They are good strategies for ascertaining the romantic worth of a man. They compel the man to show his true self.

As human beings, our personal intuition is our best guide to successful romance. Not every biological trend needs to be followed for

a woman to be happy with a man or a man with a woman. Yet each of us has greater freedom of choice as our understanding of our biological trends grows. This is true as we pursue sex and try to turn it into romance; it is true also as we try to turn romance toward commitment, then marriage.

Romantic partnerships that last beyond a year or two often reach the time of "commitment," that transition time when the man and woman say, "I think I love you," and move toward the, "I know I love you," that is required for marriage to be successful. (By "marriage" we mean long-term partnership, including "living together" or "common-law wedlock.") As relationships make the transition, they retain some of the passion that began them, and yet they transform into something else—something only possible with deep commitment between partners and a discovery in ourselves of new possibilities for our lives as men and women.

In the next two chapters we will explore the process by which men commit themselves to marriage, and we will explore the life stages of marriage. We will notice that romance occupies only stage one of a twelve-stage biological process of human relationship. We will see that most of the self-development and self-sacrifice we experience as people who love each other does not occur during romance but actually occurs in eleven later stages. The strategies and ideas in this chapter on romance and sex will apply throughout these later stages, for commitment and marriage are partially built on the powerful flow of early romance and good sex; yet commitment and marriage are something else, too, something more like an ocean than a stream. While we are in the romance phase, we think we have found the ocean of love; only later do we realize what love really is.

In the novel, *Corelli's Mandolin*, a wise father speaks to his beautiful and passionately-in-love daughter about romance, commitment, and marriage:

Love is a temporary madness, it erupts and then subsides. When it subsides you have to make a decision. You have to work out whether your roots have grown so intertwined that it is inconceivable that you should ever part. Love is not breathlessness, it is not the promulgation of promises of eternal passion. It is not the desire to mate every second minute of the day, it is not lying awake at night imagining that he is kissing every cranny of your body.... That is being "in love," which any fool can do. Love itself is what is left over when being in love has burned away. Your mother and I had it, we had roots that grew towards each other underground, and when all the blossoms had fallen from our branches we found that we were one tree, not two.

When we realize how temporary the madness is, we meet up again with biological trends in men and women. Understanding and honoring these trends can be the key to finding the soul of commitment and marriage.

PART III

What Could He *Really* Be Thinking . . . About Marriage and Commitment?

—☙—

How do you really know a man has committed his life to you? How do you ever really know?

—Kira, twenty-three, single mother

Getting married was easy. Staying married, that was the hard part.

—Sam, eighty-two, father and grandfather, retired

5

I Think I Love You: Men and the Biology of Commitment

To give himself to a woman—this was the gentleness for which he was born; if she could but convince him!

—Samuel Johnson

Sure I was scared to get married. Hell, if truth be told, I was petrified.

—Terry, fifty-two, father and husband, software designer

There are infinite ways people come to the decision of marriage. The movies often portray the man on bended knee, handing a well-cut diamond to his future wife, asking, "Will you marry me?" His face is filled with his emotions—his fear of rejection, his adoration of her. Her own face combines surprise and love, a deep sense of accomplishment, and the kind of beauty that comes from being adored by a good man. Over the years I've heard many stories from people about how they experienced the blending of romance into courtship then courtship's completion in the moment of commitment. For many people today there is no bended knee, nor even a huge jewel, but there is the same pleasure of adoration and the same hopes for the future.

In our Spokane focus group, I asked the women to recall the

moment or incidents in which they knew that their future mate had taken the leap of faith—of commitment—toward them. In each case, not surprisingly, the women were aware in retrospect of the man having passed a series of tests of commitment. The man had been saying, unconsciously, "I think I love you," for many months—or even years—testing his love. She had been testing him as well, all this going on under the surface as the couple danced the dance of everyday life with increasing togetherness.

Penny, thirty-eight, married eighteen years, with two children, told this story.

I think I knew Malcolm was ready for marriage when he got me a puppy. I mean, from the beginning we were in love with each other. That wasn't really an issue. We just bonded right away. But he wasn't ready for marriage as early as I was. He was still finding himself. The story with the puppy happened like this. He knew I wanted to get this puppy we had seen at a friend's house. He had said he didn't really want a puppy. I remember thinking, "If he can't handle a dog, how's he going to handle marriage or kids?" I didn't insist, though. Then about a month later, I came home from work and there was the puppy! Malcolm was holding her. He handed her to me and gave me a big kiss. We didn't decide to get married until a few months after that, but that's when I knew he was really committed to me.

Anne, forty-six, married twenty-one years with two children, and Claire, forty-eight, married seventeen years with one child, had similar stories of testing their future husband's commitment.

Anne recalled, "I was a nurse and Jim a doctor. I had gotten a job in South Bend [Indiana] when we met in California. At the end of his year of residency, he came out to be with me in South Bend. That's when I knew he loved me. We got married in South Bend."

Claire recalled:

Phil didn't really want to go to Japan with me at first. He had a lot going on here in the States. But I got a good job there, and it was a once-in-a-lifetime opportunity. I just had to go. Phil and I had been dating for four years. I didn't know what he would do. I was very nervous. One day he came home from work and said, "I'm going with you." I was really excited but I remember grilling him a little on why he wanted to come. I wanted him to come for the right reasons. He said, "I want to come because I love you." That was what I needed to hear. He really meant it. We went to Japan and we got married.

I think that we might have gone on dating for years without getting married. In a way, the Japan opportunity wasn't just a blessing for my career, but for our relationship, too. It forced us to make a decision. It forced Phil to completely commit to me.

When does a woman know that a man will sacrifice nearly anything for her? When does a woman know that a man is committed to love her like no other? Is there a single tried-and-true test of commitment? Is there a specific signal, like a light beacon, that universally indicates a man's full commitment to partnership?

Of course, there is not. For each couple, it will be different. One woman said, "I knew he was committed to me when I watched his efforts to get along with my father. My father was really hard on him, on all of us, but Andrew worked hard to get along. This showed me his love."

In a strikingly similar vein, another woman said, "My father is gay, and this threatened Paul, but he worked through his own issues and tried to meet my father halfway. This was a huge thing for Paul and me. Paul really wanted to show he loved me."

On this night in which we came together to discuss the dance of commitment men and women engage in during that magical time between early romance and the wedding day, two experiences were nearly universal for the women present:

- Men find ways to prove to women how much they love
  them.
- Men seem to take a long time to come to the moment
  of commitment.

Throughout our evening the words were spoken, "Why are men afraid to commit?"

Claire said, "I know for some women, it's the guy who's ready to get married from the very beginning. Like, I had a friend whose now-husband had lost his wife. He had two kids. He was really ready to get married. But in normal experience, women are ready quicker than men. Why is that? Are men just afraid to commit?"

Not surprisingly, of the fifteen women present on this night, all agreed that men were "afraid of commitment" in comparison to women. Nearly all the women knew an exceptional case, but all knew the norm as well. Men took longer to decide that this one bond of marital love would be the bond on which they formed their future life.

That men should try to prove themselves in the dance of commitment should come as no surprise to us as we recall what we've learned earlier about how men prove worth and base their lives on tests, challenges, and proofs of self. That men take longer to commit themselves than women should also come as no surprise—it is intuitive to our everyday lives. However, some of the hidden biology of commitment might come as a very interesting surprise. As an introduction to its exploration, let's look through men's eyes at the issue of commitment.

Men and the Question of Commitment

Here are some key issues for men:

- Many men hope to postpone the coming of that time in
  life when they rely on one woman to satisfy all their
  sexual needs. They are biologically driven toward sexual
  variety for reasons we already hinted at in the last chapter, reasons we'll explore more deeply in a moment.

- Many men would rather wait for engagement and marriage until they are sure they can keep their worth and status high enough for a sustained period to live up to their future family and social responsibilities.
- Many of these men watched their fathers struggle and perhaps even fail as breadwinners. This is deeply frightening.
- Many men, whose fathers were constant social successes, nonetheless know the sacrifices the father made—endless work hours, travel far away from family, high stress, and early death—and know that this sacrifice is often not fully respected by women.

     As one man told me, "Today, women seem to want from me even more than my dad gave my mom, but what my dad gave my mom was all he had. I have to think twice before falling into that trap."

- Men are afraid to become responsible for a woman's happiness. Men are very smart: They know from adolescence onward that women make men greatly responsible for their happiness. Men, especially today, know that it can easily become a zero sum game to become responsible for not only a woman's physical and financial safety once children come, but also her deep inner life, too.
- Many men fear they will not be able to completely bond with children. Men do not have the oxytocin women have by which to bond not only instinctually and socially to children, but also biochemically. Men often have to work very hard to bond with mates and offspring in order to feel parallel in their bonding intensity with women. We will develop this father-child biology further in chapter 8.
- Men biologically mature later than women—their brain development finishes later in adolescence than do girls' and women's. Thus, in some cases, the woman seeking commitment might be more psychologically mature than the man she wants to marry. She may be ready. He may not.

- Because men have no inherent biological path to worth, they often take longer than women to feel they've proven themselves worthy of marriage. They may be just as focused on the personal journey of self-worth development as they are on marriage, whereas the woman a man is courting may have the inherent advantage of inborn self-worth, and may be more focused now on marriage.
- There is no biological clock for male reproduction. Thus, a woman might feel an inner compulsion to get married and begin a family, but a man might feel no such compulsion. As long as he gets the sex and affection he needs, he may be quite sanguine with putting off having children.

In general, then, men have many reasons for not committing as quickly as women might like. Some men are simply so terrified of committing to one woman that they reflect quite well the cliché, "Men are afraid to commit." Yet men are immensely courageous, too. Especially in today's social environment, in which many females are putting not only the responsibility for their financial and material needs in the hands of men (men are still required, in most households, to earn more than women when the children come), but also the responsibility for the emotional health of the marriage, men still marry at very high rates. Men are committing themselves to romantic partners and striving to adapt and adjust to those partners. Men fear women, but know they need them. The biological compulsion to marry is still very strong, as are the biological factors that drive a man's mind and body as he passes the tests of commitment.

THE BIOLOGY OF COMMITMENT

As we've just noticed, a number of biological factors play themselves out in the time of life and love when a man tries to decide whether he should still be saying "I *think* I love you," or can honestly say, "I *know* I love you." Let's now go more deeply into this biology of commitment.

Differences in Brain Chemistry

The first and most profoundly biological difference between men and women during marriage courtship lies in the woman's dominant **oxytocin** and the male's smaller traces of the brain chemical. Women are biochemically more focused on bonding opportunities and on strategies by which to lengthen these bonds. When a woman falls in love with a man, she, more quickly than the man, tends to think of how to make the love a permanent opportunity for emotional bonding. Oxytocin pulls her toward permanence of attachment.

Men are less dominated by oxytocin and, while yearning to love and be loved, do not tend to strategize the lengthening or permanence of the bonding opportunity as quickly. As we noted earlier, they may be focused more fully on sexual bonding than permanent attachment. When women provide sexual bonding and emotional affection before marriage, men have less biological incentive to commit to marriage.

Vasopressin works differently than oxytocin, forming a biological base for the male experience. It pushes the male toward aggressive persistence in proving himself to mates, which is an outward aggression strategy, rather than pushing him toward the emotional continuation of the bonding opportunity through commitment to marriage. The man who gives the puppy or goes to South Bend or to Japan to follow his beloved is overriding—with cerebral cortex executive decision making and cingulate gyrus "I really love her" feelings—his vasopressin-driven aggressions.

Even when men seem to give themselves over to a woman completely, seeming to put the existence of their very heart into her hands, they may not move to this phase of relationship as quickly as women do. A woman may be ready, after a month, to give her lover a puppy, but it might take him two years to get there. His inward biochemical dance is one of finding proving grounds rather than soft, living beings.

Furthermore, when the time comes for marriage to be proposed or agreed upon, women may notice that the man is just as much trying to guard his independent self as he is trying to lose himself in his love of his soul mate. **Testosterone** drives independence even while his emotional need to be loved and shaped by love—a need we all have—drives him to do whatever it takes to make his potential mate happy.

As women read male signals during these months and years of relationship, they often notice that males send two conflicting signals of commitment: In the very same breath that a man seems to be saying, "Go ahead and change me to fit who you want," he is also saying, "Leave my identity alone."

The timing difference for males and females in commitment to each other is largely due to this brain chemistry and its resulting impact on human-identity development. The dual signal is less commonly sent out by women during the first years of a relationship, for female hormones and oxytocin make women malleable in comparison to male testosterone and vasopressin. Women will tend to bend and shape themselves more quickly in the first years of relationship in order to be psychologically attractive to the man they love. The man will tend to hold off in giving his core self over to anyone else.

Certainly, women today are more likely to send the mixed signal than they did centuries or even decades ago, for they now have the freedom to send signals both of dependency and independence. But biochemically, they are more likely to experience malleability than are men.

And certainly today, women can be choosier than they might have been centuries ago because of their financial independence. They do not need to marry for social survival—but still, not surprisingly, many women find themselves malleable earlier than men and often feel depression when they realize that the man will never make himself malleable. A powerful illustration of this is the woman who hangs on for years with a married man, constantly thinking that because he is in love with her, he will soon leave his other life—his wife, home, children. But, of course, many of these men never leave. They are not biochemically malleable in the way the woman thinks they will soon be.

One might think it strange that women stay with men who are

not malleable. It is even logical to think, "Wouldn't women as a group try to weed out the men like this—the higher testosterone, higher vasopressin, competitive, aggressive, independent men?" But biology is very strong, and women remain interested in the kind of men who are difficult to pin down, the same men who send mixed signals of commitment.

In *Two for the Dough*, by mystery author Janet Evanovich, the narrator, Stephanie, speaks of her sexual and sometimes romantic partner, Joe Morelli: "As a teenager, Morelli had been feral. Two years in the navy and twelve more on the police force had taught him control, but I was convinced nothing short of removing his gonads would ever completely domesticate him. There was always a barbarous part of Morelli that hummed beneath the surface. I found myself helplessly sucked in by it, and at the same time, it scared the hell out of me."

Morelli is, on the brain spectrum, at the high-testosterone and high-vasopressin end. While men like him are trying to show prowess and gain love and respect, women are hopeful that the primal male will shine through, yet afraid of that male's power.

Women who enter into romance with bridge-brain or lower testosterone males experience this inner conflict less than women who are in romantic partnerships with the average-to-high-testosterone males. Yet with every man, at some point in her relationship, a woman carries on an inner dialogue about how to let the man alone, while shaping him; let him roam free, while domesticating him; let him "be himself," while making sure attention to her needs is his first priority.

Without her realizing it, much of this inner dialogue is actually about how she is choosing to deal with his brain chemistry. How is her oxytocin going to find comfort in the midst of his testosterone? And, more than she may realize, he is assessing her love for him based on how she handles her inner conflict. If she devalues his inherent and natural need for freedom, (especially if his brain chemistry tends toward the higher testosterone end of the brain spectrum), his love for her will become difficult and, probably after a few months or years, untenable. On the other hand, if she does not try to shape him, he will also not feel fully valued, for he needs her to help him meet his commitments in their relationship and in the larger world.

With every breath and every gesture he is saying to her, "I am independent, but I am dependent on you. What will you do with this power?"

A Well-Hidden Biological Factor: Mother-Son Biology

The issue of female power goes even deeper for men during romance and commitment than immediate brain chemistry. It goes to the very biology of identity development that men experience with their own mothers. For some men, mother-son biology has very little effect on the dance of commitment; but for many men, it has a profound effect, and this effect is rarely discussed in our culture or in our loving relationships. This biopsychological reality has a potential effect on any marriage (as we'll see in a moment), and it has throughout history. The more psychologically intimate a married couple is required to be, the more pronounced its effect. When marriages were arranged for economic convenience and child raising, but not for intimacy and love, the mother-son biology was not a profound biopsychological element in the marriage. When marriages are based on intimate love, however, its chances of affecting the longevity and quality of the marriage increase manifold.

Such is the case with courtship and commitment today. Couples now strive to base their long-term commitments on intimate love, thus, the mother-son biological identity development affects the majority of today's male-female courtships.

The urge for separateness that women often encounter in men during romance and courtship is not only related to an independence biology rooted in male hormones, brain chemicals, and brain systems but also in the biology of the mother-son relationship.

HOW A MAN'S RELATIONSHIP WITH HIS MOTHER CAN AFFECT HIM

Male child biology is linked to his mother's, but as hormone and brain changes occur during adolescence, a man gains identity by successfully separating his male biology from his mother's female biology. In order to become women, girls need to separate psychologically from their mothers but not biologically. Boys need to do both, for to realize their identities they must realize that their biological path of self does not lie in the mother's body or brain system.

Clinical psychologist Michael Kirkpatrick has summed up this core identity development. First, speaking of girls, he writes: "The deep, profound, and durable female core gender identity takes its immutability from psychological interaction during the first eighteen months [with the mother]." But speaking of boys, he writes: "Boys' identity . . . begins with feminine identity [but] is driven by biological force . . . into a different masculine identity. The boy's masculine identity requires the intensity of male sexual drive. . . . It is more fragile than the girl's gender identity."

In continuing Kirkpatrick's insight, psychologist Althea Horner explains: "The course of feminine identity of the girl will be relatively uninterrupted once established. The core feminine identity originates in the early object relations matrix, whereas the boy's gender identity relies on his ability to differentiate out of the matrix."

These psychologists are connecting Freudian and other theories with biology-based analysis of identity development to accentuate a core requirement of male biological life: The male must biopsychologically leave his mother in order to become a self. Every male— even a bridge brain—must do this. A bridge-brain male, of course, will have a brain and hormonal system that is more similar to his mother's biology, so he will not be as biologically driven to journey far away from the mother's biology; but still, because of their higher testosterone and vasopressin (as well as their obvious gonadal differences), all males go through a period of biopsychological separation activity from the mother in order to discover a self.

Much of the adolescent male's social ambition, sexual aggression, and risk taking are biochemical in causation and are employed by the developing male self as aggression strategies by which to separate from the mother. While sisters will attempt to separate as well, he, unlike them, cannot find himself until he experiences a higher degree of independent biological activity. Adolescent boys become almost silent members in households. They feel overwhelmed by Mom even more quickly than girls, on average, do. They are separating their neural biology from her biological rhythms, separating their pheromones from hers, separating their cognitive vision from hers. They have discovered that independence activity calms their stress—not only the stresses of everyday life, but the developmental stress of separation from the mother. One of the reasons that adolescent boys gravitate naturally toward fathers and other older men is the need to separate biologically from Mom toward maleness.

The compulsion of the male to achieve this biological separation is so profound that when he does not, there can be serious consequences. We see examples of this when we study gender identity disorders. The majority of these appear in males. (A gender identity disorder is, from a psychologist's standpoint, a person's ongoing confusion about whether he is a male or a female). These disorders indicate the greater vulnerability of males to be unclear—both from a biological and psychological standpoint—about gender separateness and self.

Even more commonly, we find males more likely than females to report feeling afraid of commitment before marriage. When we engage in therapy with these men, we notice that, more than women, they report the fear of enmeshment. Enmeshment is a person's sense of losing the self to another person's vision or way of being. I become you and at first it may feel quite good, but soon it becomes terrifying for I have lost "me." Your expectations and projections dominate me, raising my cortisol (stress hormone) levels, and ultimately leading to my acting out toward escape from you.

During romance and courtship, both young men and young women fear becoming enveloped in each other's visions of life and the future. Both women and men fear enmeshment. But women tend to react against enmeshment in later stages of marriage. In early relationships, men are more likely to fear enmeshment, more likely to hold back emotionally once early infatuation begins to enter commitment. Men are more likely than women to fear the enmeshment of self in the woman, and neither the woman nor the man generally realizes how much of the man's sense of enmeshment resonates with his own biopsychological separation from his mother.

As I began this chapter, I quoted Penny and Claire, who told stories of men testing their own commitment and shining through. When I asked both Penny and Claire about their husband's mothers, both used these words, "His mother babied him." Both also said that their husbands' relationships with their mothers were "complex" and "strained our marriage."

Their stories, while anecdotal, provide a kind of open window to what many women experience. Often women will notice, if they are asked to focus on it, that men who take longer to pass the tests of commitment are men who have had to do profound psychological battle in order to complete their biopsychological separation from their own mothers. In most cases, neither mother nor son is malicious or wants to hurt the other. The "battle" is simply an identity-development journey that is made even more difficult if the mother does not "let go" of the son.

For a period of ten to twenty years (and sometimes for a whole lifetime), men unconsciously measure whether they have biologically separated from their mothers and developed an independent self. If the man does not feel fully gender identified ("I am a confident man of self-worth who can stand on his own"), he may well resist being committed to marriage. The greater his development of an independent male identity—the greater his sense that he has separated from the mother—the greater his ability to commit to a spouse. Things do not always work out this way, but they very often do. Even given the great variety of men in the world, it is the more confidently independent man who can be happily married for the long haul (we'll go into why this is in more depth in a moment), even though quite often, in the early years of a relationship, a woman might feel like the most emotionally malleable man is her best bet.

I worked with a man in my therapy practice who said, "Each time

I get married, I want two things: sex and security. I always get a lot more than I bargained for." This is cryptic but very reflective of what a lot of men want from marriage and of what they get. The "more than I bargained for" turned out to be mother-son separation issues.

This man had been divorced three times. A great deal of my therapeutic time with him involved helping him understand that each time he married, he felt genuine love, and he felt a need for sex and security, but at his core he was a man who lacked a male identity. We discovered this hidden issue when he talked about how, even when he wasn't talking to his mother (he and she went through periods of estrangement), he nonetheless projected his mother onto women (even down to expecting them to iron clothes a certain way). Ultimately, he made all women into his mother, occupying his relationships with the recycling of mother-son biological separation: pushing women away after a few years so that he could complete the pushing away from his mother that he should have completed during adolescence.

Male neurobiology naturally favors independence seeking, and mother-son biology requires it, creating an ongoing biopsychological difference between men and women in how closeness and separateness are approached as commitment looms. If the uncompleted separation from the mother is added onto male biology and general male psychology, stress between romantic partners as they move toward commitment, and then as marriage unfolds, can increase. It can be stressful enough just to try to make a commitment of life and marriage together; then the added stress of mother-son biology can become overwhelming.

Understanding this dynamic is often very useful, for it helps women to see that they are not being abandoned or rejected for flaws in themselves. Often, instead, they are simply part of an ongoing biological dance in the man.

Also, understanding this dance can help a woman avoid becoming an "enmesher." She can realize that the man has strived for years to separate himself from his mother's way of being. Now that he has pretty much completed his separation, he will try to remain psychologically separate from relentless emotional stimulation by women.

He will work hard for his future spouse, let her guide him in many life issues, let her run a great deal of the home and even, as years go by, his presentation to the outside world (perhaps even letting her tell him what to wear)—men will give a great deal of moral, familial, and social power to women, but they ask in return this one thing: that their emotional separateness be respected.

This male request is made even louder if mother-son separation is incomplete. In the first year or two with this man, the mother-son biology may not appear to affect the relationship. But when the stress of potential marital commitment comes into the relationship, the man might recoil, in subtle or overt acting out, and become hurtful to the woman, so wary is he of enmeshment.

Wouldn't It Be Better for Marriage if Boys Did Not Separate from Their Mothers?

In exploring both male-female biochemistry and mother-son biology, we can see some deep dynamics in male-female commitments. At a neuropsychological level, it takes a man longer to feel that he is ready for a permanent alliance with a woman because he must work so hard to leave behind his previous alliance, with his mother, and develop a concrete self. From this fact a number of elements emerge, especially a man's tendency to try to remain emotionally separate from his spouse at times and in ways that may feel, to his spouse, like abandonment. In many ways the male identity drive, manifested in adolescent changes in the mother-son bond, is the foundation of a man's commitment: Not only does the fetally coded male brain compel males to bring emotional separateness to the dance of relationship, but so too does the immensely powerful core biological need, carried out during adolescence, for mother-son separation. In contemporary relationships, we have tended to think of the man's reliance on emotional separation and independence as dysfunctional to commitments and marriage. Understanding of male biology at least forces us to ask: Are we sure it's a bad thing to rely on emotional independence in relationships as powerfully as we rely on emotional dependence?

In the last thirty years, women have discovered that independence is a good thing for women. Being utterly malleable in a marriage can have profound negative consequences for women. Yet at the same time that our culture is emphasizing independence for women, it is asking if mother-son separation perhaps could be removed from male development. The culture has experimented with saying, "Since the adolescent male's separation from mother is going to cause more male independence, wouldn't relationships between married partners be closer and therefore better if adolescent boys didn't separate from Moms?" We often see psychologists arguing (without biological proof) that men who don't separate from mothers will make better husbands.

During the 1990s, I conducted a biology-based study of male mother-son relationships which showed the falseness of this latter opinion. My research appears in my book *Mothers, Sons and Lovers: How a Man's Relationship with His Mother Affects the Rest of His Life*.

Though the man who has not fully separated from his mother will sometimes commit himself to a mate very quickly, his appearance as "a better husband" is often a temporary state. He may well give in to his fiancé's emotional vision for a few years, but then his lack of core identity will begin to undermine the marriage. Feeling enmeshed, he will tend to get emotionally overstimulated and lash out at mates or emotionally withdraw from them.

Marriages carry with them, like a picture that dominates a room, the mother-son relationship (and, as we'll notice in a moment, the parallel father-daughter relationship, too). Those influences remained invisible as the partners lived out the bliss of romantic alliances and make their marital commitments, but as marriages commence, the pictures Loom Large.

One of the great dangers to ongoing marriage today is our popular culture's acceptance of male/female ideologies that do not fit biology. We are a romance-based culture, and we think in terms of the perfection of intimacy and closeness. Intimacy of any kind is always considered a panacea. It is logical for psychologists, who don't look into biological sciences, to say: "If a man never fully separated from his mother's psychobiology, he would take better care of women, be better tuned to their rhythms, needs, and wants. Most importantly, he'd be better able to fulfill the woman's desire for a man to share his innermost self and, through that sharing, to create ongoing romantic love."

The theory sounds very good, but is unsupportable by hard science and actually disproven by human nature. More accurate would be to say that men who do not complete their biopsychological separation from their mothers often make worse husbands. As women who are married to this kind of man can often attest, the man's ongoing psychological enmeshment with his mother (or, if she's dead, with her memory) can make marriage nearly impossible. The man does not have an independent self to bring to the marriage. Only after a few years of marriage does the woman start to realize that she is living in an impossible psychological competition with the mother.

In my research for *Mothers, Sons and Lovers,* I discovered that nearly all couples report some degree of enmeshment between a grown son and an elderly (or deceased) mother. For the couples who reported severe enmeshment, that enmeshment was, for many, a cause of divorce. Not surprisingly, many women said, "If only I had known before I said 'I do' how a man's relationship with his mother would affect our life together."

Unfortunately, the enmeshment and incomplete separation of mothers and sons is growing in our culture, not dissipating, and we can expect the majority of our daughters to come up against it in their marriages, unless we reinvest ourselves in healthy male rites of passage, mentoring, and, especially, the role of the father in the lives of adolescent males. The loving father is the single most effective aid to successful male separation from mother and successful male core identity development.

This father is also a key to understanding what the woman brings to the biopsychological dance of courtship and marital commitment.

The Woman's Part in the Man's Mother-Son Dance

As a woman becomes conscious of how mother-son biology works, she is often challenged to understand the part that she, as a woman, plays in it. She is also wisely confronted by her own biopsychological issues in the dance of courtship and commitment.

The woman selected this man during the romance stage with all of her own biopsychological baggage in place. She is in the process of committing her life to him. What is the baggage she carries into this commitment?

While the man is involved in mother-son separation biology, making him psychologically more resistant to enmeshment in the female, we often find that the woman he loves is involved in father-daughter intimacy biology and is existing in an almost opposite mode: She is afraid of abandonment. Her biology is, and always has been, somewhat painfully separate from her father's biology, and she is biopsychologically sensitive to abandonment in the same way he is sensitive to enmeshment.

Men may come to the candlelit dinner and then the tests of commitment with a fear of enmeshment in tow, but women's primal fear of abandonment by male independence and distance is equally active. A woman is biologically driven toward constancy of intimacy stimulation. In most cases, her father's personality and masculinity did not focus on emotional verbal stimulation; and furthermore, her father, by necessity, may not have been as present as she wished. She might now be forming a relationship with a man whose specific desire not to give up his independence may trigger her natural and family systems–driven fear of abandonment by men. The profound difference between her developing brain and hormonal biology and her father's creates a natural sense of "distance" between fathers and daughters (this does not mean they don't adore each other), which can become disabling if the father abandoned or simply was not there for the daughter. It is unconscious but in the forefront during a woman's journey of commitment to a man.

Her lover might say, "Yeah, I forgot to call you. Sorry." Or, "Oh, right, I said I was going to do that for you, but I got really busy." Or, "You're really pushing at me. Back off a little." Such comments, which may be either natural independence behavior in the male or may be mother-son enmeshment issues, can feel like abandonment to the woman. Sometimes they really are abandonment, and her feelings are good guides of her selection process—this man might not be the right marriage material for her. Other times, though, she might simply be overreacting to his independence because of father-daughter biology.

The male brings the biological drive toward independence to his relationship and commitments, and the female brings the biological drive toward melding. In a healthy relationship, we seek a balanced blending of the drives, but that balance is nearly impossible to develop unless we understand what we're doing. It is especially impossible if father-daughter intimacy and mother-son separation were not completed. If we do not understand these biopsychological issues, we will most likely make marital commitments that later dissolve (sometimes, even before we get to the altar).

Clues to Mother-Son Separation Issues

In looking at the biology of commitment from the vantage point of both biochemistry and biopsychology, we have explored issues that hide in male-female marital commitments. We can go even further into mother-son biology by being "biological detectives."

There are three primary clues to whether a man may not have completed his mother-son separation. In providing these clues, I do not want to exaggerate the mother-son relationship as a cause—there are many other factors involved. However, if a woman can identify these characteristics in a man during the months (or years) of the relationship's movement toward marital commitment, the mother-son dynamic is a place to begin a journey of understanding, a journey which, if made during courtship, can save a marriage immense pain.

1. The man seems to have no backbone, trying to change himself to fit what he thinks his lover/fiancée wants.

2. The man is obsessively domineering, allowing the woman very little power.

3. The man, even though committed to his fiancée, moves from
   woman to woman, trying to get something—love, affection,
   power—that he never seems able to get.

If a man shows these characteristics and a woman continues to
relate to him in a committed way without the couple doing something about them, it is often safe to say that both the male core fear
of enmeshment and the female core fear of abandonment are
intensely active in the relationship and are not being dealt with.
Mature commitment often occurs when the man understands his
own fear of enmeshment and the woman understands her fear of
his independence, and they forge a partnership that is no longer
based in these core fears.

ARE MEN THE ONLY ONES WHO FEAR COMMITMENT?

As we've explored the biology of commitment, we have looked into
the hidden biopsychology of male/female dynamics in the early
stages of love (the first few years of relationship). It is important to
extend the word "commitment" to include later stages of love and
notice that men and women often break commitments they've
made, men leaving women after years of marriage and women leaving men. What might surprise people is that while men, more than
women, resist long-term commitment early in romantic partnerships, women resist long-term commitment, from a statistical standpoint, more than men.

Our contemporary society—one in which social strictures on
marriage and divorce have nearly dissolved—is a kind of laboratory.
Women and men are "free to be themselves" in a way they've never
been before. As we observe them in this freer life, we notice certain
biological trends. One of these is the tendency for men to resist
completing their socioromantic bond with women as long as they
can. When they are not forced—by shotgun, edict, or arranged

marriage—to marry at a set time, men will biologically delay it more than women will. As women become increasingly promiscuous, men don't need to marry in order to have sex.

Given their oxytocin levels and other bonding biology, including an internal biological clock set for childbearing, women will tend to seek commitment from marriageable men more assiduously and more quickly. If marriages are not arranged or forced, women will find themselves frustrated by male delay, often not realizing that their sexual generosity has helped force the delay. Furthermore, women are often unaware that with the greater financial independence of contemporary women, as well as social support systems for single mothers, women, not men, are statistically more likely to set the marital bond aside once children are born and growing. In these years, men tend to be more content in the marital framework, still desiring sexual contact and other emotional security while focusing on accomplishment, childrearing, and the diminishing of emotional expectations. Women, on the other hand, tend to hang onto their higher emotional expectations longer than men. A man might think, "Okay, I've fought my demons of commitment and decided to be her husband, now let's get to the work of making a life together." A woman might say to her friends, "Okay, I've gotten him to commit to me, but what happened to the closeness we had? That's what I want."

The majority of divorces are instigated by women. While for many women, the important focus for the future of marriage lies in trying to get men to commit to marriage during the courtship and commitment period of romance, from a male point of view, women seem to have more trouble remaining committed to a man once marriage has unfolded.

Our culture is in the middle of coming to grips with this situation, one that men often feel blindsided by. In the Spokane focus group were two therapists who both said, in different ways, something universally understood in the therapeutic community. In the words of therapist Pam Brown: "If the man telephones me to set up marital counseling, I know the marriage is finished. The woman has decided to leave her commitment behind. I know that when I meet with this couple, I'll learn that he thinks he's been a good husband, but she doesn't. The marriage only has a chance if she's the one who calls. Her call means she hasn't walked out the door yet."

Pam was certainly generalizing. Yet in her statement is one of the fears a therapist feels and certainly a confusion among men. When men have called me, it has often been the desperate attempt to hold together a marital commitment that is already gone. And nearly every time, the man who has called has been a basically good person who is confused by his circumstance.

In pointing out that men are statistically more likely to resist commitment in the first years of relationship and women more likely to absolve the commitment in later years, I am generalizing in order to ask both men and women to look at commitment differently than we have in the recent past. We have tended only to look at early resistance to marriage (usually among males) as an issue of commitment. But, in fact, marital commitment is under great stress today because of both genders.

BRIDGE BRAINS

Sue, fifty-two, married ten years, a cardiologist with three grown children, said, "From the day we met, my husband doted on me. He didn't do it in a cloying way. He just wanted to be with me. We talked all the time, long into the night. He was such a good listener. He was the one who wanted to get married right away. I resisted. I had been married before and hadn't liked the restrictiveness of marriage. I had gained my freedom and didn't want to lose it. But Bill won me over. Having Bill is like having a wife. And yet he's still all man."

During courtship and the tests of commitment, it can often feel to a woman that she has decided to marry a bridge brain. As we noted in the previous chapter, the biology of romance makes the adult brain its most flexible, adaptable, and malleable, so we all seem like bridge brains!

But have you really committed your life to a bridge-brain male? A woman probably will not know the accurate answer to this until a few years into marriage. If she has Sue's experience ten years later, she may well be living with a bridge-brain male.

Claire spoke of her husband, saying, "I know my husband is very committed to me. He shows it by buying me big-ticket items. For instance, he puts months of planning and research into the car I ought to own. He also buys the biggest birthday card out there. He treats this as a matter of research, too, picking the words carefully. But in the end, he goes for bigness. The bigger the card the better in his view. I know he loves me, and he has some wonderful 'female' qualities, but I don't think he's a bridge brain."

Claire's intuition is most certainly correct. In just these sorts of everyday subtleties we can see who is and who is not truly a bridge brain.

The biopsychological area in which the bridge brain and all other males might show little difference during marital commitment is in the area of mother-son biology. Depending on the mother's personality and on the son's journey of separation, any man can be involved in mother-son separation issues, bridge brain or otherwise.

Yet it is also accurate to say that a bridge-brain male might not need to journey as far away—biopsychologically—from his mother as might a high-testosterone male. Because the bridge brain's neurobiology mirrors the female more than does a high-testosterone male's, the bridge brain might not have to make as severe a break from the mother's biology in order to find his own.

PRACTICING INTIMATE SEPARATENESS

Whether or not to commit one's life to a man—this is one of the most profoundly important questions a woman will face in her lifetime. How amazing it is, given our differences, that men and women commit their lives to each other. How amazing, especially today, when so many protective social structures are in transition, and men and women more than ever before face the moment of engagement and commitment with the feeling of being almost alone. Except for this future mate—whose mind and heart actually operate differently from our own—we are often unsupported in knowing how to make the leap toward, "I know I love you," and, "Let's make a life together."

The practice of intimate separateness can be a support. It can help us sift through lust, romance, and love as we strive to decide who to spend our lives with.

What to Look for in a Man

While no one can say without a doubt exactly what to look for in a potential husband, there are, hidden in male biology, some clues to what might constitute a "good bet" for a healthy marriage. Within male nature itself is a kind of blueprint for what might constitute the best in a man. This "best," especially if you and the man are young, might still exist only in potential. But if you can see these things in a man, even in potential, you are probably practicing intimate separateness as you decide whether to make a life with him.

Let me list these characteristics as questions you might ask as you wonder if this man will, long after romance has ebbed, be a good husband.

1. Does he possess integrity? Is he basically honest and straight-forward in his emotional relationships?

2. Can he self-stabilize chaotic emotion? In other words, has he developed the ability to return to his center when under high stress? Find calm? Find balance?

3. Does he live with vigor and experience joy?

4. Is he at least somewhat comfortable with being a man?

5. Does he possess both kindness and firmness?

6. Is he able, not only to see other's talents, but also their vulnera-
   bilities? Even more important, is he, for the most part, able to
   nurture both?

7. Everyone feels envy and jealousy at times, but is he capable of
   returning to self-security even when he feels these emotions?

As we answer these questions, we must look for broad ways to
say yes or no. If, for instance, you define integrity in a very limited
way ("integrity means he should never look at another woman"),
nature-based thinking and intimate separateness might not work
for you, and this test might not be helpful. But if you can create in
your mind a healthy spectrum for answers to these questions, you
will be applying a kind of "nature-based" analysis to your prospec-
tive mate.

All seven characteristics are within the natural male blueprint.
The male brain and male hormones are constantly facing life as
challenges between extremes. Male nature struggles to be aggressive
yet tender, firm yet kind, honest, courageous, adaptable. As you
answer the questions above, you are asking questions of the man's
developing character. To a great extent, his nature is reflected in this
character. The psychologist James Hillman calls our character "the
soul's code." In this phrase he is saying that our very nature is
reflected in our character. The basic foundation of character is a
person's ability to show compassion. As we apply nature-based
analysis, we are hoping to peer into a man's character, his natural
ability to show compassion. We want to peer into this character
before we marry him.

When we select men for love and marriage, it is probably wise to
select first for character and second for emotional mirroring. Does this
man show compassion in his actions? This is a basic point in all other
questions. The man may not (though he tries to fool us during his
infatuation and courtship phases) have the ability to show compassion

for all our emotional needs or to show compassion by expressing himself emotionally when we ask him to. However, if he clearly operates from a strong position of character, a woman will more likely be able to trust him with her life.

Some Things You Might Not Need to Worry About

While the above characteristics are a good benchmark for what to look for in a man, women who practice intimate separateness during the courtship/commitment period often find assistance in keeping the following in mind. These are things that might seem like a big deal in the first few years of relationship—things that sometimes keep a woman from committing to a man—but actually might not indicate ongoing character flaws at all.

- Some men are very opinionated, especially during the commitment phase of a relationship. Sometimes these men go on moral rants that are best responded to with silence or few words. During courtship, men often hold a position just to prove status ("I'm right!"). These are often not an attack on anyone, even if the man uses attacking language. While it is crucial that family, society, and even mates help train both men and women away from attacking language, a man's pride and passion are often not liabilities but assets.

- During the courtship phase (and, indeed, throughout life) men often get into moral debates as a way of relating to those they love. Although the man employs his best verbal aggressions in this debate, it's useful to remember that sometimes he's arguing for aggressive bonding, and to prove himself, to keep his skills honed, and to explore verbally what he might not be able to think out silently. Rarely is he arguing with his potential mate because he wants to hurt her by disagreeing with her. He may argue to show dominance, but he is generally not judging her by whether she can either change his mind or prove she is right.

Having said that, it is also essential that women (and all friends of a man) play the role of character or "nature" mirror during the courtship phase. Men often do not think before acting. They often do not see all the consequences. They often do not realize their own power. They often need those who love and respect them to say, "You couldn't see it, but that really hurt me when you said . . ." Or, "You couldn't see it, but that really hurt your friend when you . . ." If men's flaws are presented to them as hurts they've caused, rather than through attacks on the man's character or worth, men are likely to try to do better. Men usually don't want to hurt their loved ones or friends. If a woman, during courtship, learns an effective method for being a man's character mirror and he never allows her to play that role, then he might not be the best marriage material. But if he does, at least once in a while, say, "You're right, I should apologize," his character includes the ability to do something that will be a great asset later: respond in a healthy manner to healthy criticism.

- When it is clear that a young man simply will not let go of a point until we acknowledge that he is "right," when it's clear he won't back down until we at least give him something to feel he has won, we might think, "How immature," or that maybe he has a character flaw. This might not be the case—he might just be a man with a fragile ego.

- Men and women who commit their lives to each other but have very different core value systems don't generally remain married for very long. Our moral values—which reflect our character, personality, and our very nature as individual beings—need to be in some sync with our future partner's.

However, because natural differences in male and female moral outlooks exist, as we noted in chapter 2, women often find it helpful during courtship to assess what the couple's *primary values* are—seeing if these are in sync—while allowing secondary values a wide divergence. A woman once came to my therapy practice feeling torn apart by the fact that her new husband, her son's stepfather, was a hunter and wanted to teach the boy how to use a gun and hunt. She wanted to protect her son from guns and killing. Yet it was through hunting that this boy (whose biological father was sadly distant) bonded greatly with the stepfather.

This mother had made her husband's avocation, hunting, which was really in the area of secondary values in the marriage, into a primary value in her mind. He and she loved each other and shared church life, loyalty, love of the children—these were primary values. The hunting was secondary. I helped her return it to the status of secondary value, one that she could surrender to the marriage. In the end she found this very helpful. She noted that it had been one of the things that worried her immensely during courtship, but once she saw that it was not the basis of her marriage, she felt liberated, and the marriage was less stressful.

- The practice of forgiveness is a good marker of a man's marriageability. Can you forgive the man? Does he know how to forgive you?

  Many good men do bad things in the first few years of romance and courtship. It is crucial we base our relationships with men on forgiveness, just as it is crucial that men forgive women. We need to allow a good man to do the wrong thing. We need to give second chances. We need to ascertain whether this man does the same for us. Often, women project perfection onto men (and vice versa); that projection destroys human love and gets in the way of a clear assessment of a man's marriageability.

- In many ways, women are more flexible than men. Keeping your flexibility can be a great ally to a healthy relationship, especially a relationship with a man who is at the extreme of adherence to abstract systems for self-worth—perhaps in a church, or in the military, or a system he learned from his father or mother. The wife of an army colonel came up to me at a lecture and said, "If I hadn't been flexible, our marriage would have been doomed. He didn't have a flexible bone in his body." During courtship, while she was ascertaining whether to say, "I do," she was put off by his inflexibility; yet after twenty-two years of marriage, she found that this man was lovable and did know how to love—he just did it from within a rigid pose.

- The courtship time is a good one to determine how a man handles being backed into a corner emotionally. In your dealings with men during this time, don't be surprised if, when given an ultimatum, the man chooses personal independence or a moral code rather than an emotional connection.

- Men are constantly seeking opportunities to sacrifice themselves for others or the greater good. Does your mate possess this quality? This is a good question to ask, especially before creating a family. When intimate separateness is working well, men and women value each other equally. In general, men today are striving to get better at valuing women for the many things women do that add up to their character and goodness, and women are striving to get better at valuing men for the things they do that comprise their journey toward self-worth.

Women yearn to hear men say, "Thank you for all that you do. I value you greatly." Women yearn to have men say this, not only in words, but in romantic gestures—flowers, date nights, beautiful jewelry, and loving, moral deeds.

Men yearn to hear women say, "Thank you for all that you do. I value you greatly." Men yearn to have women say these things not only in words but by managing their lives respectful of how differently men "do" things and "value" things.

During courtship, women are profoundly rewarded when they practice the intimate separateness that signals to a man, "I love you enough to let you develop freely in yourself." Just as mothers often feel fear when they raise sons and see the aggression and separateness behind the boy's eyes—aggression and separateness they, as mothers, can neither fathom nor change—so, too, are women often afraid when they see the difference from themselves that shines in a fiancé's or boyfriend's eyes.

Yet if at the core of that independence lies good character and good potential, a woman will have access to one of the most powerful forces on earth: a good man ready to commit his life to a woman. As men decide to marry women, they often think of marriage not mainly as an emotional system but as a part of their moral and character development. This is, in large part, built into their nature. As it has been with every generation, women looking for male commitment have to decide just how much "maleness" they can take during the next decades of life. Generally, if as much or more attention is paid to character as to emotional closeness, a marriage has a greater chance of not only consummating at the altar, in the bedroom, and at the births of the children, but of continuing for a very long time.

A woman who engages herself fully in understanding male nature and practicing intimate separateness during the courtship phase of life is more likely to select a mate for life. It is not guaranteed, for none of us can really predict the future. But if she practices intimate separateness during this time, moving aside romantic projections long enough to truly ascertain the core issues a man brings to marriage—where he fits on the spectrum of biochemistry, what happened in his family of origin, in relation to his mother-son biology and his fathering, what his genetic and personal character are—she will probably be better prepared to move into the next stages of the relationship, the marriage itself. She will know whether he really means it when "I think I love you" becomes "I know I love you." She will have committed herself to the actual man who is courting her, not to some other idealized man. Hopefully, in turn, he will have committed himself to the woman he is courting and then living with, not to some other idealized woman.

This kind of foundation is especially necessary when we realize that the biology of marriage itself has only begun during romance and courtship. Marriage is a many staged biological process. It is a part of human nature that benefits most from our having set it in motion during the early stages of romance and courtship with our eyes and hearts focused on what is natural to both men and women.

I Know I Love You: Men and the Biology of Marriage

The soul, to know itself, must gaze with constant love upon another soul.

—**Ancient Greek proverb**

Marriage can often be enjoyed through humor. At a recent seminar the following interchange took place—one that began very humorously but led our discussion into the heart of marriage.

"What does a man have to do to make a marriage last?" a young college-age man asked me.

I said, "Well, that's easy: Marry a reasonable woman, and then do everything she says!"

There was laughter, but the young man, a very serious fellow, looked at me quizzically. Could this middle-aged Michael Gurian really mean that? I didn't have to say anything else right away because, as if on cue, a man in his late forties called out, "Where the heck are you gonna find a reasonable woman?" This brought another wave of laughter.

A woman of about fifty stood up and said, "Don't laugh away the idea of men following a woman's lead in marriage. If men don't, especially nowadays, I think the marriage will be in trouble." In fact, as she pointed out, the research of John Gottman at the University of Washington, carried out over a twenty-five-year period, has shown that if men don't let women take the lead in a number of marital areas, the marriage is more likely to end in divorce.

When this speaker told us more about herself, we learned that she was a family therapist and had worked for twenty years with couples who faced marital difficulty. She did not want to simplify marriage, but she did want to support our exploration of what might be natural to marriage. "If we're really going to develop equal partnerships with each other, we need to fully understand our partner," said the woman, whom I learned later was named Joan Amstadter. "How else are we going to have reasonable expectations of each other?"

There were 208 people in the seminar—45 men and 160 women. In order to continue Joan's point, I asked the women to remain silent for a moment while I polled the men, who ranged from college age to retirement. I started by asking the men who had been married more than five years, the following question: "How many of you—assuming you (1) felt completely understood by your wife, and (2) felt her expectations of you were reasonable—would try to follow her lead in a majority of life issues?" Not surprisingly, the vast majority of men raised their hands (my quick head count showed 40 of 45 hands up).

"But she has to clearly understand and respect you, right?" I asked.

"She has to make that a very big priority," a man called out.

Another man, in his forties, said, "Men are very willing to give up power in their marriages if women are reasonable."

"Why?" I asked.

"Well, I'll speak for myself," he responded. "I'm not ashamed to say that I need a partner to help me through life. I need someone who's watching my back. I need a wife and a soul mate. I'll do just about anything for her if she'll give me respect. I'll let her lead me if that's how it should be. But I have to have the respect."

Another man, also in his forties, said, "I've been married eighteen years. In the first few years, there's a lot of fighting over turf. Then the kids come, and you have to make decisions about who's gonna lead in which areas, and who's gonna lead in others. If you don't, you're sunk. I have a lot of friends who've divorced, and the guy always tells me it's because his wife wanted him to be someone he couldn't be."

An elderly man said, "It took me about ten years to realize that my wife was the leader in our marriage. It only took her about two years to figure out what was reasonable to expect of me."

"How long have you been married?" I asked.

"Forty-six years," was his reply.

Inviting the women back into the conversation, I found out how many had been married more than five years. More than half had been. I asked, "Given what we've learned about the male brain over the last two days, how many of you would say your expectations of your husbands are, at present, reasonable?"

Only about twenty hands went up. One woman explained. "Before I came here and learned about the male brain, I really thought I was being reasonable, but now I don't think so."

Another woman said, "Some of what we've been learning here is depressing. It's depressing to have to change, one more time, what I thought was going to work in marriage. I'm fifty-two. I've tried everything to make my marriages work. Mostly what I've tried has been to change my husbands. I see that now. It's depressing to have to change myself."

"Not yourself," a woman near her corrected, "your *expectations*. They have to become reasonable. You're not changing yourself, just what you expect. There's a big difference."

"But what are reasonable expectations of a married man?" another woman asked. "Every man is so different."

Now a man called out, "Ladies, if you think that, we men have got you fooled. We're a lot simpler than you imagine."

This brought chuckles all around.

As our discussion continued that day, I invited the men to talk, and the women to listen. Women heard men speak of how often they tried to be dependent on and committed to women who expected them to be something they weren't. Men spoke of women who only tried to be respectful for a few months, then "their real selves showed up." Men also spoke of women who thought that they inherently understood men, as if men were just big boys.

Then I asked the women to share with us. The men listened as the women remembered their own journeys of broken promises. Each woman in that audience that day could remember the constant confusion of giving so much and feeling she got so little back. Each woman could recall the edict of her ancestors—to follow a man no matter the costs—and knew that this was an unreasonable and superficial edict, not a deep truth of marriage. Women spoke of the will to educate men as to who she was and what she needed and what she lived for; and she remembered the many men who just didn't want to listen and, it seemed, never would.

As our discussion closed, the word "trust" kept emerging, spoken by both men and women. One woman said, "I don't think men and women trust each other anymore." Each of us knew that love cannot last unless two committed people transform the bond of romantic love into the mature bond of marital trust. We all knew that men and women both want a reasonable marriage. We knew that today our understanding of a reasonable marriage is even more vital than in the past, for in the past couples had to remain married whether they emotionally trusted the spouse or not; an enforced social trust took care of that. But now marriages can't last without our deepest trust in the other, and divorce is all too common when the trust does not exist.

THE HUMAN DIVORCE

I vividly remember the moment I thought Gail and I might divorce. We sat one evening in 1989 in our car. Our best friends had just told us they were getting a divorce. We had not seen their breakup coming, nor could we believe it. Grant and Kathy had seemed to get along so well. Just as we were leaving a party, Kathy told Gail about the divorce, who then told me. I sought out Grant, and he confirmed it.

"Don't end up like Grant and me," Kathy said. "We were happy for a while, but then the marriage fell apart."

As we drove away, Gail told me that she had asked Kathy for more details. Kathy said, "Grant just kept pulling further away." There was nothing left between them.

They had been married ten years and had two children.

Gail and I, married three years, had been fighting a lot. When we had a fight, one of us would become emotionally distant from the other for days, feeling rejected; and then the other would pull away even further, as revenge. At a certain point, weeks later, we'd realize we were too emotionally distant from each other, and we'd try to talk ourselves back together. The fighting, and then these weeks of rejection, stressed our love and was putting our marriage at risk. We knew it, but we didn't talk about it much.

As we drove away from Kathy's house, I said to Gail, "We won't end up that way."

She looked at me and said wisely, "It can happen to any couple."

I looked across the small space of the car and thought of what Grant had told me at the party. "Kathy's never satisfied with me," he said bitterly. "She should never have married a man like me."

Looking at Gail, I thought, *I feel that a lot. She's never satisfied. She's so critical of me. Why'd she marry me?* Then I thought, *Gail and I are committed to each other, but maybe we will get divorced. Yes, it's probably inevitable.*

I was depressed about this for days but said nothing. One evening after we made love, Gail said, "You've been so distant. What did I do this time?"

"Nothing," I said. Then I said, "I've thinking about Grant and Kathy. You and I need to do something about us."

Gail barely missed a beat. She had been thinking similar thoughts. "Like what?

"Did Kathy tell you anything about the reason they broke up?" I asked.

"Grant would never open up emotionally," Gail responded. "He never expressed himself in a way that made her feel loved. If only he could do that, she said, there might have been hope."

"Grant didn't feel respected," I responded. "He's a man. If he doesn't feel respected, he won't trust; if he doesn't trust, he won't open up at all. That's the way men are."

Gail looked at me. "How do you know?"

"It's just the nature of a man," I said. I didn't really know if I knew it because of my work in male neurobiology or simply because I was male. "Men are transactional by nature. When it comes to emotions, we'll hold them back if we don't get what we need."

"Do you feel respected?" Gail asked courageously.

"Sometimes," I said honestly. "Do you think I'm too distant?"

She nodded. Then she shook her head in sadness. "We're just like any other couple, aren't we?"

She was right. Like most couples, we had been amazingly happy during the initial romance. From the moment Gail and I met, we felt joy in one another's presence. We had many common interests. We liked the same movies. We read each other's minds and hearts. We both wanted children. After tests of commitment, we agreed to marry. We stood up for each other. From the beginning, Gail and I had loved each other with passion. In this we must have been like nearly every young romantic couple. Then, in marriage, we must also have fit the norm. Dissatisfaction with each other set in; small things became big things. Neither of us wanted to admit we ever made a mistake. We would feel inferior to each other at times, but we were unable to voice it. We'd feel superior to each other, and we'd be unable to contain our own egos. We spent many days and nights not liking each other.

I thought of Kathy and Grant. Kathy was always criticizing Grant about something. She often told him he was wrong and responded negatively to many of the things he said. She disagreed with and competed with him in public, even though it clearly bothered him.

Grant, for his part, would often turn his head away when she spoke, or he'd get a sort of bleary-eyed expression that said, "No matter what she says, I don't really care." He didn't do the things she needed him to do in order for her to feel loved—romantic gestures, like passionate kisses or flowers, or any other expressions of his love.

He would almost always agree with her, but I could tell he no longer respected her opinion.

This—or some form of other marital stress like it—can happen to anyone. Gail and I, Kathy and Grant, and nearly every couple who has, over the last decade, come to me in my therapy practice, uses phrases like, "We've drifted apart," or, "We're not close enough anymore." Do these phrases tell the whole story?

What Gail and I did not realize back then was that before drifting apart there is an earlier step—one that goes unnoticed. The man and woman are actually not too far away from each other; rather, the opposite is true: The initial root of the problem is that they are too close.

Gail's and my relationship, like Kathy's and Grant's, was under terrible stress because we did not understand the biology of *marriage;* we were trying to carry out a marriage still locked in expectations suitable to the biology of romance. That biology drove us constantly to try to be as close and intimate as we could be. This drive, the overwhelming neural strategy that is essential for romance, the neural strategy that compels people to make the huge leap of faith into marital commitment, was, ironically, creating the destruction of our partnership for it did not fit the ongoing nature of marriage.

Let us now explore the actual biology of marriage. In it are keys to the reasonable marriage. The neurobiological transitions from romance to commitment to marriage are perhaps the most difficult transitions an adult faces, yet, unlike adolescence, it is a hidden transition for most of us. The fact that we don't understand this transition is a root cause of our present reliance on divorce to solve marital distress. The male brain, we will find, has as much to teach us as does the female brain about the biology of marriage and the natural stages of love we go through together.

THE BIOLOGY OF MARRIAGE

For a number of years, during the late 1980s and early 1990s, I surveyed developmental research, archetypal psychology, and brain and biochemical research to discover a long-term blueprint for marital partnership that was based in actual brain, biochemical, and developmental science. I was looking for a biological map of love, which began in neurobiological research of males, females, and their relationships and could be confirmed by psychological data and common human experiences. In studying scientific data and human literature from thirty cultures on all continents, I discovered that all long-term relationships occur all over the world in a very similar way: in four discernible seasons and twelve discernible stages.

Here is the biological map of marriage I discovered. I'll present it now, then explore how we can use it to develop reasonable expectations of each other and to succeed in marriage. As I present this blueprint, it's useful to remember that most stages normally last a number of years. It's also crucial to notice that many couples never leave the first few stages—the first season of love—replaying them over and over until the couple's divorce and even taking them up again in subsequent marriages.

The Season of Enchantment

A relationship is based on being biochemically enchanted with the possibilities of the partner or friend, including the possibility of altering that person to fit our projections of who we want and need as a lover or friend. Our base hormones—testosterone and estrogen/progesterone—as well as our brain chemicals—oxytocin, dopamine, vasopressin—are in a constant state of flow and flux during this time.

Stage 1: Romance. The beautiful bond is formed, and we live in its bliss for many months, generally six months to two years. When we fall in love—or even just in lust—four centers of the brain light up simultaneously, including the key love center, the cingulate gyrus in the limbic system. Increased blood flow and glucose metabolism in the brain moves in and out of these centers, and they communicate constantly, giving us the feeling of romantic love. The candlelight dinner comes to illuminate, not just an evening's passion, but a lifetime's possibility.

Stage 2: Disillusionment. In all relationships, first one partner then the other pulls away—a partner does something disappointing or experiences disappointment. The perfection we have projected on our partners inevitably dissolves into painful reality. This stage lasts six months to a year.

Many of our unresolved issues with our mothers and fathers engage our psyches during this stage. Our romantic brain chemistry is now affected by cortisol, the stress hormone. We become brains under stress. Areas of the limbic system, like the cingulate gyrus, that were somewhat more disconnected from judgment centers in the frontal lobes during stage 1 now reconnect with the top of the brain. We become very judgmental.

Stage 3: Power struggle. While this is a normal stage of marital development, one that many couples move through—lasting two or more years—it is also the most likely stage for divorce. Nearly every divorced couple has become locked for many years in this stage of relationship until stress-hormone levels for each person become so severe that one or both initiate divorce.

In this stage, partners attempt to deal with disillusionment and disenchantment as well as the stresses of general human life—work, raising children—by trying to change the core personality of the partner or the self. During this time, the brain exists in a confusing trauma of hormones, brain chemicals, and brain centers. Hormones and brain chemicals that build romance and lust no longer dominate, though we try to rely on them. Judgment dominates, but we want the dominance of the bliss-producing brain chemicals again. We are in a neural limbo that manifests itself in our struggle over power and our primary strategy of getting the partner to change in order that—we hope—our own brain chemistry will return to the bliss of a few years ago.

The Season of Awakening

The first season of our marriage is a wild ride of enchantments, disillusionments, and psychological battles. In stage 2, we try to get off the roller coaster. While many relationships end in a power struggle, for just as many people there is a time of psychological awakening in which we realize our marriage can't last if we keep arguing over turf or trying to change the other person. This is the time Gail and I moved into when we confronted the divorce of Kathy and Grant. In this season there is a concentration in the brain on combining limbic functions with frontal lobes. We seek a new rhythm for our relationship. Neurally, the top of the brain wins the struggle between hormones/chemicals and the thinking centers in the neocortex. Organization of neural impulses wins out over the chaos of romantic love and sexual lust.

Stage 4: Awakening. In moments of epiphany and insight, we feel an immense relief to realize that we can become adults who care deeply for each other rather than child-adults who constantly project romantic idealizations and illusions on our partners. We gain a kind of bliss during this stage—an increase in endorphins, a pleasant bonding echo from oxytocin increases—but it is not the supercharged bliss of stage 1; it is the bliss of insight, of seeing reality for what it is. Over a period of months, usually with a lot of communication about the awakening itself, we set ourselves to the hard task of really learning how to love one another. We say things like, "Relationships don't have to be a war," and, "Wow, I think I finally understand what's going on!"

We gain insight and awakening just in time because suffering greater than our own marital power struggle is coming our way.

Stage 5: The second crisis. In all relationships, crises arise. A partner loses a job, a child is badly hurt, parents become gravely ill. Crisis and trauma are natural to the life journey, and struggling with them as a couple is also a natural part of the marital journey. While no one knows exactly when a crisis will hit, the kind of external or larger family crises we're discussing here seem to intersect with marriages after about five years. We can't say that human nature seeks out crisis, for we don't really know if that is what the brain is doing. We do know, however, that every marriage faces a series of crises over a lifetime.

This map for marriage has four major crisis stages in it (by "crisis" we can mean a number of problems over a period of months or years). The first was composed of fighting with each other, creating a crisis of disillusionment and power struggle. Just as that first one challenged our marriage with raised cortisol levels—high stress and conflict—so does this second major crisis. The first crisis is one we can resolve by moving into awakening or by divorcing. The second major time of crisis imposes a new focus of marital difficulty. We no longer focus on "how to be in love" but on how to find deeper courage as individual selves and as a couple.

During any time of crisis, the brain goes into trauma reaction and stress hormone increases. If a couple has constructed a strong base of love by this point, including awakening, the individual selves can rely on each other's strength, compassion, and guidance during the crisis, and stress hormones more easily dissipate. If major crises occur in a marriage before the couple has even moved out of the crisis of disillusionment and power struggle, it is very difficult for the marriage to survive.

Stage 6: Refined intimacy. Surviving power struggle and then surviving life's hardships together can bring a couple into a common marital rhythm. Perhaps seven to ten years of marriage have passed now. If the relationship has not broken down by this time, it has probably become stronger. If, after seven years, a relationship is still a high-stress struggle, then the couple is probably still in stage 3. If, however, it is a relationship each person looks forward to at the end of the day, the couple will now enter a time of great refinement, especially in communication and conflict management. The skills of love become polished and refined. Much of the trauma that has emotionally affected the limbic system of the brain has become resolved. The amygdala, for instance, at the base of the limbic system (where aggression responses are often housed) is less activated now when the partners come in contact. The temporal lobe at the top of the brain, where spiritual functioning occurs, is more active. The issue of "reasonable expectations" becomes a matter of important conversation. The partners value each other's opinions and ideas.

In this stage the brain is often moving into greater sync with the other's brain. This match of brain rhythm is not like the pheromone-induced in-sync quality of early romance but is more of an earned happiness. Partners learn to read each other's biological signals and act accordingly. When one partner has the flu, for instance, the other partner knows what he or she needs. When one partner says a key code phrase in daily conversation, like, "I don't feel valued," the other partner responds not with immediate reactivity ("Haven't I done enough for you," "What are you talking about?" or, "Well I don't feel valued either!") but instead with the phrase or gesture the saddened partner needs. Partners work hard to be honest, not manipulative. They know what it's like to have their relationship dominated by romance chemistry, then by stress chemistry, and they work toward a more refined balance. Relationships in stage 6 are not a struggle as they were before—though it is always hard work.

The Season of Partnership

By the time we achieve the rich partnership we dreamed of in our youth, we are generally in middle age. Men may have reached midlife—that time in their lives when it is a doctor, not a policeman, who tells them they should slow down. Women will probably have given birth to all of their children by now, and those children will be in various stages of growing up. Couples will have worked out a rhythm for most key elements of partnership—sex life, parenting, work life, home life.

Perhaps the key to understanding this landmark on the map of marriage is to notice couples who have been married well over ten years. They seem, for the most part, to have worked out who they are and what they need from the other. They have probably learned that they can't get the majority of their personal needs met by the other, but they need friends, careers, and communities in which to develop a midlife self. They have learned that their love relationship is unique—there is no "correct" way to be partnered.

More than half of our marriages today do not reach this biological season of partnership. In many cases, a couple married for fifteen years is actually still in power struggle.

For those people who do arrive at the third season of marriage, biology becomes, as always, a clear marker. Especially as the partner enters midlife biological transitions—perimenopause then menopause for females, and male menopause for men—couples must draw deeply on their secure base of partnership to weather a number of biological storms. Even as we struggle to weather these, we may notice that our marital partnership has become not only life sustaining for us and our children, but also deeply useful to our community. Our brains experience our love for the other as a "whole-brain" activity. In one earlier stage, the frontal lobe dominated, in another, the hormones in the hypothalamus. But in the season of partnership, blood flow in our brains is more equally balanced between necessary brain centers.

Stage 7: Creative partnership. After a decade or more of marriage, couples often find themselves content (at least for a time) with career, child raising, volunteering, and other creative endeavors; they realize that they can gracefully be creative because of their marriage. Marriage is the secure base with which to accomplish their goals. Certain goals will have to be sacrificed and human limitations accepted, but a couple knows it is in stage 7 when there is a base of contentment even when creative goals are relinquished in order to keep the marriage and family strong.

These are years in which couples might achieve some financial and personal success, and will feel good not only about their relationship but about how it gives them the ability to do what they each feel spiritually called to do during this decade. In a neural sense, two individuals have by now so completely learned to enjoy each other's neural rhythms that they are able to finish each other's sentences and even think each other's thoughts. Unlike in the first season of a relationship, this almost uncanny dissolving of self and knowledge of the other's inner world does not create power struggle but, instead, generosity of self.

Stage 8: The third crisis. Inevitably, this season of life is challenged by crisis and tragedy. As in stage 5, crisis challenges the couple to sustain their marriage through hard work, good communication, and reasonable expectations. If a child dies or one of the partners has an affair, the marriage might break up at this point. Or the relationship might continue beyond these difficulties, its fragility and the pain of life bringing the partners close again. Many of the hormones that ruled early love and romance are less active partners of relationship at this stage. Male testosterone levels are in decline. A man's social ambition and sex drive may decrease. Female hormones enter menopause, a time in which everyday affection and stability is made difficult in the face of profound mood alterations.

The ability of a couple to survive crisis during this stage—both external tragedy and internal hormonal shifts—will often be equal to the completion of former stages of biological development. The human brain, especially in ongoing love of another, develops rhythms in stages of completion. If a couple faces the death of a child before they have reached stage 7, it may be harder for them to stay together through that tragedy, for they may not have laid a strong enough foundation. If, during hormonal shifts, one of the partners has an affair, the couple might still elect to stay together; they may be more ready and capable of this gesture if the first two seasons of marriage have successfully completed. If, however, the couple has been involved in a low-grade power struggle for the last decade, making some advancements into later stages of life but their marriage remaining very fragile, the hormonal shifts of stage 8 (which can last around ten years) or the external tragedies can more easily break them apart.

Stage 9: Radiant love. Couples who, as they survive tragedy, crisis, and normal hormonal development, find their love constantly reignited become the couples that others come to admire greatly. Their love seems to radiate from them. In this stage, the couple and their marriage become role models. In stage 7, they might have been seeking inventive and creative endeavors that reaped financial and other rewards; in stage 9, humbled by tragedy, fate, and their own midlife biological changes, they may now focus mainly on service, without needing much material return. They may well have every-thing they need, their kids grown. They may well become people of whom others say, "They know who they are."

The Season of Nonattachment

Many decades have passed by now. Couples advance into their elder years, entering a time of memory and detachment (some couples may be in second or third marriages). They love their grandkids, but they also enjoy returning them to the parents at the end of the day. They are entering a time in life when they tire more easily but sleep less. Circadian rhythms are changing. The hypothalamus is less active, more detached, lacking the compulsion to process waves of hormones. Men become more tender. The body is engaged in the slowing down that comes with age. Brain cells fire less quickly. Some people will fear this time in life, hoping to regain youth. These people, by the way, often have higher testosterone flow than average for their age. Most people who have moved through nine stages of a relationship are generally focused, by this time, on accepting who they are. Power struggles that were submerged in the relationship might reignite now, and some people in their third or fourth decade of marriage do divorce, but most marriages, having made it through the previous stages of biosocial development, remain intact.

Stage 10: Acceptance of solitude. As the brain's circuitry begins to slow down, certain centers of the brain nearly shut off. Most cen-ters of the brain lose gray-and-white matter at faster rates than ear-lier. Depending on the person's genetics and life choices (e.g., smoking, drinking), decay of the brain occurs at different rates of acceleration.

During this time, as the brain destimulates, relationships come to include a great deal of solitude. Daily projects are still enjoyed. Sex lives can be active. Life can be quite full. But the sense of a deep drive to create, invent, conquer is being replaced by a need to

listen and hear. In the aging brain, blood flow away from the parietal lobe where spatial orientation occurs, can make a person feel
less connected to the everyday activities of the world. If both partners are still alive, they have probably been married three or more
decades by now.

Stage 11: The fourth crisis. All seasons of life are marked by traumas, tragedies, and crises. The late nineteenth-century Russian nov-
elist, Fyodor Dostoyevsky, wrote: "Suffering is the origin of
consciousness." The map of human biology seems at least in part to
bear out his wisdom, for even in our late stages of biological growth
and relationship, crisis and pain affect the brain. In this case, generally the most obvious crisis is the sickness and death of our spouse.
Caring for a spouse whose brain and body are in decay affects our
own brain chemistry—cortisol levels, blood flow between the limbic
system and the frontal lobes, effects on our own memory centers, are
all profoundly felt.

In this stage of life, we and our spouse and friends may talk a lot
about our ailments, sicknesses, the ailments of others. We have
faced many crises in our lives—deaths of others, losses of work, lost
relationships, mental or physical illness, fights with our children,
economic ups and downs in our nation, assassinations of our leaders
and heroes, the sacrifice of our children to war—and now these
crises are part of what gives our neural web the strength to survive
the loss of our spouse and the diminution of ourselves toward
death.

Stage 12: The end of life. The last stage of any relationship is the
death of the relationship. Our spouse dies and then we die. The
neural web shuts down. All the tugs and pulls of brain stem, limbic
system, neocortex disappear. As we're dying, perhaps we say, "I have
lived a full life; I'm ready." Perhaps we say, "One of my greatest
accomplishments has been this: that I have learned how to love." Or
perhaps we simply move on, the brain, the self, the soul closing
down, awaiting the next stage, which our sciences have not yet been
able to chart.

A MAP FOR MARRIAGE

In presenting a marital map that emphasizes biological development, I hope I've presented a recognizable picture of human love. As
you look at it you might think, "Do most of today's couples ever live
out the whole journey?"

This biology-based map of marriage is not obvious on the candle-
lit table in romance, yet it is the map we commit to when we commit to each other. Religions often hope to help us commit to it;
priests, ministers, and rabbis standing before us when we marry, saying, "Do you, Michael, promise to take care of Gail the rest of her
life?" Most people, even in responding affirmatively, do not realize
there are at least twelve biological stages of marriage to commit to
in the first place; yet as couples make a home together, they begin to
lay the map of marriage out on the kitchen table: Their early discussions of marriage are replete with plans for the future.

We can do better than this once we understand the actual biological map of a marriage. Unless we do better, as a marriage progresses, what little we know of our own biological development as a
couple may get lost or buried under a bed, a carpet, an old dream.
We may get stuck in a power struggle, distancing; disdain may take
over human love, the candle-lit dinners and wonderful sex and
mutual dreams and the map of love all just memories a few years
down the line.

When men and women feel sadness (neural depression) at the
disillusionment that sets into their struggling marriages, they remember lost intimacy quite vividly. As they remember, the hippocampus
and temporal lobes become engorged with neurotransmission. The
candle light, the sex, the long conversations, the commitment to
marry, and all the other moments of closeness and intimacy rise up
for them as on a movie screen. They begin to remember times of distance during the romance phase. They think, "Oh, look—the relationship was already disintegrating; I just couldn't see it." Or, "If I'd
only been smarter, I'd have realized he didn't love me like I thought."

Our memories—whether positive or negative in feeling—hold
closeness and intimacy as their standard of quality. When a memory

of separateness creeps in, it is judged immediately as a harbinger of the present doom we feel in an unhappy marriage. It is *closeness* we want; it is closeness we want to remember. Even as we contemplate divorce, it is closeness we believe can save our marriage, if our marriage can be saved. "If only we could be close again, like those moments at the candle-lit dinner."

After five or ten years of marriage, we are looking back for solutions to the first stage of the partnership: romance. When our mate comes home or we sit at the dinner table with him, we'll feel the anxieties and tensions of the power struggle. For perhaps five or ten years we are locked in the first season of human love; locked in this season, we are conditioned to project onto our present, complex love the romantic expectations for closeness and intimacy with which that love initially began. We are still not focused on the whole map of marriage, the whole biological blueprint of who we are.

Human development has only arrived at this general state of marital distress in the last century. For the most part, our ancestors spent little time brooding in stages 2 and 3 over the lost closeness of stage 1. Marriages were forced to last by religious edict or other social values. Personal understanding of a biological map for marriage was not really necessary.

Nowadays, we spend inordinate time living in lost romantic illusions. This is one of the primary drivers of lost love today. If the biological map of marriage teaches us one thing, it teaches us the necessity of not just trying to be close, but also searching for answers in another kind of intimacy. This kind of intimacy—intimate separateness—winks at us constantly, trying to get our attention, throughout our life stages. Let me give one example of how confusing, and yet liberating, it can be to notice biological stages in married life and the kind of intimate separateness that makes all the stages possible.

SHE SAYS: "I FEEL FAT." WHAT SHOULD HE DO?

A couple came to see me in my marital practice. They had been married twenty-two years. Among the issues they faced was this one.

He:

Sarah said the other night, "I feel fat and unattractive. Sometimes I just want to give up." As you know, she's in perimenopause, and she's gained weight. She used to do weight bearing exercise and do aerobics, but she no longer does those activities. She has become more sedentary than she was, and she's gained about thirty pounds.

When she told me how she felt I said, "I can see what you mean. It does kind of seem like you've given up on yourself. You've gained weight."

"You're still attracted to me, though, right?" she asked. "Sexually, I mean."

I told her the truth. Maybe this was a mistake, but we've been married twenty-two years and we've talked about this topic before. I said, "I love you as my mate for life, so I'm not going to stray on you, if that's what you mean. But I'm definitely more sexually attracted to you when you're not overweight, when you're working out. You kind of glow when you're active and in charge of yourself. When you're not, that glow isn't there."

Sarah got really mad at me and cried and said I was completely unsupportive and hurt her feelings. I guess, in this case, the truth wasn't a good idea.

She:

The other night I said, "I feel fat and unattractive." I wanted Trace to tell me I looked fine, but he was in one of his "brutally honest" moods and told me he didn't find me sexually attractive anymore because I don't work out as much as I used to. I've gained a few pounds, but I don't look bad. I was so offended, so hurt, by what he said. He was basically telling me he didn't want me anymore. It's been a week, and I don't know if I've forgiven him yet. He keeps insisting he's trying to

help me, or motivate me, or something. I just feel like he ran over me
with a truck. I wish he could be supportive of me.

Many of the biological differences between men and women are
revealed in this incident. Both males and females can separate love,
commitment, and sex when they functionally need to, but they do
this very differently. Men, more often than women, will choose a
strategy that brings independence or a seeming lack of intimate support to a relationship; women, who are oxytocin driven, find this very
confusing. Yet there is a wisdom in what the male brain is doing.

Trace was indeed being honest when he said he didn't find Sarah
as physically attractive because she didn't have "the glow." This
phrase encompasses his sense of what is attractive in his spouse,
what stimulates him sexually. As couples get older, males who are in
love with their spouses adjust to their spouse's growing and changing
body. Still, males have an internalized range of what they find attractive. When a spouse moves out of that range for a long period of
time—gaining perhaps twenty pounds would not spur Trace's comment, whereas thirty pounds might—the male becomes less sexually
attracted. In some romantic alliances, including marriages, this can
contribute to his "looking elsewhere," especially if it goes on for
many years.

This is a biological fact that we cannot hide from. Males and
females, if married to a spouse whose appearance *significantly*
changes, can stray sexually from that spouse. Sexual and physical
attractiveness are locked into our brain stems. When Trace spoke of
it honestly, he was practicing intimate separateness. He was saying,
"I'm intimate with you, but I'm not you—I'm me, and as me, I agree
that you are looking less attractive."

When Trace said that he loved his wife but did feel less sexually
attracted, Sarah heard this as a complete rejection of her, a complete
abandonment. It is hard not to feel sympathy for her point of view.
If Trace had said, "Honey, what are you talking about, you look fine,"
a response that would have carried a blanket intimacy, at least on the
surface, she would have probably felt not only much better about

herself but also about the romantic alliance. However, Trace did not say those things. He valued honesty and, from a male point of view, was being supportive. He tried to motivate her by making her feel bad so she would want to change things—which is a very male strategy, one men often use with their mates when they perceive that their mate's own strategies have not worked.

"I love you as my mate for life, but . . ." Men may well think the spouse is not doing her part in the marriage if she "gives up" or "loses the glow." Males often feel that remaining sexually attractive is a very important part of a female's commitment to romantic longevity. In fact, I have often heard men say, in the privacy of my therapy practice, "Women tell us to talk about our feelings and do everything they want romantically, but then they don't take care of themselves physically." Romance is a transaction for both males and females, and males often focus on protecting the transaction. They often watch closely what a woman brings to the romance, judging her romantic abilities, not by whether she buys him flowers, but by whether she takes care of herself physically so that she remains sexually attractive.

Everything we've said here, of course, has less bearing for men and women who are postmenopausal. As testosterone decreases in men, sex is still enjoyed, and romance is still a pleasure, but many of the issues that faced the man the first twenty-five years of marriage are not the same issues in the last. But in the case of Trace and Sarah, this was a big issue in the marriage. The issue was not only that Trace agreed with Sarah about her lack of attractiveness, but that, as Sarah put it, "Trace doesn't know how to be intimate. He's always finding some way to pull away from me."

Over the last three decades, books on marriage have seemed to cover absolutely every facet of married life. Yet if you review those books, you'll find they mainly cover marriage as an "intimacy system" that, in order to work, needs more intimacy. As you can see, I am taking a different course here, one based on brain science.

Marriages, in order to work, need as much separation as they need intimacy. The human brain needs independence just as much as it needs dependency.

We May Be Too Close

It has been popular to say, "Women are mature, men are immature." Indeed, the male brain does complete its adolescent development later than the female, and especially if a couple is aware of a man's incomplete separation from mother, there is a temptation to engage in shaming language about male immaturity. Certainly, some men are immature. But sometimes, also, the male drive toward independence behavior is objected to and labeled as immature.

Yet it might be this very drive that helps a marriage mature to later stages of life. Independence, as we hinted in the last chapter, can be a very useful and maturing influence. Instinctively, men know that independence is a great stress reducer.

Being Too Close Is a Bigger Stressor Than We Realize

In the last decades, increasing numbers of women have experimented with the male approach to "maturity" by striving to achieve more independence. Some women have even said, "Women don't need men at all. Women can be happy without a man." This can be an empowering idea and crucial to a healthy life, especially when it is eventually balanced by the intuitive realization that a woman may, indeed, need a man—an intuition that becomes the fullest biological reality when she has children and is faced with the challenge of raising them alone.

When women live life and deal with stress, not with oxytocin-driven bonding but rather with testosterone-driven independence, many can be saved from relationship-stress depression—and can be protected from their inherent fear of abandonment.

In the human brain, marital problems are "attachment and bonding stressors." Marital problems increase cortisol (stress hormone) levels, increase functions in the adrenal glands, and increase other physical markers that fit a person's particular genetic composition—including heart palpitations, anxiety attacks, depression, and addiction. The brain-in-love experiences stress and attempts numerous strategies to mitigate the stress. The brain seeks to free neural activity from the stressful enmeshment of the self and other selves; it will try to regain neural independence, get a rest from intense neural activity, and then try relating to others again.

The woman turns away from her husband's request for sex, hoping to push him away so that she can regain some of her own power. The man spends twelve hours a day at work, hoping to free himself from the sense of being trapped in his wife's expectations, needs, desires, and dissatisfactions. These scenarios can be applied to either gender.

Two crucial levels of the human dance go on simultaneously— enmeshment and independence separation. Divorce, the dissipation of sexual relations, or the escape into work are separation activities. A key question we must ask is: What got the man and woman to the point at which they had to rely on those separation activities? What brought the man and woman to high cortisol levels and stress was not just distance but closeness, too. While striving to meld themselves together, two adult selves lost their independence. In neural terms, the brains and the bodies (including hormonal and chemical functions) became absorbed in emotional stimulation, which was pleasing at first, then became overwhelming.

As we suggested earlier, the male brain will tend to seek a return of independence as a stress reducer more quickly than the female, but both brains engage in seeking independence as a stress reducer. In that seeking is a clue to what we mean when we say, "Maybe marriages are in trouble today as much because the man and the woman are too emotionally close as they are because the man and the woman are too emotionally far away."

WE ARE TOO CLOSE. CAN WE COME TO TERMS WITH IT?

This enmeshment—the destructiveness of this emotional overstimulation—has been glossed over in the last few decades. Pushing for

emotional closeness as the romantic ideal of marriage, women's culture has supported female attempts to be independent of men while
disparaging male independence. Female culture has done this without understanding that male independence is part of what makes a
marriage work. Cognizance of the need for emotional independence
is one of the best things the study of male nature brings to human
marriage; along with this cognizance comes an insistence on separateness and independence.

Once armed with a knowledge of male independence–based
biology and how it benefits a marriage, women are armed with a
new skill to help keep marriages strong. Couples make it through
the twelve stages of relationship as much because they can reduce
intimacy stress through independent lives as through intimate connection itself.

Many marriages will not be saved by a woman's or man's decision
to leave early romantic idealizations and parental projections
behind, for many men (and women) will never do their part to keep
a marriage going. But there is immense power when a woman, for
instance, takes the step of leaving behind her disillusionment that
constant intimacy is not occurring and begins to judge her relationship by how well it dances between intimacy and independence.

In my therapy practice, I often saw women leave marriages because they could no longer function in their fear of their husband's
independence, distance, and separateness. These women rarely tried
to discover their own independence within the marriage. In fact,
they tacitly believed that their independence would have meant failure as women, lovers, and wives. They were not "empowered" to create social independence in their lives.

I also witnessed women who left their husbands behind once
they developed social and emotional independence. These women
were not afraid of commitment during the romance and commitment stages but had trouble as the couple moved toward later stages
of marriage and the need for separateness. Often, these women
reported feeling emotionally unfulfilled by the man. Ironically, many
of these women went from divorce to divorce, constantly dissatisfied. They had gained social independence but not the emotional

independence they sought. Later in life some of them looked back with regret, realizing that the very man they left was the man who gave them the emotional safety in which to develop their sense of independence.

In many cases, these women did not understand that the new emotional independence they felt in middle age came in large part from changes in their own hormonal biology. As female androgenic hormones (testosterone) shine through, women biologically feel more independent.

More marriages than we realize dissolve in these sorts of confusing life circumstances. In most cases, marriages do not dissolve because of abuse or alcoholism; they dissolve because the partners become dissatisfied, and the power struggle of this dissatisfaction wears them down. Among women, the most common dissatisfaction is lack of romantic and emotional fulfillment by men. My therapy practice taught me that while lack of emotional fulfillment is definitely a marriage breaker, at least half of its effects can dissolve in the empowerment of a woman who understands separateness as well as she understands closeness. In a moment, we will explore in depth how to practice this understanding.

Women face a great challenge when they understand male biology. They see that a man's insistence on independence, distance, and separateness is actually a blessing. Women realize that they need more of that independence. The woman who idealizes romance and cannot go beyond that mind-set can feel quite alone. She may very well blame the man for her loneliness. In the awakening stage of a relationship, many women realize that their own sense of loneliness is at least half theirs to carry, and they see that to move to later stages of marriage, they must find other people, not necessarily their spouse, with whom to feel many of the emotional bonds and moments crucial to an oxytocin-based neural system. These women make time to relate to women friends and community, building their part of the relationship's evolution to radiant love.

In saying this, we do not mean to say that independence behavior is the only key to a successful relationship. If a man and woman become too independent of each other, their marriage is often doomed. If a man and woman interpret independence as meaning two selves in a power struggle, their marriage is probably doomed. If a man or woman abuse their hard-won independence—by having sexual or romantic affairs, for instance—the marriage is often doomed. But if the male way of being married exists in balance with the female way, the future looks bright for marriage, and the later stages of human love are immanently achievable.

BRIDGE BRAINS

The bridge-brain male is more female in his emotional processing, and his independence needs may not be as strong as other males. He might stay at home more, spend more time in the nest. He is probably higher on the verbal end of the brain spectrum, so he might enjoy the kind of conversation a woman does.

Many women married to bridge-brain males report immense satisfaction. One woman joked at a seminar: "I'm married to a bridge brain. It's like having a wife. It's great." Another woman wrote, "My husband is not only my best friend, he's like a girlfriend. I talk about everything with him, tell him every secret, and we laugh and giggle. We see the world in exactly the same way."

The bridge-brain husband is perhaps the ideal for many women—at least in theory. Yet in actuality, for many women a bridge-brain male is too "soft."

The freedom and diversity of present society, while creating more confusion for most men and women, is creating a better chance of happy marriage for bridge-brain males. Old gender stereotypes, which emphasized provide-and-protect and high testosterone, are less universal, giving bridge-brain males more of a chance to compete successfully for females. As the level of testosterone in some women continues to increase, the need for lower testosterone and bridge-brain males will naturally increase. Human adaptation has a way of catching up to itself.

Simultaneously, male testosterone levels are also on the rise. We can expect the bridge-brain male to remain more an exception than a rule during the long length of a human marriage. And even if a woman is married to a bridge brain, power struggle can still occur. Intimate separateness is still necessary.

PRACTICING INTIMATE SEPARATENESS:
TURNING MARRIAGES AROUND

In the last decade of teaching nature-based theory, I have been lucky to help turn my own marriage around and to help facilitate positive changes in many other marriages. As Gail puts it, "Understanding what each other was *really* thinking saved our marriage."

Our love for each other is still a mystery, and there are parts of each other that will always remain unknowable; but we understand each other, and the happiness of our marriage is based more on that one effort than any other. Gail and I have been able to break down illusions about each other—especially illusions about how things *should* be between a woman and a man. During the last eighteen years, we have come to see each other, and we made the decision to like what we saw. The compassion our marriage needed came to us from the world of science—brains, hormones, bodies, minds—and from that compassion came the daily acts of love that every marriage needs in order to flourish. When we fight, or need time apart, or go through life passages that are stressful, we return to sanity and common sense by considering the key we *both* hold to the doorway of a happy marriage: an understanding of human nature. While I enjoy focusing on Gail's nature as a woman, she enjoys focusing on my nature as a man.

In our roles as marital therapists, Gail and I have been able to help many other people. Here are testimonials from people who have enjoyed turnarounds in their marriages.

Joyce, thirty-five, said:

We fought a lot. He was emotionally distant. I left him once, which shocked him. It was like he couldn't see it coming. He decided to work hard to give me what I needed. It's not like he's a bad man. He's the father of my children. But he just didn't come through, and I didn't know what to do.

I took your advice and decided to stop waiting for him to figure things out. I took it upon myself to figure things out. The "ah ha" came for me when I learned about the male brain. My husband and I changed our lives, working together on our marriage as a "project." This worked for him. Men like projects. It took us over a year of work, but things really turned around.

We're the same people now, but we have a very different relationship. I think our love shines through. You told us we deserved to be happy, and you were right.

Carrie, forty-four, from Minneapolis, wrote:

My husband and I are religious people. We believe in staying married no matter what. But we just couldn't get along. We talked about divorce, which was terrible. I went on medication for depression.

When we heard about the so-called "nature-based" approach to marriage, we looked it up. We heard you speak and realized what you're talking about. You're talking about getting to know who the other person really is, the soul of the other person. The soul of my husband is what I've been trying to understand all along. I thought I had understood it. Now I think I really do. We're much happier.

Layne, forty-seven, said:

I was a radical feminist, then I had a son. I'm still a feminist, but I know how different boys are from girls. There is such a difference! But I still didn't want to admit how different a man is from a woman. Or maybe it's just that I knew it but didn't want it to be important. I tried to be openminded. But I've struggled in my marriages. I go through phases of blaming the men. Now I'm older. I understand that blaming and shaming get me nowhere, but that still didn't help me. And it sure didn't help men understand me.

I'm with someone now whom I really love. A friend told me about this nature-based approach to marriage. I was skeptical at first, even angry about it. I'll admit I figured you were just saying old, patriarchal stuff about men and women. But I'm hooked now. There's a kind of superficial reaction a lot of women have to the idea that they have to understand their husbands in order to be loved by their husbands. But living it is something else. It really works! My husband and I have been together six years. This is the most equal partnership I've ever had.

Darren, forty-one, wrote me:

I'm divorced, two kids. I'm living with a woman. We moved in together three years ago. It got so bad between us that she walked out.

I begged her to come back and she did. We decided to change our relationship. It was her idea. She got into "nature-based marriage." I never knew it could be fun to understand her better. We changed the way we talked with each other. We changed what we expected of each other.

Darren's fiancée, Sherry, thirty-nine, agreed:

I've been divorced for ten years. I've been looking for love all my life. Now I think I've found it. I think marriage is different in our generation than it's ever been before. A lot of what my parents based their marriage on, I can't use. But I want to feel like my husband loves me and will take care of me. I think all my life I've been waiting for him to come to me, even though I thought I was the one giving everything up for him. Now I see that I have the power to shape my own marriage, and it's my power. I don't have to compete with him for his power. I've never understood a man like I understand Darren.

I'm not in the dark anymore about men, and it's helped me be in love.

These success stories are not evidence that every marriage can be saved by increasing human understanding. But having lived these circumstances myself, I am heartened to know that intimate separateness is being practiced by many people with great success.

But What If a Woman Is Married to a Deeply Wounded Man?

Having mentioned success stories, we all know that many marriages cannot be saved. We know that some men, like some women, are so wounded by childhood trauma or previous marriages that trying to relate to them only seems to lead to pain.

What success can intimate separateness bring with men whose neural development has been severely damaged? Since there is hardly a man or woman who has not been psychologically wounded in some way, this is an important question.

All human beings have suffered traumas to the neural web, for we flourish in life by meeting stresses and adapting to them. All of us grow up with some form of low-grade posttraumatic stress—what is now popularly called our "baggage." These wounds are part of our stages of life, part of who we are, part of our character and being. To a great extent, these neural traumas—these wounds—have been integrated into the self, becoming motivational, educational, and worthwhile. They can actually help us. They don't have to negatively affect our marriage. But when we speak of an emotionally wounded man or woman in the context of marital stress, we are not speaking of the normal attachment and separation stresses of childhood, nor are we speaking of just any wounds to the psyche, the brain, the heart and soul. We are speaking, specifically, of wounds that become primary neural drivers.

The brain of a severely traumatized person, when scanned, will show dark spots in areas where we would normally see healthy neural activity. The hippocampus might constantly recycle the memory of trauma through the limbic system, which in turn keeps the stress cycling through neurotransmission in the brain. When the right trigger occurs in the environment, the brain explodes with overwhelming activity. The centers of the brain that should calm this re-creation remain dark. When we study the wounded brain from an endocrinological point of view, the posttraumatic memory and resulting rise in stress hormone and adrenaline might not have a tangible daily effect on the person's life, but when the right trigger comes, the stress hormones rise, along with adrenaline, and the person enters a baseline fight-or-flight response. Areas in the top of the brain remain dark, but lower brain areas explode with activity.

A man might live in the same house with his wife while projecting onto her his posttraumatic stress memories. When the posttraumatic brain condition we are calling "the wound" manifests itself, it is almost always a manifestation in response to a trigger. The trigger could be a substance, like alcohol or drugs; the trigger could be a movie, a nightmare, an everyday experience; the trigger can also be the love relationship itself; the trigger can be the wife's actions. And we must remember, always, that everything we are saying about men applies to women. When a person is wounded, he or she reacts in somewhat predictable ways.

If a female partner is a dominant personality, there is a great chance a male will see his dominant mother in his wife. If his mother's dominance greatly impinged on his developing identity during boyhood, there is a great chance that he will stand, like a soldier, against dominance by his wife, though he may learn how to mask his projection of his mother. He may acquiesce to his wife for a number of years—buying her what she wants, satisfying other needs of hers—but he'll withhold from her whatever is the very heart and soul of love she most wants. In today's marriage, that will probably lead to divorce.

What should a woman do in the case of marriage to a deeply wounded man? Women have the power to choose what to do. They can choose to continue the behavior that triggers him, or they can change the behavior.

In living with wounded men it is natural for a partner to say, "I do not cause him to push me away; the wound does, so why should I have to alter my behavior?"

A wife might say, "If only his mother hadn't done such-and-such, we'd have a better marriage."

Or she might say, "This is all about him, not about me; he's the reason we got the divorce."

If power comes from being right about these things, then we have the power we sought. But if power comes from managing human relationships to a point of success and longevity, power comes from rethinking. Whatever the man's wound, the attachment stress that wounded him is already a part of the man's brain system. If the man is full grown—in his twenties and beyond—most of his brain development is complete. The man's brain is wired the way it's wired. Some changes can be expected, and hard work in therapy can help, as can medication, but the plasticity of the brain by the mid-twenties is limited. The man is very much who he is.

Nature-based theory encourages reasonable marriage, *especially* with men for whom wounding is a prime neural driver. Reasonable marriage is reality based. It assumes that neither the wounds of men or women will be completely healed during the marriage. Excluding cases of obvious danger, couples can discover the twelve stages of relationship if they adapt to each other's wounds; the man and woman must become conscious of each other and understand the dynamic between them. The full healing of the other's self is usually an impossible expectation, but it is very possible to manage a marriage through a balance of oxytocin-driven closeness needs and male testosterone-driven independence needs. Generally, the most relationally intelligent couples are those who use careful timing in their application of each strategy.

Often in my therapy practice, I have had to point out to women that the relational intelligence—the timing of talk and nontalk, eye contact and non eyecontact—-they apply to long-term relationships with their women friends does not work, much of the time, with men—especially wounded men. Since women think of relational intelligence from a female point of view, they are often surprised to discover the male side of relational intelligence.

Nowhere was this better brought home than with a couple, in their thirties, who came to me before the birth of their second child. The husband, Frank, had problems with anger. He had been in anger management during adolescence and early adulthood. He had never struck a girlfriend or child, having successfully learned to take his anger out on inanimate objects; he struck walls, slammed doors— once he drove his car into a railing. His wife, Anne, loved him, as he did her, but she was worried about the marriage. She entered therapy, bringing him along, "in order to help him stop being so angry."

In talking with Frank and Anne, I discovered that Frank had been abandoned by his parents, brought up in foster care, and been in trouble with the law during adolescence. He had discovered help from many circles—from social services, from mentors, from religion. He was successful in business but, in Anne's words: "When he gets angry and I try to help him by getting him to talk about it, he gets even angrier and this scares me. I can't live with that. What if he really goes overboard one day and hurts me or our child?"

Anne's fear was very real, and Frank admitted that he knew he became immensely frightening. He was much bigger than she and much stronger. He had punched a hole in the wall in the bedroom about a month earlier.

"I don't like this about myself," he said, "but I just can't take it when she's in my face, talking to me. I can't take it!"

In this comment was a clue to what was going terribly wrong in this marriage. In the area of his own wounding (the loss of attachment and the resultant attachment stress during childhood and adolescence), Frank was (even if unconscious of his wisdom) relationally more intelligent than Anne. He was trying to say: Leave me alone when I get angry. He knew that his neural drivers when he became angry were drivers he had to take care of independently. Anne, seeing things from a female point of view, wanted to get him to talk to her when he was angry. "I try to help him talk about what he's feeling," she said. This was exactly the wrong thing to do.

I explained that Anne's method of helping Frank was actually the wounding trigger that made their relationship difficult. To make sure my suspicion was correct, I asked Anne, "When he starts out feeling angry, do you think he would hurt anything or anyone?"

"No," she said, "it's when the anger *builds*. Then I get really afraid."

"By the time his anger builds, have you said anything or have you remained silent?"

"I've tried to help him by then, yes. He just can't seem to help himself."

My suspicion was correct: Without realizing it, Anne was cocreating her own suffering in this aspect of the marriage and her own fears for herself and her unborn child. There were many things Frank could do differently; but in this area, which was the most compelling for Anne, it was she who needed to alter her approach. She had to realize that when the darkness on his brain became his neural driver, his mental wounding was not her province to alter or reshape.

I described how Frank's brain, which had experienced so much childhood trauma, was probably now wired to handle intense stress: When he was triggered by a significant stressor in the outside world—a problem at work, perhaps—his amygdala filled with blood flow. In the brain of someone who processed anger with less physicality, that neurotransmitter overflow in the amygdala would be more quickly guided to move toward the frontal lobe, where the frontal and prefrontal cortex would help calm it. Because of Frank's childhood attachment stresses, including genetics—his mother had a temper—his brain was wired for a slower process of neurotransmitter movement up to the neocortex and more rapid movement into the spinal fluid of the brain stem and then through the physical body. Instead of quickly shutting down his own anger, he was more likely to gather the energy to lash out. He would then need more time than many other people would to calm himself down.

When Anne saw Frank get angry, she instinctively tried to help his brain move neural energy to the cerebral cortex. She did this by trying to talk with him. She tried to get him to process what was going on. His brain, his whole relational intelligence at that moment, was crying, "Leave me alone!" She did not realize that she had to do just that—give his brain time. She tried to rush his neural process. By trying to rush him toward the words produced in the cerebral cortex, Anne was making him even more dangerously physical. If she said nothing, stood back and gave him space, he was not more likely to hit something but, in fact, less likely. His amygdala and other brain functions would get the extra time they needed to complete the management of anger in his wounded brain.

As she listened to this nature-based scenario, Anne experienced an "ah ha" moment. She understood the part she played in her marital problems. Over the months, Frank engaged in therapy on many issues, and Anne discovered gaps in her relational intelligence. She discovered that she had selected Frank, unconsciously, because of her idealization of her angry and abandoning father.

When I saw Anne and Frank at a hockey game two years after they had ended their therapy, they were happy, and their new child was flourishing. We talked and Anne volunteered what she thought had helped the most. "He gets mad and I let him be. Things are so different now because of that one thing." Her own fear of abandonment, she confessed, was no longer triggered by his anger so she no longer needed to save herself by saving him. Frank confessed that life was much easier for him now and for the whole family.

In dealing with wounded men, happy endings like Anne and Frank's are not always guaranteed. There is no single magic bullet. But understanding the mysteries of the male brain can be life changing for many couples. That understanding can make the enjoyment of later stages of love more possible. Seeing the wounds as a part of the life process, gaining relational intelligence, not only from the female style of relating, but also from the male—this is the practice of intimate separateness, and it is a most natural way to help love last.

What Is a Soul Mate?

When two people understand each other's natures, they can embrace the soul of the other person, accommodating the soul's need for both closeness *and* distance.

All of us search for a soul mate. When we are in love, soul is felt to be the hidden *nature* of the person, the hidden depths of the person. We want to be close to that deep nature during a marriage.

But we can get too close.

From a nature-based point of view, we each marry for three primary reasons:

1. To care for and protect children, should we have them.

2. To give and receive unconditional love.

3. To fulfill our personal calling in the world from the position of safety and confidence that a secure home gives us.

Each of these are well within the purview of why people say they want to find a soul mate. When we divorce, we experience a disintegration in one of these three areas. Generally, the movement toward divorce comes when a person feels he or she is not getting enough unconditional love. Nature-based theory notices that enmeshment of ourselves in our own and the other's idealizations undermined the roots of the marriage; also that we did not notice the source of the problem because the relationship endured for three or five or seven more years. Many of us can go decades—from marriage to marriage—never realizing that when we say, "My marriages always seem to drift apart," or, "I can't find the love I need because I can't find a man who knows how to be intimate," we could also be saying, "We never got to the stage of marriage where we learned to keep just the right separateness. No matter what, we tried to be close, and that was often just too close. That's what pulled us apart."

Women are very smart. Many women in the last decade have come to the realization that a one-shot approach to marriage—intimacy at all costs—might be incomplete. Every woman, at some level, knows that she has immense power in her marriage; and women know when what they're doing is inherently unsuccessful. Marriage, which has changed so much in a hundred years, is poised, I think, to change again, toward a nature-based approach. We are poised to truly learn what a soul mate is in our everyday lives.

Though in some marriages, women are treated terribly by narcissistic men who cannot and will not change; though problems like alcoholism, substance abuse, and violence do make many marriages impossible; though some men are, simply, hell to be married to, I have observed that most broken marriages are alliances defeated, not by the fact that the man has a massive character/emotional flaw, but by the fact that the woman and man have not discovered true power. In the male partner's case, he is in a shell, trying to relate too much from the I-am-independent/I-am-separate modality. In the female partner's case, she has not yet become that reasonable woman— respectful of independence and needing her mate to care for her through action more than words—to whom the man would like to give emotional and marital power. The couple remains locked in a power struggle until they divorce. Even if, over the years, she has been able to develop a confident personal identity, she has not been able to step out of romantic idealizations of men and discover reasonable expectations of the nature of men themselves.

When a woman understands her husband's nature, she understands the soul of the man she loves. Her expectations become clear and reasonable because she understands who her husband really is; she transcends her own projections of manhood, of her own father, and of her social idealizations of a man. She, and often he along with her, fully grow up. She and he have a greater chance of moving beyond a power struggle into the experience of knowing a soul mate.

This transcendence is a road to awakening, actual power, actual love, and the combination of personal independence and mutual dependency that a marriage needs to be. When a woman takes the time to answer the question, "What could he be thinking?" her mate has a much higher chance of noticing that her expectations of him are reasonable, *and he likely will yearn to meet them*. Meeting her reasonable expectations becomes a life challenge for him. He will quite often bend over backward to make her happy; he feels understood and loved, and most people who feel loved become great gift givers. His expectations of himself also become clear, and he tries to express them in the marriage (though, more rarely than she'd like, in words).

In this expression grows an even greater miracle: Now, understood by her, he wants not only to care for her, but also to understand *her*—for who *she* is. Men who feel respected come out of their shell. They don't have to force, to dominate, to withdraw in order to protect fragile ego and self. They can listen, they can admire, they can enjoy.

In their social and personal idealizations of men, women often think, "My husband should want to understand me and live for me no matter what I do. That's what unconditional love is: No matter what, he should adore me." Women might think, "Hey, he says he loves me so let him love me. Why should I have to have 'reasonable expectations' in order to get him to love me? A woman should have the highest expectations, and a man should meet them. That's how he proves he loves me." This point of view makes sense, but if we're searching for a man who will be a soul mate, is it practical?

The Transactional Nature of Male Bonds

Let's go into this a little more deeply.

One of the most important things that male nature brings to marriage and to the idea of "soul mate" is a powerful sense of transaction. Men are transactional people. They seek a soul mate who understands this and with whom, through this strategy, they can make the many-staged journey of life and love.

At a biological level, as we've discussed, men experience life as a journey of personal quest in which they meet others and transact. In the work world we would say, "with whom they do business." While men can be immensely self-sacrificing—for example, running into a building to save others with little regard for their own safety—men also tend to withhold the emotional self unless it is coaxed out of them transactionally. They tend to give emotionally what they receive transactionally. Women are built differently. Female hormones and brain systems tend to keep giving and giving until the day comes when, exhausted, they seek liberation.

Women and men often tell me that the "transactional" male nature is painful to hear about, but it needs to be said: When the infatuation and courtship stages of love are over—within about one to two years—men enter emotional stasis, waiting to see if they will be respected, understood, and treated with deep compassion by their mates. If they receive these things, they are much more likely to come out of their shells. If they do not, they dig in deeper. They come to therapy talking about "not feeling respected." This comment is a clear warning sign of the possibility of divorce.

Wonderful things happen in a relationship just by the female partner's understanding of the man's sense of the transactional marriage. Even when the man just "doesn't get it" in a marriage, or "just doesn't want to work on this marriage," if the woman does, marriages still can change immensely. His "not getting it" and her "getting it" is not as optimal as when a man and a woman engage in equal and mutual understanding, but it is more effective than many women realize.

"He's oblivious," a woman told me after a workshop, "but at least now I'm not. As a couple, we've worked out how to get by in our marriage. We have good times. It's not perfect, but it works. *A lot more of the success of our marriage has to do with what I do and think than I realized* [italics mine]. I'm glad I understand how to use my relational intelligence better now. Before, I resented him for not having much relational intelligence of his own." Women who understand the transactional nature in men find their own relational intelligence more excited by marriage rather than tormented by it.

While no one likes to say, "A marriage can work even if the man is oblivious," I'm glad people come up to me and admit that sometimes it is true. All of us who care about successful marriage need to keep working on men to increase their ability to practice the female version of relational intelligence, but we don't need to give up on happiness and marriage just because a man does not ever really seem to get it.

Putting the Transaction to Work

Having made the case that marriage can be happy even when the man is not skilled in relational intelligence, I do not want to make the case for marriage in which a man does not do his part in the transaction. He can remain relatively unintelligent in an emotional sense, but he can fulfill responsibilities for the stability of the marriage in his deeds, even if not in words.

In my marital practice and seminars, I often ask men to agree to a list of "marital needs." The list follows. I hope you'll modify this list, during a date night, perhaps, on which you take on the task of making the marriage a very conscious, and uplifting, transaction.

I, as a man, agree to:

1. Do my part to provide for the family.

2. Do my part to help you and the children feel safe.

3. At least one of three times, respond to what you've said with, "I hear that," or another paraphrase, before I problem solve, critique, or talk about myself in relation to the issue.

4. Participate in couples' ritual times with you: talking together after kids are in bed, going on dates.

5. Show I love you in sensual ways—such as by giving you flowers—at least five times a year.

6. Give you time off from your responsibilities to enjoy yourself in solitude or with your friends.

7. Call home every day when I am away on trips and speak to you and the children at least briefly.

8. Participate in the children's lives as a father (see chapter 8), not as a mother.

9. Remain loyal to you, understanding that this loyalty is a show of respect for you.

10. Find opportunities to tell you that I value what you do for me, the children, and the world.

Most men can agree to these terms of the transaction. Can women agree to let this be enough? As women and men come together to make these transactions, it is useful for women to make a list of their own responsibilities in the transaction. Some will mirror the men's, but some won't. Husbands will be called upon not only to agree to the reasonable terms of transaction, but, like women, to agree that the meeting of those terms are enough.

A NATURAL OPTIMISM

Over the years I have heard people say, "Gurian, you're way too optimistic about men." My overarching idea—that men want to be good husbands, want to move through all the stages of love, want to give power to women if the marital transaction is complete for them— falls, at times, on disbelieving ears.

Yet I stand by it. There are certainly men who are dangerous and who cannot be husbands, but these men are not the norm; they are the exception. If a woman uses good intuition during romance and courtship, takes into account the genetics and family system from which a man comes, and blends a careful sense of intimate separateness with the mysteries and passions of her love for her partner, I would estimate that at least four out of five men will turn out to be successful matches. By successful, I mean, they will turn out to be reasonable mates—loving, caring, compassionate in their own way, and able to meet women's reasonable expectations.

Both women and men benefit by recalling that most men were brought up by their mothers to take care of the first woman in their lives, and therefore all others. If the mother overemphasized this attachment at the expense of normal adolescent separation, the man faces terrible complexity in marriage, which will require a wife to become an even finer master at intimate separateness. Yet even in these cases, the heart of the complexity is the man's desire to care for a woman—to understand her, to be cared for by her, to give back to her.

Some women have said, "I don't want a man who will take care of me; I want a man who will treat me like an equal." These two things are not mutually exclusive. The soul of a married man yearns to give the gift of love to the soul of his wife. It is wired into our brains to care compassionately for those we love

I am optimistic. I believe in men. I believe in women. I believe we are each striving to respect our own nature and the nature of the other. Men are, by nature, good people. I have faith in them. I hope this book will increase your faith in them, too.

PART IV

What Could He *Really* Be Thinking . . . About Home and Children?

Some of the things he does around the house . . . I just can't believe he's serious. But he is. Who is this person I live with!

—Jessica, thirty-six, married eight years, one child

Whenever I'm tempted to think that my husband doesn't have as close a relationship with the kids as I do, I watch how they follow him around. They just love being with him. Someone asked me the other day how come my kids turned out so well. I told them because they had a good father."

—Christine, forty-eight, mother of two grown children, married twenty-six years

The Male Brain at Home: Men and Women Living Together

*We love people for their foibles, even their defects,
not just their good qualities.*

—Jacques Maritain

A man sent this E-mail to me:

My wife kind of gets a look in her eye when she thinks it's time to clean the house. Our sons, 9 and 11, and I both see it. It used to be she'd say, "Boys, it's time to clean your rooms," and then she'd give me a room to clean, too. I'd clean the living room, then the dining room. I'd clean a bathroom. She'd be cleaning the den. Maybe a half hour later, the kids and I would say, "We're done." We'd be proud, or at least just relieved. Then she'd come look at what we'd done and she'd get a different kind of look, a frown. Sometimes she'd just get mad at us. "You call this clean? How can you call this clean? You do this on purpose! I should just clean the whole house myself."

217

Well, to make a long story short, she sort of does clean the house herself now. It was so frustrating for her (and for all of us) for the house cleaning to just not be the way she wanted, so she took it over. The boys still clean their rooms, and I help with basic picking up of rooms and so on, but basically she does the rest so that the house gets done just the way she likes it.

An E-mail by a woman echoes this man's situation.

I talk to my women friends about their husbands and the house-cleaning. Why can't he see that the house is a mess? He's looking right at dust or papers everywhere. The floor clearly needs vacuuming. The kitchen floor needs sweeping. But it's like these guys just refuse to see what needs to be done. Sometimes I think my husband wants me to work two jobs so he can sit in front of the TV and laugh at me. If I hear him say one more time, "The house isn't a mess—it looks fine," I think I'll scream!

So many of us can recognize the situation of the people who wrote me. There is a trend in relationships and marriages toward extreme emotions—often frustration!—about what's going on around the house.

In this chapter, let's look at some of the nature-based reasons that a man's approach to certain important aspects of home life are so different from a woman's. Some of this material is humorous, and at the same time, it reveals some differences between men and women. What speaks more to the depths of who we are than our homes?

THE BIOLOGY OF THE HOME

As we explore home life, we'll be noticing how the following "facts of nature" affect the way we live together as women and men:

- **The differences in the way we process sensory information.**
- **The spatial-kinesthetic male brain.**
- **Fine-motor and gross-motor activity in the brain.**
- **The abstract-mechanical male brain.**
- **Rest states in the male brain.**
- **The hippocampus.**
- **Our hormones and brain chemicals.**
- **The amount and rate of blood flow in the brain.**

Our homes are a place where "who we are"—our identity and nature—show up very clearly. In our homes, where we are safe and our life energy is so deeply invested, we live out our internal imperatives, proclivities, and psychological truths.

To help us explore the male brain at home, I'd like to start with a question I hear very frequently.

WHY CAN'T HE SEE THAT THE HOUSE IS A MESS?

The female brain takes in more sensory data than does the male. As we've noted, there is a biological tendency in women to see more, hear more, smell more, taste and feel more through their skin and nerve endings. Having just sat down on his couch, it is more likely that a man will not neurally register the bit of paper, the dog hair, the children's toy shoved into the couch; it is more likely that his wife will do so. While a man may not smell the urine odor from the cat's litter box, his wife is more likely to do so. This fact about the brain is not a worthwhile excuse for a man to neglect duties he has agreed to, but it does partially explain why he doesn't see or smell or sense around him the same mess that so disturbs his spouse. It also partially explains the common phenomenon of men staring right into a refrigerator and not seeing what's right in front of them. They don't register details, like color and texture, as well as women, which makes men more likely to stare and not see.

Furthermore, even when buying the very house in which they will live, men do not tend to attach as much importance to the "fine details" of the place. The male brain tends to seek out gross motor activities more than the female, inspired by larger quantities of conductive spinal fluid in the brain, and is less interested in fine motor activities. In a similar way, the male brain is less interested in fine detail and more inclined to larger physical movement and gross detail. The female brain is more likely to sense the book that is awry on the coffee table, the dust on the end table, the bed not made as she'd like it, and so on and so on until the woman might become frustrated by the sheer accumulation of mess. Her husband may well just plunk himself down in the middle of it and grin, or wander outside to mow the lawn.

We are not saying that men don't care about fine detail at all. A man can seem almost obsessive about building the model of a tiny ship inside a relatively small glass bottle. But in that instance, a different dynamic is at work. He is focused on doing whatever it takes to succeed in reaching his goal—building the almost toothpicklike ship. As he sits in his living room reading the paper or listening to his child's speech or talking on the phone, he doesn't experience the mess in the house as a challenge over which to triumph.

It's fair to ask: Why can't he get his brain to see that the neatness of the house is as important as that delicate little ship? Herein lies another secret of human biology.

The human "nest"—a biology-based word now used to describe our homes—has not historically been the space that occupied male-brain development. For millions of years, males spent their time in space *outside* the nest, involved in activities of larger abstract design, like hunting. Just as so much else in our present male/female brain development has become wired into the brain from so many years of separate activities, the trend toward men not seeing the need for housework in the way women do is probably a result of millions of years of men not doing it and thus not developing their fine motors, their sensory centers, and their attention to it.

Though it can be frustrating for women to work two jobs—in the workplace from nine to five and then in the home at the end of the day—men are often equally frustrated by how strangely focused their wives and girlfriends become on the minutiae of home and surroundings. In this area, men and women are notoriously confused by each others' foibles. Often men think, "She just worked eight hours and now she comes home and instead of relaxing for a second she immediately starts working again. Why does she care so much that the house is a mess? It doesn't matter. Why doesn't she just relax with me on the porch?" Just as many women think men have strange priorities, many men often find women's busy attention to the details of the home to be counterproductive at times.

For many women, personal well-being is experienced in how the home feels, and personal identity is associated with the way the home looks. It has been so for millions of years and may well be for many more.

Once, when we were preparing for a gathering of good friends and Gail was busy cleaning the house, I asked her, "Gail, these are our best friends—why would they care if the house is a mess?" To me, being with good friends, meant being relaxed and carefree.

Gail said, "Mike, for a woman, it doesn't matter who's coming over. People will notice if my house is a mess. I want it to look good. That's that." For her, it was impossible to relax if the house was a mess.

WHY CAN'T HE LOAD THE DISHWASHER THE RIGHT WAY?

How can we talk about home life without talking about the strange disease men have—their inability to load a dishwasher properly? Sometimes men won't even put everything away that they unload from the dishwasher. They just put things on the dish rack and leave them there.

When I've given talks on the male and female brain, many people have come up to me and said versions of the following:

A man: "I load the dishwasher and then she comes around and changes what I've done."

A woman: "He'll load the dishwasher and say he's done, but I just have to come and change it all anyway, so I might as well have done it myself."

This recent invention, the dishwasher, is filled with the beauty of male/female brain difference. He sees the dishwasher as something just to get loaded and run. Even when he unloads it, he seems to leave some of the dishes sitting around, rather than put them away. While he's unloading it, he doesn't seem to notice as well as his wife if the dishes come out with spots or tiny bits of hardened food. Rather than rinsing the dishes first, he just shoves them in and turns the machine on. He thinks: "Why was the damn machine invented anyway if you have to clean every dish before you put it in? Just rinse 'em a little, get them in there in a relatively ordered way, and be done with it. Move on to something more important."

But for her, this is the important thing in this moment. She will more likely notice the hardened bits of food or the spots. She will more likely worry that someone else will notice. These dishes, these glasses, are extensions of her home, and thus, more than he realizes, parts of her identity. She feels a great deal of pride in making sure the dishes her children will use are clean.

A woman in her forties wrote about her husband:

He never uses soap when he washes the dishes. This drives me nuts! I catch him washing the dishes and I see there are no soap suds in the sink.

"Honey, are you using soap?" I ask patiently.

He says, "Yes," but lowers his eyes, a game between us. Or he says, "No," being honest. Sometimes we argue about it.

"Why can't you use soap?" I ask. "We've got two kids. They need clean dishes."

Once he said to me, "Look, if we go camping, we don't use soap. We just wash the dishes in the stream. If you think about it, we don't really need soap, you know. It's not a necessity."

I couldn't believe it. What could he be thinking?

In this humorous interchange is a beautiful secret: In a sense, many men are always "camping." In a biological way we can easily understand the male proclivity toward "roaming" and seeing the world through the eyes of a camper. Even a man who has never camped a day in his life may well live the neural imperative of his ancestors: to look out of the home rather than into it for his sense of how life really ought to be.

WOULD IT KILL HIM TO PUT HIS LAUNDRY AWAY?

A New York executive, president of a major corporation, told me this story.

"I was talking to my best friend the other day. She's in her fifties, like I am. She noticed that no matter how often she asks her husband, he just won't put his laundry in his dresser drawers. She'll leave his clean laundry in the basket, all folded for him, and he'll throw the basket in the closet and want to live out of it. It's like he wants to live out of a suitcase! His dresser's just a few feet away, but he won't put the clean laundry in his dresser drawers!"

"My husband's just like hers. I'll bring the laundry basket upstairs, or I'll ask him to, and he'll do it, no problem, but then he won't fold the clothes. Not only that, when he needs something, he'll just go to the basket, yank out what he needs, and then for him it's like, 'Oh well, I guess the clothes will fold themselves!' I gotta tell you, I used to get so mad at him; but now, after talking to my friend and realizing men are just like this sometimes, I just roll my eyes and laugh."

It is difficult not to want to grab these husbands by the arm and yell, "Put your laundry away!" And yet, from their perspective, there is some sense in what they're doing. The "sense" is similar to what we alluded to with "camping."

The executive who shared the following story with me had recently gone to see the wise and funny stage event, *Defending the Caveman*. She said, "It does make sense, if you think about it. These husbands are like nomads. They use the cave as it's practical to use it, but they figure pretty soon they'll be using another one anyway so why waste a lot of time in this one?"

Certainly there are many men who like their clothes neat and put away in drawers. And of course there are those men who specifically don't deal with laundry because they think "it's women's work." But most men do not act toward their clothing the way the New York executive described just to make trouble for their wives. Rather, they "live out of the suitcase" because it feels good, it feels familiar, it feels free. The messiness seems fun rather than a problem. When you look at it from inside a hunter's brain, not a nesting brain, folding the laundry seems very low on the priority list. It is something that can be put off, even for weeks, because, as one man wrote me: "You know, if you think about it, I'm just gonna use the clothes again anyway. Why worry so much about getting them all in place just right when I'll be pulling them out of the drawer tomorrow?"

There is a further reason that men have a biological tendency toward this kind of "logic" in the home. Often fiercely independent by nature, the minutiae of home life is something to be resisted. Folding the laundry, washing the dishes perfectly, focusing on fine motor tasks—all the while knowing that your spouse not only wants you to do them the way she wants them done, but she may also want you to value them and feel about them as she does—is something that many men will naturally resist. No one, male or female, child or adult, wants to be forced to feel a certain way about something that he or she does not inherently value. Men often are very sensitive to the hidden agenda in the female psychology of the home which is to get the man to value the interior of the home as much as the woman does so that she can feel even more secure about his presence, commitment, and loyalty to the home, and therefore to *her*.

Women often intuit that their identities are neurally, emotionally, and even spiritually connected to the home in mysterious ways, but often they do not sense that they would feel just a little safer in their relationship with their husband if they could convince him to be neurally, emotionally, and even spiritually connected to the nest they have made.

Men often do not understand why they are resisting their wife's psychology of the home, but often it is very much their sense that being "house tenders" is not natural to them but imposed on them by a spouse who has a hidden psychological agenda. This unspoken, often unexplored, tension rising between men and women can debilitate a marriage, a relationship, and ultimately the happiness that is possible in the home they have created together.

In previous generations this was less a problem for marriages because male/female divisions of labor did not really allow the hands-on care of the home to become a psychological or romantic identity issue. In the majority of families, women ran the homes the way they wanted, and men stayed out of the way. Today, our different neural impulses regarding home life can become very large issues.

WHAT IS IT WITH MEN AND THEIR CARS?

"He goes out after work and washes his car," a woman wrote me from Des Moines, Iowa. "It seems to relax him. Sometimes he pays our son to do it. But most of the time, he just wants to do it himself. He treats the car better than anything else in his life! He scrubs it, he waxes it, he buffs it. My brother's the same way about his car. What is it with men and their cars?"

Could there be reasons, in brain science, for the love relationships men have with cars, motorcycles, trucks, and other vehicles, which are, from a women's point of view, just vehicles of transportation?

In the way a woman might love and care for the inside of her home, a man might care for a vehicle. This could be a boat or other big-ticket vehicle, not just a machine on wheels. Men are wired to care for these objects of freedom and of power. A hormone- and brain-driven urge to roam is one neural reason for a male's love of the vehicle and respect for its power and possibility in his life. A great dream among adolescent males is to get in a car and take a road trip. The young men yearn just to drive, explore, roam. They want to discover, experience. They want to be free. The young men feel an inherent respect for the far-reaching, goal-tending, sacred quality of the car.

A second reason for men's love of these vehicles is "emotional" in its content and thus neural. The relationship with the car or motorcycle or boat is a relationship with an object of care and love that does not emotionally complicate life by being loved and adored. A man came up to me at a seminar and said, "You know why I love my '68 Thunderbird? Because it just takes me for who I am. I take care of it, and it takes care of me. No complications like you have in a marriage."

Often women don't realize that male/female intimacy is overwhelming for a husband or boyfriend. Sometimes, a car or other machine object of care, is simply easier to deal with than a spouse and yet quite rewarding. If we just think about one aspect of male-brain development, this will become even clearer.

The male brain, as we noted earlier, seeks more opportunities to go into a state of rest than the female. Talking to a spouse about a problem, or being emotionally attentive to a spouse, are not rest states. The man who goes out to wash his car every day after work may be exhausted from work, going outside to do something that allows most of his brain to rest. While the water washes over the metal and his hand moves along with the soapy sponge, the rest of his brain can simply close down.

This way of relaxing holds less appeal to a woman's brain. A pleasant state of mind might come for her in doing the very thing that overstimulates him: communicating, talking, emoting after a day at work. She wants to connect emotionally and verbally with him. He wants just the opposite. In the end, she might want from him the very thing that his mind cannot give without negative stress consequences: to talk about how he feels and what he's done during his day. If he gave her this, her oxytocin levels would increase, which would in turn increase her sense of well-being; but his own stress-hormone levels might also increase. He doesn't want that. So he steers clear of the kind of communication she wants, which seems like rejection to her. It is logical that she would then think, "He values washing his car more than talking to me." Though he may value the care of the car at that moment more than talking, it is not true that he values the car more than her. He simply goes to the low-stress area of care that best tends his brain.

Of course, there are bridge-brain women who don't want all that talk and who may care about a car more than their husbands do. There are bridge-brain men who can't wait to come home and talk and emote about their day. Some men couldn't care less about cars. Some women are bored to death by hearing their husband come home and go on and on about what happened to him. There is great variety among individuals.

Yet we can also say that there is a biological tendency for men to seek a set of care objects that allow for brain rest and the pleasure of independent relationship without the stimulation of emotional con-versation. A car is, not surprisingly, an object of choice for many men. It is the quintessential "spatial object," one that moves through physical space with utility and grace. At the same time, the car or other vehicle has the potential to make a clear statement about per-sonal status and self-worth. Great worth is attached, not only by the man, but by all of society to the vehicle a person travels in. Not sur-prisingly, the more materially wealthy many men become, the greater the chance that they will try to show their status in an even fancier spatial object by which to rest, roam, and be known.

WHAT ABOUT THAT REMOTE CONTROL?

The television remote control has been both the butt of many jokes and the source of many male/female conflicts. It is also a wonderful object for studying and enjoying male/female brain difference.

Perhaps everyone has noticed a tendency in men to "take control" of the remote. Let's say that a man and a woman decide to zone out in front of the TV one night together. It's a nice bonding time. The children are in bed. The couple can cuddle on the couch and relax, but herein lies a dilemma. The man and the woman know that to enjoy the experience certain TV programming will be most useful to each of them—but the preferred programming may not be the same. Also, the method of channel surfing between programs may differ. For his brain, jumping from show to show might feel relaxing; for her brain, focusing on one show might feel better.

Logistically, the man often gets to the remote control first, perhaps because the woman took more time getting the kids to bed or clearing up some other details she had, or perhaps because he puts pressure on her to give him the remote. Once he has control, she notices that he channel surfs to shows that are not of as much interest to her. When he happens to light on a dramatic program in which people are talking to each other about their relationships or emotional life, he moves on to something else. He just surfs between shows as if they had no content.

She might say, "Honey, wait, stop there. What was that woman saying?"

Or, "Hey, stop bouncing from channel to channel."

But he doesn't like to linger. He prefers moving from a sports channel to one where things are getting blown up and guns are being shot to one where lawyers are arguing with each other or police are chasing criminals. Out of respect for his wife or partner, he might surf back to the program she wanted, but he'll be antsy to get away from it once she has heard just a few lines of dialogue. This becomes very frustrating because she just got enough information to become interested! But off he goes, back to objects getting blown up, criminals, cops, and sports.

In some marital relationships this is happening because the couple is conflicted, and television use can be part of a psychological struggle in a marriage. Most of the time, however, this difference in TV use is an internal, neural matter.

The female brain has 15 percent more blood flow moving

through it and more neural pathways to verbal-emotive centers of the brain. Enjoying a human conversation, especially an empathic one that involves emotional processing, can increase oxytocin levels; it can make the female brain feel good, feel relaxed, feel connected.

This condition is often oppositional to a greater proclivity the male brain has toward seeking rest states. While the female brain certainly seeks rest states, it does not do so as much as the male. Also, emotive stimulants don't "wake up" the female brain as much as the male. They can feel like second nature to a woman. But emotive stimulants and long conversations force the male brain to wake up. His brain, late at night, or at whatever time of exhaustion or personal renewal he uses to sit in front of the TV, probably does not want to wake up. It simply wants to rest. Since the male brain goes into a rest state in ways the female does not, it has what we might call "the luxury" of resting. There are advantages to being male and resting the brain is one of them. A man knows that if his wife gets hold of the remote, he probably cannot rest his mind. He will have to watch a program that forces his brain to wake up, which is exactly what he does not want.

We might logically ask, "Okay, so he wants to go to a rest state, but why does watching things blow up and watching guns shoot off give him rest? Why don't these things agitate him?" "Certainly," a woman might say, "watching people die on television and property getting destroyed agitates me."

When the male brain goes into a rest state, it tends to settle more of its blood flow in the brain stem than does the female brain. The brain stem is the elemental part of the brain, involved in fight-or-flight instincts as well as other basics. It is not an emotionally sophisticated part of the brain. During a rest state, it does not link well to the frontal lobes at the top of the brain where empathy and emotive processing can be refined.

Since the male brain rests here, it should therefore not surprise us to find men "zoning out" in front of violent action movies. The fighting is actually reflective of and soothing to the part of the brain where much of the male blood flow lies. This does not mean the male will get up and hit somebody. It simply means he is more likely to shut his brain off at his brain stem and take a break from areas of the brain that utilize empathy, emotion, and higher verbals.

WHY DO MEN LOVE TO TINKER AROUND WITH GADGETS AND ELECTRONICS?

A man wrote: "My wife thinks I'm a little crazy, but I just love my model train set. I'm wondering if you can help me explain to her why it makes me feel so good to work on it."

A woman wrote: "He's always tinkering with something in the garage. He seems to like to work with wood, so he's always building something. He loves to whittle objects for the grandkids."

With some frustration, a woman told me, "My husband loves to play around with gadgets or his newest electronic marvel. He'll spend lots of time with his DVD player or his sound system. But when I give him a honey-do list, he puts off doing those things. I end up having to do a lot of those projects, along with everything else I have to do to keep the house running."

These letters and comments reflect two crucial elements of the male mind: the love of gadgets, including electronic ones, and the tendency to tinker in areas that bring personal satisfaction. To a wife or partner, these areas might not seem necessary.

While there are bridge-brain males who couldn't care less about train sets, models of airplanes, woodworking, a new kind of light bulb, the latest ratchet set, a sump pump, a riding lawn mower, a power drill, the difference between types of fuel, the newest computer software, a new video game, or a DVD player, many men get endless satisfaction from acquiring, using, storing, reusing, inventing, collecting, and teaching others, especially children, about their gadgets. Not surprisingly, these gadgets are generally objects moving in space—whether in real or virtual—that appeal to the spatial-kinesthetic centers of the brain, even the aural rather than the verbal. In other words he wants to hold these objects of utility in his hands or build them or put them together and then display them once finished. He gets connection with the objects by their physical utility and their trophy value.

Also, especially in their home environments, men tend to want to *choose* which gadgets or objects they'll use or build. They generally don't want to be told what objects and inventions to focus on. Men feel that too many people have told them all day at work what to focus on and now they just want to have some time to "be themselves." The man often wants to shut down the rest of the world's demands and feel the freedom of using the ratchet or the whittling tool and building something really cool.

There is an historical marker in the male brain regarding this biological trend. This marker involves a concept that archetypal psychologists, like Carl Jung, began applying to brain studies many decades ago: "the sense of magic." Every human being seeks areas of magic in him or herself—areas of specific talent, areas of life in which the person's identity shows clearly. Obviously, men and women often do this differently.

While females have biologically gained identity by the magic of birthing and caring for children, males have often gained identity by the magic of inventing and utilizing tools. Tools are a very male way of feeling magic, the mysterious transformation of an object or self into another object or self. The word "magic" is not used lightly here. Females have an inherent and inborn neural path to universal magic; they themselves transform, physically, into mothers; the fetus within them transforms into a child.

Males, being more spatially, kinesthetically, and mechanically oriented, and not possessing this inherent path to transformative magic, have tended to try to become the magicians of tools and tool making. In our day and age, electronic and other gadgets are neural equivalents to the tools of our ancestors. When a man puts together a complicated sound system or builds a model airplane, he feels magical. He discovers in himself a magician he always sensed deep down but could not activate except in this tool-using way. Just the feeling of making, building, and creating can bring him magical satisfaction by increasing the transmission of such feel-good neurons as endorphins in the brain; if his building, his invention, his capacity to utilize a tool brings him some greater notice, a sense of showing off his trophy, a sense of worth, all the better. Step one is playing with, using, and creating with the tool. Step two is often the display of the object created or manipulated by the magic of self and tools. "Honey, come look at my new sound system!" Or, "I've got the new turbo on the lawnmower. Let's see how it runs."

As men focus on gadgets and tools, we notice that they carry an internalized limit on how they want to create, manipulate, and use their magic. In his home life, a man might find his wife or girlfriend saying, "You love gadgets, you love to work on this or that, but you won't do these chores, or repair that sink, or . . ." Especially around the house, and especially after long work days and long work weeks, men often need the time to work on the magical acts, objects, trophies, and gifts that they themselves choose—they often resist those chosen for them. A man may not get to items on the honey-do list on his wife's timetable but, rather, on his own.

A social trend has emerged recently that needs to be discussed along with this biological trend. Many men are now involved in work through which they experience no magic. The jobs by which they earn money may carry little or no status. They may be rote jobs that break the back and soul. They may be so boring that a man wakes up every day realizing he has nothing to show for his life, but he must keep on working at the job because his family needs him to do so.

And he will keep on. But he is wired to hunt for the magical world, and he will seek it somewhere. Especially in the case of this kind of man, working in soul-boring conditions, the self-worth, self-esteem, and simple pleasure he gets from building the model airplane or train set can be of far more emotional and spiritual worth than might be the accomplishment of the chores for a given day, or even a given week, or, in the end, a lifetime.

A woman can utilize the male's search for magic. The very chore on the honey-do list he has resisted for weeks might become the one he actually wants to accomplish once he finds, or is given, the new gadget by which to accomplish it!

DOESN'T HE REALIZE THAT GOD IS IN THE DETAILS?

We've talked about gadgets, remote controls, cars, laundry, so many vital areas of identity and magic, but now let's get back to human conversations in the home! Does this one sound familiar?

Woman: "How'd the doctor's appointment go?"

Man: "Okay."

Woman: "Well, what did he say?"

Man: "Not much. Gave me some medicine. I have some skin disease like we thought. I'll be fine."

Woman: "What else did he say?"

Man: "Nothing."

Woman: "You were there an hour. Didn't you learn why you have it, where it came from, all that?"

Man: "It's nothing, really."

Or how about this one:

A man has revealed that he saw some of his wife's friends that morning downtown.

Woman: "What did Sheri say?"

Man: "She said to say hi."

Woman: "Just hi. She must have said more than that. Didn't she tell you about Mark?"

Man: "She talked awhile. Al says hi, too."

Woman: "What did you guys talk about?"

Man: "This and that."

Woman: "Like what?"

Man: "I don't know. I don't really remember."

It can be so frustrating for women and men to sit in their own homes trying to relax and yet find that their life partner wants to obstruct them. For him to relax, he'll often want to *not* be interrogated. He'll want to sit back and not have to try to pry memories to fit specific words said or clothing worn or details of location. These things are harder for his memory because of his smaller hippocampus, fewer neural pathways from sensory centers to hippocampus, and less verbal memory.

For her, relaxation can often specifically mean *more* detail, *more* sensation, *more* memory, *more* conversation. What was the person wearing? How did she look? Did she ask after me? Did you tell her about the kids? What was she buying? All these questions are blank spots in her mind that she needs filled in. A woman would almost rather her husband did not bring up the moment of running into friends if he won't tell all about it! Often she will just wish she could have gone to the doctor with her husband if he's not going to tell her what went on. His health is part of her home life; her friends are part of her web of relationships. She needs and wants the facts, and much more.

The field of neurobiology has been able to identify elements of our hunting-gathering history in these male/female differences.

When we think of men playing sports or working on a job-related project, we can see the elements of a hunting activity—each man individually, and as part of a hunting team, pursuing an object. When we think of shopping, we can see the elements of a gathering activity. Laden in the female brain is the desire and efficiency to gather goods for the home in the same way women used to gather tubers and roots, searching among leaves and undergrowth, chatting with friends while doing so, or storing up details for future gathering.

The female brain loves to store up details and loves to gather details and, often tragically, the male brain does not. At this basic neurohistorical level, it is not surprising to hear conversations like those we just outlined. While the husband was talking to Sheri and the others, his brain did not store up details. He kept a simple neural outline of people and objects. Were his wife there with him, she would have stored up details not just outline and then been able to share them later with others. While the male patient was at the doctor's, he was goal focused: making sure he was going to live and getting the right medicine. Were his wife there at the doctor's, she would have paid attention to the nuances of how the doctor talked about the illness. She might even have thought to herself—based on how the doctor looked—that the doctor himself might be losing too much weight or might need a vacation. Her husband would be focused on the goal, not on the person.

Whether it is the doctor's office, a chance meeting, or an emotional encounter, we can definitely expect men, on average, to pick up on less detail than women. The female brain tends to want to make conversations longer and richer in order to deepen and further the connection with others. Deepening these connections through words and shared memories stimulates her oxytocin, her bonding chemical, to secrete further and make her feel good.

The irony is that the constant verbal connection she wants might be the very thing that makes her husband or boyfriend recoil. He might say, "Stop bugging me! I don't remember anything else!" To her, it feels as if he is rejecting the very core of her being.

How painful, and yet how logical this is, from a neural sense. From the point of view of the brain at work, rejection is not the issue. He is living out how his brain functions and often feels unable to do anything else but employ a rejective behavior in order to protect himself.

BRIDGE-BRAIN MEN AT HOME

When a woman lives with a bridge-brain male, this kind of rejection happens less often. If the male partner is a bridge brain, with more hippocampal memory than average, more neural pathways from emotive and sensory centers to the hippocampus, and higher-than-average verbal-emotive skills, a woman will tend to get more detail from him and even more personal motivation to share emotional and sensory detail. He tends to enjoy, more than average, the giving of the details and the bonding through that conversation.

He may tend to like to channel surf the way she does.

He may tend to enjoy housework and the dishwasher's subtleties as she does.

His brain may not go to a rest state as much as the average guy's, and he may enjoy multitasking as she does.

He and she may not face as many of those moments that feel like rejection to her.

When a woman does not live with a bridge brain, she may be

faced with a personal decision: How much rejection can I take? Con-
comitant with this is the question of how much verbal-emotive difference can our marriage take? Often she finds she needs others in
her circle with whom to engage in the detail-oriented conversations
that stimulate oxytocin levels. Her husband or boyfriend will stimulate her core self in other ways and is not required for this one.

But if she is living with a bridge brain, she'll probably enjoy long
conversations.

How does a woman know if she's living with a bridge-brain
male? Short of doing an MRI—taking a picture of his brain—perhaps she can make a guess, not only by focusing on the above qualities, but also by considering the following four questions.

Why do men and boys spit so much more than women and girls?
Spitting is, like urinating, a territorial marker, linked to testosterone.
This is true of men and women both—women with higher-than-
average testosterone spit more than women with less testosterone.
Bridge-brain males on the other hand, tend to employ territorial markers less than other males because, in general, bridge brains may have
average-to-lower testosterone. All human beings can control and project spit, thus showing prowess. Males, driven by higher levels of testosterone, will tend to rely on it more than women or bridge-brain males.
In spitting, men are unconsciously saying, "Here I am, here's my terri-
tory, here's my power."

Does he think the dish will wash itself? A woman wrote, "My husband works out of our home. He'll go upstairs to have leftovers for
lunch, dirtying a dish. But he never cleans the dish. He goes back
downstairs to his computer. When I get home the dish is still dirty. I
confronted him on this and he said, 'Honey, before we go to bed I'll
get it done. Don't worry about it.' I did a test, leaving the dish. Sure
enough, he did clean it with the evening dishes. I guess he got me
there."

Men, on average, will tend not to feel the imperative as quickly as
women to wash dishes, to set things right in the living room. This is
primarily a matter of less sensory input in the male brain and thus

greater tolerance for things gone awry. A man who is neat by genetic personality or parental training may not fit this pattern. Also, a bridge brain may not fit it; with greater sensory processing, he may gravitate toward dealing right away with a detail that is awry.

Why does he have to play the music so loud? "My family and I had pulled up to a stoplight and suddenly our own vehicle began to tremble," a woman recently wrote me. "Beside us was a young man in his early twenties playing his music so loud that we thought we would go deaf."

" 'Why does he have to play his music so loud?' my daughter yelled.

"Her older brother answered, 'He's just gotta show how cool he is.' "

The most obvious reason a male plays music louder than female is that on average, his auditory abilities are less sensitive. Thus, in many things, males need louder sensation than females in order to enjoy hearing. Even in important marital conversations this is true. Often a woman feels frustrated that a man isn't listening to her when he might simply not be hearing her as well as she thinks, especially if she is a soft talker. Men, among other things, do not hear soft voices and background noise as well as women. Also, loud music, beyond its hearing component, is, as the son intuited, a way of showing prowess. The boy or man who blares his music for everyone to hear is saying, "I'm here, I'm cool," and "I'm powerful," i.e., "I just dare you to tell me to turn it down."

For bridge-brain men, there is often an opposite reaction. They may have more auditory ability and thus hear well. They feel little compulsion toward this kind of public show of prowess.

Maybe I should give my boyfriend a visual shopping list, rather than a written one? A school counselor came up to me at a lecture. She had seen a TV commercial for a digital camera in which the husband was walking through a grocery store unable to remember what his wife wanted him to buy. In the next scene of the commercial, his wife walks around her kitchen with a digital camera taking pictures of what she wants, then she cuts and pastes the pictures and creates a visual shopping list. Now there is great bliss in the grocery store! He buys all the right things and is happy. So is she.

While this commercial connotes, unfortunately, that men are totally incompetent, it also provides a valuable illustration. For many men, the neural difference between a visual and a written stimulant is profound. For bridge brains, less so. The male brain is, on average, a more spatial and mechanical brain system than the female brain and also more visually inclined. A man will certainly, on average, remember better if he is *seeing* the object. But a bridge-brain man might not experience any difference between a visual and written stimulant. He may even find this commercial ludicrous.

Also, while many men might not spend a lot of time in the kitchen—enjoying repetitive stimulant memory there, they remain unfamiliar with the brand name of a specific product that a spouse wants—the bridge brain may be very familiar with it. When his spouse asks for flour, expecting a specific brand, he knows just what she means.

PRACTICING INTIMATE SEPARATENESS IN HOME LIFE

As we've answered each of the questions in this chapter from a neurobiological point of view, we have hinted at the importance of practicing intimate separateness at home. Sharing the same small space together is a major stressor on both the male and female brain. Some of the stress created is "good stress." But some of it is not and can break marriages and relationships apart.

As we've explored messy houses, remote controls, gadgets, and other aspects of the nest couples create together, we've explored issues of identity for women and men. In the pursuit of independence and freedom that men bring to many aspects of life, including the home, we have a very male lens into the practice of intimate separateness.

Men are on a quest. They constantly seek to measure and ensure their self-worth. They'll make great sacrifices of life and limb, blood and brain, and even of their own happiness, to establish their worth and value. There are certain environments that they will associate with their own value, self-worth, and identity. They'll yearn to enter those environments every day and prove themselves in them. While the home is certainly an environment of great worth to men, it may not be the center of their identity. It probably is not their primary environment of *challenge*.

For women, on the other hand, the home may well be the place where the very challenges of identity are confronted. The home may be the key worth and identity marker for women, while for men it is a place to be relaxed, safe, and to escape from troubles, but it is not a place in which to say, "Most days, in this small space, I am measuring who I am."

When the home is a definite identity marker for men, it is generally an identity marker in terms of its value: "Here is my large home that shows what I have accomplished in the world." While a woman might certainly feel proud of the home's gross value in this same way, there may still be a difference. For her, the *interior* of the home might be a place that reflects her identity; the interior is a place of "fine value," as opposed to the "gross value" the male is after. Unfortunately, the fine value, or interior, of the home is so often a much smaller part of a man's quest and identity than women would like.

It is reasonable, then, to notice that men don't see what's needed as much around the house nor value the care of the nest as much as women do. For some men, our noticing this biological trend is "just another excuse to stop helping around the house." For most men, however, our noticing this is an insight into the male mind and has inherent value in the practice of male/female relationships. Just acknowledging our profoundly different approaches to identity and to home can liberate our relationships from a great deal of stress.

To be even more practical: If men are not as biologically entranced by the home as women, yet the home needs the whole family's help in running itself, how do we make home life better for all of us and live together happily?

Here, again, intimate separateness can help.

Use your sense of humor. One of the best ways to make it work is to attach nearly everything around the house with a family's sense of humor. A woman might say, "Nice vacuuming there, honey. You didn't notice the dog hair, though? Can I just move that dog hair to the center of the room for you?" Practiced without venom, and in a loving way, satire, fun sarcasm, healthy jesting, and jibing can be used in marriage to get a message across in a nonstressful way. If they are used, the man can't be the only butt of jokes. Women have to let themselves be satirized as well.

He might ask, "I finished vacuuming, but I might have missed a speck of dust somewhere. Do you want to come look?"

Use lists and goals. It is also useful to practice intimate separateness by making lists and setting goals. A man and a woman who live together can come to agreement on five to ten tasks he needs to do around the house every week. If he agrees to them, he has entered in a transaction and his integrity will be at stake. He is likely to want to meet the goals he has agreed to. These goals need to be reasonable to him, and he needs to be able to do them his way. While she probably holds the ultimate standard for how well the task has been done; and while she has the perfect right to come around and "clean up" what she feels he has missed, she does not have the right to say, "You aren't doing your part." He is doing his part, whether or not she likes how he does it.

Division of labor. Division of labor is crucial in making this work. And bridge-brain thinking fits here very well. For instance, in our home, Gail is handier with a screwdriver than I am. She likes to put together dressers and bookshelves. She also likes to paint. She's something of a bridge brain with a screwdriver. I admire her greatly and get out of her way. We've agreed that she'll do the building of items that come in kits.

I'm handier when it comes to cars, lawnmowers, etc. She lets me do that labor. When either of us faces a situation we can't individually master—I tend to be a little more stubborn about admitting I am stumped!—we call on professional help, or the help of a family member or a friend. We don't create a conflict with each other when there are others in our relationship network who can help. Labor is not only divided between man and woman, but also between the family and extended family.

Avoid hovering. One key to success in this practice is to avoid hovering over each other's tasks. It is important to avoid constantly saying, "Try this, try that." Each person is an individual who must make mistakes and accept the consequences. In this regard, the biological tendency of the more independent male brain can be helpful. More than females, males generally do not think of household tasks as crucibles for intimacy. Men just want to get them done. It's good to lean, sometimes, toward this male end of the brain spectrum and just let go of having to develop intimacy through household jobs.

Appeal to his sense of duty. In all relationships, there is a center point at which men and women both yearn to meet. Even when they appear to hate each other, some part of them wants to come together. The word "duty" is a good word that both men and women use, with all its attendant feelings. Women feel a duty to do certain things for men; men feel a duty to fulfill certain things for women. This sense of duty is part of the transaction of marriage and relationship that bears fruit later.

Sometime it is useful to cast some household jobs in the role of duty. These tasks can then sit in the center point of a relationship as part of the quest that love is. If we speak to a man's moral sense of duty and are reasonable in the tasks we ask him to associate with duty, he will often feel that his importance is being measured and defined, and he'll want to succeed.

Throughout a woman's practice of intimate separateness are these objectives:

1. To be reasonable, given what she knows about profound differences between men and women. Certainly, it is crucial that he is reasonable as well.

2. To realize she cannot change his feelings about housework or other tasks.

Women, more than men, work a "second shift" at home. The resentment over working a second shift does not have to be danger-ous to a marriage. It can be joked about in humor and even spoken of in irritable conflicts. Men will never, on average, value what women do in the home as much as women do. Nor will they ever, as a group, understand the level of identity women reach through the minutiae of their activities in the home.

When a husband is neglecting to help out at all, even at yard work, sticks to little or none of the tasks within his or her division of labor, and devalues the work that is done by the spouse, then there is a problem. This is probably a marital pattern that has more to do with psychological and relationship power struggles than it does with male/female "home" differences.

If the long-term stability of human intimacy is of the greatest value in our lives as men and women who love each other, then we will prefer intimate separateness to the desire to change our spouse's brain. A woman can help a man change his habits and even some of his desires; she can affect his goals by encouraging him to do more by appealing to the best side of his character. But she will generally fail at changing that which his brain biologically attends to. While this failure can create a deep, hidden cycle of resentment that can destroy human love, we do not have to get to that point. Human nature is our friend, even as it confronts us with mysteries.

8

What a Father Knows:
The Nature of Being a Dad

It is a wise father who knows his own child.

—William Shakespeare

L inda, thirty-three wrote:

I think my husband's favorite line is, "Don't worry, honey, the kids'll be fine." I try to get him to back me up on stuff, and what do I get? "It'll be okay." Or "Don't worry." Last week I told my twelve-year old son he was too young to go to the mall with his friends. "Too many things can happen there," I told him. "Jim," I said to my husband, "don't you agree?" Jim said, "You gotta trust him sometime," and shrugged his shoulders. It drives me nuts! Sometimes I think I'm the only safety patrol in this house!

Grace, sixty-seven, wrote:

> Things have certainly changed since I was raising my kids. One thing that's really changed is fathering. It used to be moms were glad the dads were out of the way, especially when the kids were young. Now, fathers want to be a part of everything. I think the new trend is good. I think it's great for my grandkids. But I've noticed something. No matter how involved dads are—my son is very involved with his kids—I think dads are just dads, too. They're not moms. They just do things a different way.

In the United States today, 69.1 percent of children are raised with two parents in the home, 22.4 percent with a mother in the home but no father, 4.2 percent with a father in the home but no mother, and 4.1 percent with neither parent. Outside the United States, the statistical likelihood that a child will be raised with both a mother and a father in the home is even higher. In developing countries, where most of the world's population lies, when a father is missing from the home one or more extended family members is likely to move in or live in close proximity.

Throughout the world, the human biological trend toward providing children with more than one parent is very strong and promises to continue that way. No matter the social experimentation with family structures a given generation engages in—our present interest in single-family systems is one example—protecting a child's brain and physical development, as well as providing social and psychological security, tends to be the responsibility of at least two parental caregivers.

Human nature pulls us toward this trend with internal instincts, supportive social mandates, and also social reaction against experiments that counteract our natural drives. For example, after a brief social experiment that proposed fathers weren't necessary, more recent research has shown how psychologically and intellectually damaging it can be for children to be raised without fathers. In the United States we are now especially intent on protecting a father's role in the raising of children, because studies like David Blankenhom's *Fatherless America* have shown that all child-safety and personal-development statistics are affected by the lack of the father in the home. Government studies have shown the same thing. The role of the father is becoming even more crucial to human development in countries like the United States because, while in the past, grandmas, grandpas, aunts, uncles, godmothers, godfathers, neighbors, and other tribe members did a great deal of parenting, they are doing less parenting now, and more mothers work outside the home, increasing the importance of the role of the father exponentially.

THE BIOLOGY OF FATHERING

Let's explore the depths of fathering from the lens of everyday life and from the seat of that life, human biology. Fathers are, by nature, fathers just as mothers are, by nature, mothers. The mind of the father is natural to the man. The act of fathering is, in many ways, a biological crucible. Nearly every biological and nature-based factor we've explored in the previous chapters of this book are crucial to fathering.

- **A father's brain chemistry sets him up for a different kind of parent-child bond than the mother experiences.**
- **Testosterone and vasopressin mix with the male brain to create a particular kind of parenting called *paternal nurturance.***
- **Fewer verbal centers and more spatial kinesthetic tend the father toward a predominance of physical play over verbal empathy, side-by-side connectivity over eye-to-eye contact.**
- **Abstract-mechanical cortical functioning tend to weave through a dad's training of his children's skills and**

proclivities, providing children with mechanical and design challenges they might not get except from a dad.

- The need for constant self-worth assessment drives a father, and thus a child, both boosting and challenging the child's self-worth and sense of self-esteem.
- A father's ethical biology is crucial, especially to risk-taking adolescent children.

As this chapter progresses, we'll explore these and many more natural tendencies in depth. Sometimes, humorous comments by fathers, mothers, and children can be like a doorway into the hidden male mind. Here is the first of these.

DON'T WORRY, HONEY, THE KIDS'LL BE FINE!

Though there is immense variety among men, there is also a biological trend in males that makes the statement, "Don't worry, the kids'll be fine" a more "male" comment than a "female" one. Fathers tend to be more hands-off, more wait-and-see-what-happens, more intent on teaching independence through example and edict. Women tend toward hands-on parenting, "doing-things-for-children-right-away," immediate empathy, and more dependency building.

A dad wrote: "About some things, I'm almost obsessively moral and strict, but about a lot of things, I just don't worry as much as my wife."

A mom writes: "One of my husband's favorite comments about me and the kids is, 'Don't make such a big deal about it.' I used to be hurt when he'd say that, but I learned he didn't mean anything personal. A lot of stuff with the kids really isn't as big a deal to him as to me. I think I just see more negative possibilities than he does. And you know what, I think he just bonds differently with the kids than I do."

At a biological level, human males do bond with offspring differently from females, which leads to profound differences in nurturing techniques.

One clear scientific way to begin an observation of male/female differences in bonding with offspring is to look at other animals. Among many mammals, a father's biological role is not as complex as it is among humans. The lioness, for instance, does most of the parenting of children; the lion, much less. During certain developmental stages in the lives of gorilla and chimpanzee children, the mother spends more time with children and does more parenting.

In these situations, not surprisingly, the lack of a "hands-on" father is rarely felt by the child because these mammals rely heavily on such social structures as packs, herds, and groups. Offspring are raised by the mother and the pack, of which the father is a part; when the father is wandering in search of food, other males and females are close by.

Among humans, however, the father's biological role is the most comprehensive in any known species. Our fathers bond more directly with their offspring than do most male mammals. The human father's bond with offspring is one of the primary reasons humans flourish as a species. Human nature has adapted the father's biological role to parity with the mother's, and human children have advanced beyond the other mammals in their abilities, skills, and confidence.

Yet even as human fathers bond as powerfully to children as human mothers, the nature of the bond is different.

The Bonding Difference

When a woman becomes pregnant, her hormonal system changes to accommodate the gestation of her child. Her progesterone levels, for instance, can rise more than twenty times their previous levels. Her estrogen system alters, which alters other brain chemicals, like serotonin and dopamine. Her oxytocin levels change. In total, her hormonal and brain-chemical alterations are responsible for her neurochemical interest in imagining, caring for, protecting, and nurturing her child and her home.

Men share with women the instinctual connection to children. Men also share social, emotional, and psychological bonds with offspring. All human bonds in some way involve brain chemistry, so it is fair to say that the male brain attaches acutely to children.

However, that brain system does not undergo significant alterations in progesterone, estrogen, serotonin, oxytocin. Since the male body does not go through physical pregnancy, male hormones, brain chemicals, and bodies don't significantly change. Female chemistry forms its bond with offspring more quickly than does the male's and with greater biochemical input. This biological difference in bonding is the primary reason that 90 percent of young males who impregnate teen females abandon the mother and the child. It is a primary biological reason that a society that does not legislate marriage will face a problem with "deadbeat dads," men who leave their offspring behind and form new families or just abandon their fiscal responsibilities. It is a primary biological reason that fathers have more trouble adjusting to and respecting a physically or mentally disabled offspring. And it also explains why married men have so many extramarital sexual affairs during their wives' pregnancy.

To point out this biology is not to exclude other reasons for each of these trends. Males who impregnate teen females tend to be in their late teens and early to mid-twenties—so they lack psychological maturity. Men as a group are often less trained in empathy and so do not have as many internal resources for being empathic to offspring who disappoint them. Deadbeat dads often do not want to pay for offspring because of a lack of certainty as to paternity, fear of exploitation, and sometimes, as revenge against a former spouse.

Simultaneously, a behavior does not occur without starting out as a series of brain chemicals and neurotransmitters interacting inside the brain. So while it is true that males bond with offspring, it is also true that their bond is biochemically different than a woman's bond. This biochemical-bonding difference leads to a father's tendency toward paternal nurturance, a parenting style that is crucial to children's growth, but often somewhat different from a mother's.

Paternal Nurturance

Paternal nurturance is a term used to describe a particular way the male brain approaches children.

- Primarily because of lower oxytocin levels, males don't tend to bond as much with offspring through immediate empathy attachment as females do. Mothers will tend more quickly to say, "Are you all right?" and pat the child, or get a Band-Aid, or hug the child. Fathers tend to hug a child for less time than a mother and tend to say or signal nonverbally, "You're fine. You'll be fine," more often than mothers.

- Paternal nurturance tends toward a "respect" model more than an "esteem" model. A mother of three, who is also a family therapist, put this statement in the "question" box at a training I was giving. We had just been exploring, as a group, how to help boost self-esteem in kids:

  "It is important to differentiate self-esteem and self-respect. Self-esteem is fluid. We need to allow the fluid to flow. We need to be very hands-on to help it flow in kids. Self-respect is different. It's earned over time through achievement. It needs failure as much as success, painful feelings as much as pleasant ones.

  "I think women tend to focus more on self-esteem and men more on self-respect."

This is a crucial distinction between the way the male and female brains accommodate the raising of children.

Mothers attempt to keep the flow of good feelings going, trying to make sure things are smoothed out as much as possible for kids. Fathers tend to turn children toward greater competition, where they must experience failure.

Mothers tend to do more things for children—pick up their dropped fork, help them over a small impediment on the sidewalk, speak for them with others. Fathers are more likely to say, "Do it yourself," or "You don't need my help; you can do that."

Mothers often keep children's activities within a smaller physical, psychological, and social space, in which they are less likely to fail and/or feel alone. Fathers tend to extend children's activities into larger physical spaces ("Honey, let them go over to the park—it'll give us a break and they can run around more."), psychological spaces ("It's just all part of growing up. Kids get hurt by friends. She'll get over it."), and social spaces. A colleague recently provided a stunning example of this. When his first child went to junior high school, his wife was depressed for a number of days about the passing of an era in her and her children's lives. One day she sobbed, "My baby's growing up. Soon she'll be gone." Her husband, almost simultaneously, said to himself, "How great that my first child is becoming independent and going into the big world. Good for her."

Though this man certainly felt the passing of time and childhood in his own way, he was not as emotionally devastated by his children's growing up and away from him as she was, and he was more immediately celebratory of their independence.

The essence of paternal nurturance can be found here. Fathers often try to build greater independence into many neurochemical aspects of a child's life. Nature seems to have intelligently designed family life so that children can get both the intimacy imperative from maternal nurturance and the independence imperative from males.

This generalization in no way negates the thousands of times a mother drives the child toward greater independence than the father. Nor does it negate that fathers are more overprotective than mothers in certain areas of life. This can especially be true of fathers who curtail their daughters' pulls toward independence, fearing that girls are too fragile to survive "out there." However, when all social trends are counted, males still tend, on average, to lean toward paternal nurturance.

Given the aggressive male-hormone base, male-brain chemistry, and the more spatial and abstract male-brain system, we hear, "Don't worry, the kids'll be fine," more often from fathers than mothers no matter the culture we visit.

Given a woman's hormonal connection with the child, Moms

tend to feel that the child is a part of herself—she finds it difficult to turn away from him or her. Whereas men approach childrearing with the attitude that while the child has his love, he or she needs to earn his respect. If the child doesn't earn that respect, Dad may well turn away from the child in order to compel performance. Dads tend to push kids out of the home earlier than mothers.

Fathers will probably continue to seem to "do less" for children and mothers to "do more." Since fathers tend toward more psychological distance in their parenting, they are less likely than moms to say, "When my children aren't here, I lack purpose," or "It seems as if I spend every day just doing things for my kids." We are more likely to hear fathers' verbalizations—and notice their relational energy focused—on more abstract and systemic issues of the self, "I put my family first by being a good breadwinner and father."

Both maternal and paternal nurturance seem essential for human development. Maternal nurturance has been the more greatly celebrated in the public consciousness, but during the last decade, paternal nurturance is beginning to make a comeback. As it does, our children will be generally safer and better cared for.

DON'T YOU EVEN CARE HOW THE KIDS FEEL?

This question, uttered by many mothers at some time during their children's upbringing, can seem harsh to fathers. They'll often hear it and think, "What does she mean? I care. I just care about the important stuff. All those feelings don't seem that important."

Given the male brain system, men don't have the same relationship to their children's feeling life that mothers have.

Marianna, fourteen years old, wrote me:

"Can you help me understand my father? He's a great guy and all, but he doesn't care about my feelings. He's into his own stuff, or into me following rules, or he's into sports—he really wants me to get good at tennis so we can play together—but he's not into *me*. By me, I mean how *I feel*. Ever since I was a kid, whenever I got hurt, he'd just say things like, 'Hey, don't cry. Be proud. You've got a war wound.' That stuff just doesn't work for me!"

A mom, Jennifer, sent me this E-mail:

> I don't think my husband realizes how he hurts the kids' feelings. For instance, the other day my son, Brandon, who's nine, was sitting on the couch doing a project. His father came over and brusquely told him to get off, then settled down for a nap. For the rest of the afternoon, Brandon was in a bad mood. I could tell he was hurt. Mike, my husband, didn't notice right away, but then near dinnertime he got irritated with Brandon for being so moody. He asked Brandon what was wrong and I helped Brandon tell his dad he felt hurt about the couch. His dad said, "Okay, I didn't realize I was rough on you." That made Brandon feel better.
>
> Later I was talking to Mike about how hurt Brandon can sometimes get and how harsh Mike's tone can be sometimes. He heard me but he said, "You know, I get all that, but Brandon saw me coming, knew I wanted to lie down there, which I do every afternoon, and just wouldn't budge. Maybe I hurt his feelings, but he knew what he was doing. He was testing what I'd do. It's part of the game. Sometimes stuff's not about feelings, it's about respect. I wanted some respect."

This is an example of a paternal form of nurturance. Both cases reveal a male tendency in prioritizing feeling-life in children. The male brain, on average, does not sense as much, feel as much, rely on as much processing feelings with kids as the mother's brain generally does.

Also, with children of all ages, mothers tend to encourage the expression of complex emotion more than men, thus extending the life of feelings and emotions in the brain. Among other things, greater levels of oxytocin in the female brain guide women toward greater interest in immediate "bonding echoes." Bonding echoes are the coos, smiles, tears, laughter, words, and tactile feelings that occur when a woman talks to a baby, talks to a spouse, hugs a child who is crying, sits over lunch with a friend chatting. Echoes of the bonding experience itself are felt throughout the extended emotional experience. Mothers more often guide children toward the extension of emotional life in large part because the women themselves are provided such good feeling from the bonding echoes.

Fathers, on the other hand, are generally more "male brain" in their tendency to end emotional content more quickly. They don't tend to create verbal opportunity for expression of feelings between father and child but instead focus the child on learning how to control and manage and thus stabilize emotions.

In our generation, which is presently absorbing female brain-based thinking into a culture that previously suppressed female thinking, we have often come to the conclusion that the male "non-feeling" way with children is inherently defective or even dangerous to the child. Though some men are so emotionally repressed as to be a danger to themselves or children, the male biological trend is not defective. From a natural sense, this aspect of paternal nurturance is especially helpful in the parenting of adolescents.

Fathers have a tendency to instigate a redirection of the child's emotions toward a moral or social goal, like respect, which finishes emotional processing in favor of starting moral, character, or self-discipline processing. The paternal nurturer is helping the child to move neural stimulation out of the limbic system and up to the prefrontal cortex more quickly. This cessation of emotion in favor of thinking—this repression or shutting down of feelings and prioritization of character development—reveals a male tendency to repress emotions in children. Because it is repressive, we've tended to condemn it. We have missed how this form of stabilization is of great value to impulsive children. It forces children to learn to "grow up" in a way that the constant expression of feeling fails to do. It compels children to pay attention to moral development, which is crucial for adult life. Fathers help train the child for success later in life when the child becomes an adult who must "do the right thing" no matter how he or she feels. Fathers model and teach processes by which to "close out what you're feeling and just do it." There are a million times in a person's life when "just do it" is more important than "take time to feel it."

Both the maternal and paternal forms of emotional development are essential to human growth and adaptation. If the paternal form becomes too dominant or abusive, it can be defective and dangerous. If maternal and paternal maturation of children's emotional life is relatively balanced, the child has a good chance of growing up with the ability to be empathic and reserved, able to lead and to follow, emotionally stable and yet capable of joy.

The age of adolescence appears to be a time when the lack of the paternal approach to emotion is especially hard on children. Adolescent boys raised without adequate fathering tend toward greater violence than boys raised with adequate fathering. Adolescent girls raised without adequate fathering tend toward more emotional disorders than adolescent girls who receive adequate fathering. What paternal nurturance does to the brains of adolescents seems to be very useful. The adolescent has a "high-risk" brain—prefrontal lobes, which control executive and moral decision making, grow more slowly than the limbic system, which compels impulse and physical and emotional risk—thus it is important that children get the stabilization and repression many fathers bring to the dance of childrearing.

Saying this in no way encourages mothers or daughters to repress their feelings about their husband's or father's emotional obliviousness, but it does beg women to see that fathers actually help mothers control, manage, and mature our children just by "being a dad."

DIVORCED FROM THE MOTHER, BUT STILL A FATHER

Scott, a father of three, divorced four years, wrote:

"With their mom, my kids are always saying, 'I want this, I want that.' They do it with me a lot, too, but finally I said, 'Let's hear what you *need*.'

"One of my kids said, 'Dad, you could be a little more sympathetic!'

"I looked at him and said, 'Yeah, and you could grow up a little more.'

"At first he got angry, then he started to grin. He said, 'Yeah, I guess.'

"Then, a few minutes later I heard him say to his mom, 'Mom, I want . . .'"

When children experience the divorce of their parents, the parent from whom they are most likely to lose emotional, physical, moral, and parental touch is the father. This fact lies at the heart of many of our social problems, as has been well documented during the last ten years. The average divorced father spends two to four days a month with his biological offspring. This fact in itself indicates how profoundly the biological attachment of parent and offspring changes once divorce occurs. Children are no less hardwired to attach to their parents when a divorce occurs than they were before its occurrence; but when their environment changes considerably, their hardwiring is less supported.

In situations of divorce, fathers may stay involved in their children's lives but lose their full role as father. They become what I call half-fathers. This father, after a divorce, systematically loses his biological bonds with his children—mainly because of lack of physical proximity—and feels like half a father. Not wanting to lose that half, too, he foregoes much of who he is as a father—he gives up at least half his paternal identity, hoping to gain the identity of "friend." This carries immense dangers for the child, the society, and even for the mother, who within a few years will often discover that her children are acting out more than they were and presenting a higher incidence of mental and other disorders.

If the father has helped stabilize emotion, divorce does not change the need for him to do that. The child still needs him for that. If he becomes a half-father, living in another city, or only seen every other weekend, he may still pay bills and provide safety, but he may well not focus as much on this aspect of fathering. His children have lost a great portion of their developmental security.

If the father has taught self-respect, he is still needed for that. He teaches independence, assertiveness. He provides and protects. He is biologically driven to care for his children and his children to be cared for by him in the ways already established in the family system. When he becomes a half-father, the child loses a great deal of developmental direction. The child's brain, quite literally, becomes confused.

For Scott, part of the family's biology involved the distinction between "needs" and "wants." Scott has continued to value his own way of being, and his ex-wife and children seem to value it, too. He has worked hard to remain a full father. He has found a way to keep this biological tendencies as a father intact postdivorce. In his case, a joint custody arrangement has helped considerably.

Though some men quickly abandon their children after a divorce, and still others are alcoholics, mentally ill, or otherwise dangerous to children, most fathers are good dads who find themselves half-fathers because of an inadequate cultural understanding of the father's and child's nature. Part of our civilization's future will depend on mothers, fathers, extended family, judges, case managers, lawyers, and all others involved in divorce, becoming trained in parent-and-child biology and thus revising our divorce and postdivorce systems.

Scott wrote at the end of his E-mail: "That I can be a real dad has helped my ex-wife. We're friends now, and she's said to me, lots of times, 'I couldn't do this alone. Thank God you're so much a part of their lives.'"

Scott's ex-wife, even if she does not use the words of science, has a keen understanding of the importance of the biological role of a dad.

THE BIOLOGICAL ROLE OF THE FATHER

When we think of "the biological role of the father," we might think of semen and sperm. When we think of the words "a father's role," we might think of *Leave It to Beaver* and then the cultural backlash against that kind of father. Neither the reproductive biology nor the sociopolitical views of "a father's role" are the whole biological role of Dad.

When we take on the topic of a father's biology and try to understand his biological role, we are confronted with a wealth of information, more than enough for many books and for constant controversy. Fortunately, a great deal of what we need to know about a father's biological role lies in our own experiences. People living out brain science in everyday life understand a great deal about the father's role even when they lack the scientific knowledge to describe it.

During the last decade, I have collected comments from men and women about what the biological role of the father is. Many of the comments have carried what we think of as traditional role values: "To provide, protect, and be the breadwinner." Others have carried more contemporary language: "To help children see beyond strict gender roles." The traditionalist and the contemporary ideas are well within the biological role of the father. If treated separately, each is limited, but put together they begin to speak of the father's role. Yet they only begin. Providing food, shelter, and clothing are crucial, but not enough. Helping women change human attitudes is important, but not enough. These are not complete markers of the variety and complexity of the whole father. Can we get a better glimpse of this whole father?

From mail I received during the four years I wrote a newspaper column on this subject, then from ten years of mail concerning my books, I have gained a great deal of information on what parents and others consider to be the biological role of the father. Let me present the eight most popular ideas, then provide comments used to express what people from many places and situations felt about the father and his biological role.

1. The father needs to start being a father even before the child is born.

2. The father has to be able to grow with the children.

3. The father must communicate with his children that he loves them unconditionally.

4. The father must help children build their confidence and character.

5. The father has to show his children how to be proud of who they are.

6. The father must help children find mentors and other ways of being successful in the world.

7. The father must teach children how to become respectable and responsible people.

8. The father must share his emotions so that children can see how men feel.

"A father is the one who goes out and plays soccer in 100 degree weather, and when you ask him why he would do that to himself, he says, 'Just to see if I can.' Then he looks over at one of his kids and winks, and his eyes say, 'If an old guy like me can do something hard this, kid, then you can do *anything.*' "

"My father was all man, but he was also very 'Mediterranean.' He cried, he talked a lot, he hugged a lot. He taught me there are lots of ways to be a dad."

"A father's the one who looks at the favorite doll his daughter left out on the floor, and when he sees how the new puppy tore it up and he sees his daughter in tears, he gives her a hug, then he says, 'I guess you won't leave your doll out for him again, huh?' "

"A father's the one who says, 'Hey, do that yourself. Your mom's not your servant!' "

"Dads like to show their love by just driving in the car with you."

"Fathers like tools, so kids get to like tools, too."

"My father was definitely more emotional than my mother. He was always telling us he loved us. I knew my mother did love me, but it was great to have a father say, 'I love you.' There's nothing like it."

"Fathers let kids run wild, then rein them in. Kids learn to become like rubber bands, able to stretch."

"My father taught me to face my fears. He just wasn't satisfied with me staying afraid of anything for long."

"Fathers teach children to make it in a competitive world."

"My dad challenges me, pushes me, and makes me work.

"Fathers are inconsistent, but that's okay. Kids learn that life's inconsistent, and they just have to make their own decisions."

"If it weren't for my father, I would have ended up in prison. I just needed more than my mother could give me."

"My dad is more self-centered than my mom, but I don't think he's more selfish. He's just different from her. It's hard for me to really describe what I learn from him. It's easier to talk about my mom. But I know I learned just as much from him."

"I remember when I was a kid reading the story about the minotaur in the labyrinth. I felt like I was in a labyrinth when I was a kid, especially in school, but my dad always seemed to help me find my way out."

"Fathers toughen kids, and that's not such a bad thing. My father can be really gentle, but he makes me tough, too, and I'm glad he does."

From the point of view of biological research, all these statements are tenable. The role of the father is a highly adaptive one, built on the foundation of biological trends and capable of adaptation.

Today, fathers are under incredible stress to adapt. They will generally accept that stress and make adaptations to their children as quickly as they can. When they feel inordinate stress to adapt to what the children's mother wants of them in relation to the children, they may not adapt as quickly, especially if the mother seems to be trying to get the father to alter himself to the maternal style. Fathers unconsciously assess what the mother is already giving the child and then carve their own way with the child that is true to their own basic nature. While there is overlap with the mother's parenting style, fathers will generally try to be fathers, not mothers. This process is somewhat dependent, as so many things are, on how the mother handles it. If she understands what a father's potential is and helps him and the children toward that unique potential, it is generally the case that she ends up better supported in parenting than if she tries to change the father into a mother.

Having said this, it is also just as tenable, from a biological point of view, to hear some people report that their fathers were like mothers.

We are speaking, of course, of bridge brains.

BRIDGE-BRAIN FATHERS

A father wrote: "I think I must be one of those bridge brains you talk about. From the second my wife told me she was pregnant, I was thinking, 'When can she go back to work and I can have the kid to myself.' I'm joking, you know, but I'm serious in a way. I just couldn't wait to have babies. My wife says sometimes she thinks I'm going to spontaneously lactate."

A mother wrote: "I'm married to a man who hasn't had any problem staying home with the kids while I've worked. I'm the primary breadwinner. It's been this way since we got together. He's the homebody. It works out great for us. He's even better at multi-tasking than I am."

These men are probably bridge brains, just as a man teaching second grade is probably a bridge brain. Teaching the lower grades, like the hands-on, stay-at-home parenting of infants, requires high amounts of patience, empathy, hands-on caregiving, eye-to-eye contact, and, not only the ability to do many different tasks at once, but also to do different kinds of tasks simultaneously—talk, listen, supervise an activity, complete a previous task, begin a new one. Biochemically, the bridge-brain fathers and teachers may well have higher serotonin levels than average, making them less impulsive; higher oxytocin, making them more interested in bonding echoes; less testosterone and vasopressin, making them less socially aggressive. Their brains are probably formatted with a larger-than-normal corpus callosum, allowing more cross talk between hemispheres and multitasking. These men probably do verbals in more brain centers than the average male and may have more neural pathways to the hippocampus from the limbic system, giving them greater ability to pick up sensory-emotive cues and store them in memory.

If a father is staying at home from economic necessity but finds the task very difficult, then he is probably a man who is trying to adapt to life circumstances as best he can, but he is not a bridge brain. Any human brain has the ability to adapt, especially when children and family are at stake. If the man loves to teach second grade or would like to spend much or all of his time in the bonding echoes that care of young children provides, he may possess a brain and hormonal system that bridges between male and female quite obviously.

Human males are gaining increased skill in many of the areas human females used to dominate, but we don't have evidence that there is a mass change in brain functioning. Stay-at-home dads, for instance, while a growing population, will not become 50 percent of the stay-at-home parents in the foreseeable future.

There is also no evidence that bridge brains have not always existed. We tend to think of "traditional fathers" when we think of the past, but there were also many men who gave hands-on care to their young when wives died in childbirth, and they found themselves completely at home in the role.

Social thinkers have pointed out for about two decades that social and gender roles are changing, allowing fathers to do more of what mothers do, and women to do more of what men traditionally did. Often when these thinkers talk about these "gender transitions," they do so in praise of the new gender roles. While the statement is accurate, and the new gender roles can be freeing, this kind of discussion is generally incomplete. It also demonstrates a tacit idealization of the bridge-brain dad and a derision of the father who leans more toward the masculine end of the male-brain spectrum: the dad who will probably never fit the bridge-brain modality.

Women are moving into the workforce and are finding it generally compatible for their brain systems. They are also, gradually, altering workplaces to accommodate their brain systems. The home—the place men are encouraged to enter with more vigor now—differs from the corporate workplace in one primary way: Family life is not a place set up to manufacture, build, or invent something; it exists to emphasize bonding and attachment. The male/female bonding difference more greatly affects families of small children than it does a large workplace. We are not seeing as many men take over the "female-dominated" profession of early child care as we are women advancing into the corporate or career world. A woman does not generally need to be a bridge brain to be a professional or office worker, but a man probably does in order to become a full-time, hands-on caregiver of young children.

Though we are creating a society that respects bridge-brain fathers more than some previous societies did, we are not living in a society in which the biology of fathering is becoming the biology of mothering. This is a crucial thing to keep in mind as we try to be the best parents we can be to our children.

THE PRACTICE OF INTIMATE SEPARATENESS

If it is true that men have expanded parenting skills and made room for women at work, even explored "the more feminine side" of themselves, but still remain predominantly male brain, then we are faced as a civilization with how to value fathering and paternal nurturance for its strengths. One way to make sure children get access to the very important biology of fathering is to engage in the practice of intimate separateness.

A mother of two sons, and a clinical psychologist, sent me an E-mail with this insight:

> We were at the beach and I watched a dad and a son, about thirteen, doing wrestling moves on each other—half nelsons, take downs. The mom said, "Boys, stop it!" and I thought about how I've said that very thing to my husband. Or I'll say, "Take it easy," or something like that, thinking he lacks tenderness with our son, even how violent these guys are. But watching this other family, I thought about how infantilizing it is when a mom says, "Boys, stop it!" These are men being tender to each other—men, not boys. And there's no doubt in my mind that these half-nelsons, these hits and scratches and yells are actually very tender gestures between men, they're just weird to me. I don't think I understood this in my own professional training. I think, finally, now that my sons are teenagers and my husband is the father of teenage boys, I'm getting my education.

So much of human life might be summed up in this paragraph. It can often take most of our offspring's childhoods to realize what subtleties the father brings to the family. There is often a tendency to infantilize the physical aggressiveness of males. There is often a fear that the father lacks tenderness and will harm his children. The biological truth is that children are equally harmed by both mothers and fathers, and by the lack of mother and father. The idea of intimate separateness can help us give children the best of both parents.

Dividing labor. Often, understanding the hidden nature of the father (and mother) can help women and men divide parenting labor. Agreements can be reached as a woman is pregnant, as each child comes along, and as family adaptation is required during child development. The female and male parenting perspectives can be equally honored. The supervision of adolescent boys is a prime example. Many young males will especially need the father to take a profound interest in them during puberty in the same way the mother did during infancy.

Deference. Intimate separateness requires mothers and fathers to defer to each other when the other is clearly right on a parenting issue. For example, if a father knows his wife is right about curfew times or amount of television use, but withholds deference because of a power struggle over intimacy issues, the children will suffer. Intimacy-marital relationship issues need to be separated from parenting issues. Especially in situations of divorce, parents tend to mix relationship and parenting issues. It can be difficult to separate them, but it is essential to try to do so.

Family conferences. It can be useful to make lists and have family conferences to promulgate and agree to the lists. If men have a list, they inherently work toward fulfillment of the list. They understand that they are involved in a transaction that requires their attention. With the subtler parenting joys and sorrows, like "My father makes me be fearless," or, "My father seems selfish and yet also selfless," this kind of list is not possible. But with basic parenting discipline, morality development, child care, a list is a very useful tool.

Letting nature take its course. Often the transactional nature of a household can be seen not only in dividing labor but in allowing nature to take its course. Men who feel free to parent in ways they feel are important often give back great gifts to the household.

An example of this came to me through a family who were my clients. The father was a video game afficianado as was the son. The father and son bonded, in some part, through video games. The mother wanted no video games in the house, having learned that they can stunt brain development if abused and that violent video games can cause violence in young males. Yet certainly she wanted to support bonding.

As the family's therapist, I found much to agree with on each side. A compromise was reached—one of intimate separateness—in which both parent's points of view were acknowledged.

1. When mom was gone, video games were okay. When mom came home, it was time to put them away.

2. Violent video games were only allowed for twenty minutes on a weekend day, none on a school day. Since this child was on Ritalin for hyperactivity, school days needed regimentation and extra care.

3. No video games were allowed if homework and chores weren't done.

4. If grades fell, reading was not getting done, or schoolwork and intellectual development suffered, the video games would be put away until the situation changed.

This family worked out a solution that benefited all. The solution required both to give something, as is generally the case in the practice of intimate separateness.

Intimate separateness, as it pertains to fathering, does not mean a father is given carte blanche to do as he pleases or to make excuses for a job not well done.

Intimate separateness is not about anything else except mutual understanding. If a man fulfills his biological role, he is living within his nature. Every woman is faced, at some point, with deciding whether her husband's actions as a father—his living out his own nature—is enough for her. In this she has a great and profound responsibility for the future of her children.

THE BEST FATHER

Let me end this chapter with this poignant letter from Johannes, forty-six:

I try to be the best father I can. When I was young I promised I would be different from my father. He was a German-Dutch, very rigid. He did not speak of his love for his children. He was a strict disciplinarian. I turned out well enough indeed, but I always missed him. Even when I was with him I felt like I missed him. When he died, I cried, and my son said, "Papa, I love you," and I hugged my son and I hoped my father knew I loved him, too. I know he loved his children, a father always does, but sometimes with fathers these things are not so clear. I want it to be different with my own children.

Epilogue

There is more in a human life than our theories of it allow.

—Jarnes Hillman

I hope you have enjoyed this scientific view of the male-mind. As we delve deeply into who a man is, we are participating in one of the great acts of civilization. We are each doing something incremental to help shape the role of men. We all know that without those men and their role, we would be lost.

Our men represent our past and our future, our strengths as humans and our weaknesses. Men are prepared to carry nearly any burden given to them if they can get back some sense of worth. Even if they get nothing back, so often they carry the burden anyway.

Men confound us. Men make us better people. One of the most profound acts of self-preservation we can engage in is to under-stand men. As a culture, we've made profound mistakes in the last few decades by assuming that men were unnecessary. Many people have even gone so far as to negate or dismiss what is at the core of a man.

I hope as we've examined the male mind we are also aware that a man is more than we've discovered. Science hates limiting human discourse. Science wants the great expansion of the human mind, the increase in adaptation and invention. Science drives us to discover things we didn't know and to avoid being limited by those new discoveries.

The vision of this book has been nature based, for there is no other realm as limitless as the constantly adapting world of nature. Yet this book is only a reference point for the ongoing discovery of the nature of men.

Let me end by quoting the philosopher Aman Motwane, who says, ". . . nature does nothing inattentively. Every moment, every action, every step is orchestrated to create the most productive outcome possible. Every available resource is mobilized, every necessary ally is commissioned to ensure success and survival. Nature exacts a very high price for inattentiveness. If we want to create a meaningful future, we must emulate nature."

This is good advice when we don't know what to make of the man we are trying to relate to in a given year, month, day, or moment.

It is good advice as we answer one of the great questions of our time: What could he be thinking?

Notes

Introduction: What Could He Be Thinking?

Anecdotal research from two different focus groups is referred to in these pages. One is the smaller women's lunch group, with whom I have been in conversation for almost two decades. The second is a larger group of women called together specifically for this project by Gail and myself.

Though both groups are comprised of friends and acquaintances, I have long made it a practice to change people's names when I use them in books, mainly for the purposes of privacy and compositure. Thus, names of all of the focus group members have been changed, with the exception of the therapist Pam Brown.

The real names of the focus group members can be found in the acknowledgments. Again, I would like to thank these women very much.

Whenever my client's names are used, these names have been changed, and their stories altered enough to retain confidentiality but not to diminish applicability. I have also changed the names of people who have written E-mails and other correspondence.

The Science of Manhood

Gender biology: The nature-based philosophy in this book is grounded in biological research that you can access in more detail in many interesting books, including the groundbreaking work, by Anne Moir and David Jessel *Brain Sex* (Dell, 1990), as well as Barbara and Allan Pease, *Why Men Don't Listen* (Broadway, 2001); Deborah Blum, *Sex on the Brain* (Viking, 1997); Anne and Bill Moir, *Why Men Don't Iron* (Citadel, 1999); and Dianne Hales *Just Like a Woman* (Bantam, 1999).

Like these authors, I am beholden to the primary researchers in brain and hormone biology—Ruben and Raquel Gur, Laurie Allen, Roger Gorski, Camilla Benbow, Deborah Sichel, Daniel Amen among them—whose work in clinical laboratories, with PET scans, MRIs, and biochemical trials have changed the way we think of ourselves.

Over the twenty years I have been researching male and female biology, I have had to develop a method by which to discover what biological research is most helpful and accurate. I begin by learning what primary researchers in various countries have discovered through their clinical trials, then I see if these facts in their hard science fit cutting-edge research in soft sciences like psychology, anthropology, and sociology. I've learned that in studying both hard and soft science, it is crucial not to stray too far from people's real lives or from good common sense. Thus I try to match what we've learned in clinical trials and other research with people's everyday lives.

The Nature of a Man

D. W. Winnicot, *Human Nature* (Schocken, 1988), an example of a very useful psychological approach to the topic of what is natural to human beings. However, it spends less time on the actual biology of human nature than we can now spend. I hope that as we analyze human nature in the future—equipped with new sciences and technologies—we will be able to pursue the topic without having to step aside, or step over, the actual biological nature of men and women.

PART I: THE MALE BRAIN

Chapter 1: What's in His Head: A Friendly Look at the Male Brain

Videotapes of Anne Moir and David Jessel's books, *Brain Sex* (Dell, 1990), are available from The Learning Connection, as well as from Films for the Humanities and Sciences (www.films.com, 800-257-5126).

See also my work *The Soul of the Child* (Atria, 2002).

The Male Brain
Two outstanding books on the composition of the brain are: Mark Bear, Barry Connors, and Michael Paradiso, *Neuroscience: Exploring the Brain* (Williams and Wilkens, 1996); and by Eric Kandel, James Schwartz, and Thomas Jessel, *Essentials of Neural Science and Behavior*, (Appleton and Lange, 1995).

The Power of Natural Identity in Our Relationships
See my *The Wonder of Boys* (Tarcher/Putnam, 1996); and *The Wonder of Girls* (Pocket, 2001).

Chapter 2: How Nature Answers the Question, What Is a Man?

The Despair of Men and the Core of Manhood
See Susan Faludi, *Stiffed* (Bantam, 1999); Robert Bly, *The Sibling Society* (Addison-Wesley, 1997); Christina Hoff Summer, *The War*

Against Boys (Simon & Schuster, 2000); my book, *A Fine Young Man* (Tarcher/Putnam, 1998); Samuel Osherson, *Finding Our Fathers* (Fawcett, 1986); Aaron Kipnis, *Angry Young Men* (Jossey-Bass, 2001); Warren Farrell *The Myth of Male Power* (Simon & Schuster, 1993); and David Blankenhorn *Fatherless America* (Harper, 1995).

See also: William Pollock *Real Boys* (Random House, 1998); and Michael Thompson and Daniel Kindlon *Raising Cain* (Ballantine, 1999).

The Biology of Male Identity
See Simon Baron-Cohen *The Essential Difference* (Perseus, 2003); and Shelley Taylor, *The Tending Instinct* (Times Books, May 2002).

Men Seek a Calling
The quotes from Deshimaru and Eric Gill can be found in *The Soul Aflame*, edited by Phil Cousineau (Conari, 2000).

Statistics concerning men, women, and the workforce appear in Anne and Bill Moir's *Why Men Don't Iron* (Citadel, 1999).

Bringing It All Together: Men Are on a Quest
See Allan Chinen *Beyond the Hero* (Tarcher/Putnam, 1995); and Robert Wright, *The Moral Animal* (Vintage, 1994).

PART II: WHAT COULD HE *REALLY* BE THINKING?

Chapter 3: What Could He *Really* Be Thinking... About Feelings and Emotions

The Male Mode of Feeling
See Gale Berkowitz et al. "Female Responses to Stress: Tend or Befriend, Not Fight or Flight," *Psychological Review* (2000).

To access a new study on men, women, and emotional difference, you can go to www.pnas.org. There you can see the Proceedings of the National Academy of Sciences. Look for a study by

Canli, Desmond, Zhao, and Gabrieli. It is fascinating to see these MRI scans of the male and female brain as they do emotional tasks so differently!

For greater knowledge of how PET scans and MRIs can be used to understand a brain's emotional functioning, the reader might enjoy Daniel Amen's *Healing the Hardware of the Soul* (The Free Press, 2002).

A Bottom Line: Women Trust Feelings More Than Men
See Martin Buber, *I and Thou*, Trans. by William Kaufman (Scribner, 1970).

Research on prolactin, crying, and tear glands has been spearheaded by William Frey, a biochemist at Regions Hospital in St. Paul, Minnesota.

Chapter 4: What Could He *Really* Be Thinking . . . About Sex and Romance?

The Biology of Sex and Romance
For further study in this biology see: Helen Fisher, *The Anatomy of Love* (Norton, 1992); Robert Jay Russell, *The Lemur's Legacy* (Tarcher/Putnam, 1993); R. Robin Baker and Mark A. Bellis, *Human Sperm Competition* (Chapman & Hall, 1995); Carl Sagan and Ann Druyan, *Shadows of Forgotten Ancestors* (Random House, 1992); and Lyn Margulis and Dorion Sagan *Mystery Dance* (Summit Books, 1991).

What Are Reasonable Romantic Expectations of One Another?
See David Popenoe, co-director, *The State of Our Unions 2001: The Social Health of Marriage in America* (The National Marriage Project, Rutgers University, 2001), Rutgers University, and the Bureau of Statistics.

Practicing Intimate Separateness
See Mary Batten, *Sexual Strategies* (Tarcher/Putnam, 1992).

Turning Romance into Commitment and Marriage
See Louis De Bernieres, *Corelli's Mandolin* (Vintage, 1994).

PART III: WHAT COULD HE *REALLY* BE THINKING . . . ABOUT
MARRIAGE AND COMMITMENT?

Chapter 5: I Think I Love You: Men and the Biology of Commitment

The Biology of Commitment
See Janet Evanovich, *Two for the Dough* (Pocket, 1996).

How a Man's Relationship with His Mother Can Affect Him
See Althea J. Horner "The Role of the Female Therapist in the Affir-
mation of Gender in Male Patients," *Journal of the American Acad-
emy of Psychoanalysis* (1992). Michael Kirkpatrick is quoted from
this article.
    A. Davis Henderson, Thomas V. Sayger, and Arthur M. Home,
"Mothers and Sons: A Look at the Relationship Between Child
Behavior Problems, Marital Satisfaction, Maternal Depression and
Family Cohesion," *The Family Journal* (January 2003); and see my
Mothers, Sons and Lovers (Shambhala, 1993).

Practicing Intimate Separateness
See James Hillman, *The Soul's Code* (Warner, 1997).

Chapter 6: I Know I Love You: Men and the Biology of Marriage

The Human Divorce
See Scott Stanley, Howard Markman, and Susan Blumberg, *Fighting
for Your Marriage* (Jossey-Bass/John Wiley, 2001); Linda Waite, *The
Case for Marriage* (Doubleday, 2000); and Constance Ahrons, *The
Good Divorce* (HarperCollins, 1998).

The Biology of Marriage
I am often asked how I developed this twelve-stage system for understanding marriage from a biological perspective. As in all my work, I am combining biological data with personal observation of marriages in my clinical practice, as well as the work of other thinkers in the area of marital development. From Freud and Jung onward, the field of psychology has been trying to develop a staging framework for individual development. I hope I have added a staging framework for marital life that will stand the test of future scrutiny.

A Map for Marriage
See my *Love's Journey* (Shambhala, 1994).

She Says: "I Feel Fat." What Should He Do?
John Gottman's "Marriage Survival Kit" is an example of a practical tool that accepts how different men and women are as they approach marital conflict.

The work of John Gray, especially in *Men Are from Mars, Women Are from Venus* (HarperCollins, 1992), has been profoundly helpful as couples face nitty-gritty issues of marital conversation.

For couples facing issues of male/female difference of a sexual nature, John Gray's *Mars and Venus in the Bedroom* (HarperCollins, 1993) is very helpful.

Practicing Intimate Separateness: Turning Marriages Around
See Thomas Moore, *Soul Mates* (Harper Perennial, 1994).

PART IV: WHAT COULD HE *REALLY* BE THINKING . . . ABOUT HOME AND CHILDREN?

Chapter 7: The Male Brain at Home: Men and Women Living Together

Why Can't He Load the Dishwasher the Right Way?
I have not had the good fortune to see *Defending the Caveman*, however, having heard so many good things about it, I am anxious to do

so! Humor is a profoundly important tool in helping us enjoy male-female differences.

Chapter 8: What a Father Knows:
The Nature of Being a Dad

See the following: David Blankenhorn, *Fatherless America* (Harper, 1995); Kyle Pruett, *Fatherneed* (The Free Press, 2000); my *The Prince and the King* (Tarcher/Putnam, 1992); Neil Chethik, *Fatherloss* (Hyperion, 2001); and Mark Bryan, *The Prodigal Father* (Three Rivers, 1997).

Epilogue

The quotation from Aman Motwane's *The Power of Wisdom* appears in *Discoveries* (August 2002).

About the Author

Michael Gurian has published eighteen books in seven disciplines. A pioneering social philosopher, he has authored five national bestsellers, translated into fourteen languages, and been credited with bringing a new understanding of human nature to the national dialogue.

His ground-breaking *The Wonder of Boys*, was credited with inspiring a "boys movement," which led to international interest in how our sons become men. Michael has been called "the Dr. Spock for boys" and has provided studies of male emotional and moral development in the *A Fine Young Man* and *The Good Son*, as well as father-son and mother-son relationships in *The Prince and the King* and *Mothers, Sons and Lovers*.

Michael's work in female development has been heralded as rev-

278 About the Author

olutionary. In his bestselling *The Wonder of Girls* and *Boys and Girls Learn Differently!* his call for a rethinking of girls' and women's lives sparked national debate.

His counsel as a family therapist has been sought by couples and families throughout the United States. His speeches and seminars (www.michaelgurian.com) have been attended by thousands over the last decade. The cofounder of the Michael Gurian Institute (www.gurianinstitute.com), he has spearheaded a national effort to provide teachers, parents, and couples with training in male and female learning styles.

Michael's work has been featured in the international media, including the *New York Times*, the *London Times*, the *Washington Post, USA Today, Time, Newsweek, Good Housekeeping, Le Monde*, as well as *The Today Show, Good Morning America*, BBC, CNN, CBC, PBS, and National Public Radio.

Michael lives in Spokane, Washington, with his wife, Gail, who is a family therapist, and their two daughters.

Men Are From Mars, Women Are From Venus

John Gray Ph.D.

Get seriously involved with this classic guide to surviving the opposite sex

You can't live with them – and you can't live without them! First published in 1993, this book has gone on to become one of the most famous non-fiction publications of all time.

A classic and lively book on successful communication between the sexes, many millions of readers all over the world have been able to work out what makes members of the opposite sex tick, learning to understand their verbal and non-verbal language, ultimately reaching a point of harmony where it becomes possible to live, work and love together.

- Motivate the opposite sex and get what you want!
- Avoid arguments and promote fruitful communication.
- What will really impress your mate? Score points with the opposite sex …
- Learn about the real emotional needs of the opposite sex and the behaviours associated with these needs.
- Discover the keys to keeping love alive – and staying together long term.

Make
www.thorsonselement.com
your online sanctuary

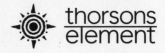